evangelical awakenings
in EASTERN ASIA

evangelical awakenings
in EASTERN ASIA
J. EDWIN ORR

BETHANY FELLOWSHIP, INC.
Minneapolis, Minnesota

Published by Bethany Fellowship, Inc.
6820 Auto Club Road, Minneapolis, Minnesota 55438

Printed in the United States of America

Library of Congress CIP Data:
Orr, James Edwin, 1912-
    Evangelical awakenings in Eastern Asia.

    Bibliography: p.
    Includes index.
    1. Revivals—East (Far East)—History. I. Title.
BV3777.E18077   269'.2'095   74-30353
ISBN O-87123-126-3

TABLE OF CONTENTS

Introduction   vii

1   Awakenings and Pioneers, 19th Century   1
2   The Fifth General Awakening   12
3   Taikyo Dendo in Japan   21
4   The Korean Pentecost   26
5   The Chinese Quickening   34
6   Southeast Asian Revivals, 1900—   42

7   Years of War in Japan   46
8   Light in Korea's Darkest Days   50
9   Despair and Recovery in China   57
10 Awakening Beyond the Wall   64
11 Awakenings in North China   69
12 Shanghai and Central China   76
13 Revival in the South and West   82
14 China in Revival, 1927-1939   92
15 Southeast Asian Revivals, 1920—   97

16 Post-War Evangelism in Japan   103
17 The 1947 Quickening in Korea   109
18 The Curtain Falls in China   120
19 Taiwan, Hong Kong, and Overseas   135
20 Conflict and Revival in Southeast Asia   140

    Conclusion   149

    Notes   157
    Bibliography   175
    Index   179

Introduction

EVANGELICAL AWAKENINGS

An Evangelical Awakening is a movement of the Holy Spirit bringing about a revival of New Testament Christianity in the Church of Christ and in its related community. Such an awakening may change in a significant way an individual only; or it may affect a larger group of believers; or it may move a congregation, or the churches of a city or district, or the whole body of believers throughout a country or a continent; or indeed the larger body of believers throughout the world. The outpouring of the Spirit effects the reviving of the Church, the awakening of the masses, and the movement of uninstructed peoples towards the Christian faith; the revived Church, by many or by few, is moved to engage in evangelism, in teaching, and in social action.

Such an awakening may run its course briefly, or it may last a lifetime. It may come about in various ways, though there seems to be a pattern common to all such movements throughout history.

The major marks of an Evangelical Awakening are always some repetition of the phenomena of the Acts of the Apostles, followed by the revitalizing of nominal Christians and by bringing outsiders into vital touch with the Divine Dynamic causing all such Awakenings—the Spirit of God. The surest evidence of the Divine origin of any such quickening is its presentation of the evangelical message declared in the New Testament and its re-enactment of the phenomena therein in the empowering of saints and conversion of sinners.

It is more than interesting to compare the characteristics of the Awakenings of various decades with the prototype of evangelical revivals in the Acts of the Apostles, a perennial textbook for such movements.

Our Lord told His disciples: 'It is not for you to know the times or seasons which the Father has fixed by His own authority. But you shall receive power when the Holy Spirit has come upon you; and you shall be My witnesses . . . to the end of the earth.' Thus was an outpouring of the Spirit predicted, and soon fulfilled.

Then began extraordinary praying among the disciples
in the upper room. Who knows what self-judgment and confession and reconciliation went on? There were occasions
for such. But, when they were all together in one place, there
suddenly came from heaven a sound like the rush of a mighty
wind and it filled all the house. The filling of the Holy Spirit
was followed by xenolalic evangelism, not repeated in the
times of the Apostles nor authenticated satisfactorily since.

The Apostle Peter averred that the outpouring fulfilled
the prophecy of Joel, which predicted the prophesying of
young men and maidens, the seeing of visions and dreams by
young and old. He preached the death and resurrection of
Jesus Christ. What was the response? The hearers were
pierced, stabbed, stung, stunned, smitten— these are the
synonyms of a rare verb which Homer used to signify being
drummed to earth. It was no ordinary feeling; nor was the
response a mild request for advice. It was more likely an
uproar of entreaty, the agonizing cry of a multitude.

Those who responded to the Apostle's call for repentance
confessed their faith publicly in the apostolic way. About
three thousand were added to the church. Then followed
apostolic teaching, fellowship, communion and prayers.

What kind of fellowship? Doubtless the words of Scripture
were often used liturgically, but it is certain that the koinonia
was open. What kind of prayers? There are instances of
individual petitions of power and beauty, but there are also
suggestions of simultaneous, audible prayer in which the
main thrust of petition is recorded, as in the prophet's day.

The Apostles continued to urge their hearers to change
and turn to God, which they did by the thousands. And no
hostile power seemed for the moment able to hinder them.
Persecution followed, but the work of God advanced.

The events recorded in the Acts have been repeated in
full or lesser degree in the Awakenings of past centuries.
From the study of Evangelical Revivals or Awakenings in
cities and districts, countries and continents, generations
and centuries, it is possible to trace a pattern of action and
discover a progression of achievement that establish in the
minds of those who accept the New Testament as recorded
history an undoubted conclusion that the same Spirit of God
Who moved the apostles has wrought His mighty works in the
centuries preceding our own with the same results but with
wider effects than those of which the apostles dreamed in
their days of power.

Although the records are scarce, there were Evangelical Awakenings in the centuries before the rise of John Wycliffe, the Oxford reformer. But such movements in medieval times seemed very limited in their scope or abortive in their effect. What was achieved in the days of John Wycliffe—the dissemination of the Scriptures in the language of the people —has never been lost, nor has the doctrine of Scriptural authority. Thus the Lollard Revival led to the Reformation, which would have been unlikely without it; and the principle of appeal to the Word of God in the matter of reform has not been lost either. The Reformation thus led to the Puritan movement in which the essentials of evangelical theology were refined; and the Puritan movement prepared the way for the eighteenth, nineteenth and twentieth century Awakenings occurring in more rapid succession.

A student of church history in general and of the Great Awakenings in particular must surely be impressed by the remarkable continuity of doctrine as well as the continuity of action. Anyone could begin reading the story of the Gospels, continue on into the narrative of the Acts of the Apostles, then without any sense of interruption begin reading the story of the poor preachers of John Wycliffe, the itinerants of the Scottish Covenant, the circuit riders of John Wesley, the readers of Hans Nielsen Hauge in Norway, or the Disciples of the Lord in Madagascar.

Not only so, but the student of such movements would find in the preaching of the Awakenings and Revivals the same message preached and the same doctrines taught in the days of the Apostles. But non-evangelical Christianity, with its accretions of dogma and use of worldly power, would seem a system utterly alien to that of the Church of the Apostles, resembling much more the forces both ecclesiastical and secular that had opposed New Testament Christianity.

The reader of the Acts of the Apostles must surely notice that the Church began to spread by extraordinary praying and preaching. So too the 'upper room' type of praying and the pentecostal sort of preaching together with the irrepressible kind of personal witness find their place in Great Awakenings rather than in the less evangelical ecclesiastical patterns.

The first three centuries of progress were followed by a millenium of changed direction when the Church was united with the State and political force compelled the consciences of men. These centuries are rightly called the Dark Ages, though they were not entirely without light.

Before the fifteenth century, a change began, commencing a progression of awakenings that moved the Church by degrees back to the apostolic pattern and extended it all over the world. Not only were theological dogmas affected and missionary passion created, but society itself was changed.

From the times of the Lollards onward, the impact of the Evangelical Revivals or Awakenings was felt in the realm of personal liberty— knowing the truth made men free, and made them covet freedom for all. Thus the Social Rising of 1381 championed a charter of freedom based on evangelical conviction. Its daughter movement in Bohemia defended its freedom against the forces of tyranny for a century.

The consequent Reformation that soon began in Germany caused such a ferment in men's minds that a rising became inevitable— but it was crushed, only because some of those responsible for the hunger for freedom betrayed it. The hunger for righteousness of the early Puritans brought about another attempt to establish freedom under the law, but, like various ventures before it, the Commonwealth failed because it relied more upon secular force than persuasion.

In the eighteenth, nineteenth and twentieth centuries, the revived Evangelicals re-learned an earlier method. New Testament counsel began to prevail, helping persuade free-thinkers and Christians, traditionalists and Evangelicals, that freedom was God's intent for every man, everywhere. Thus the nineteenth century became in itself the century of Christian action, taking Good News to every quarter of the earth, to every phase of life. Those whose hearts the Spirit had touched became the great initiators of reform and welfare and tuned even the conscience of unregenerate men to a sense of Divine harmony in society.

Yet Christians believed that the horizontal relationship of man to men was dependent upon the vertical relationship of man to God, that social reform was not meant to take the place of evangelism, 'so to present Christ in the power of the Spirit that men may come to put their trust in Him as Saviour and to serve Him as Lord in the fellowship of His Church and in the vocations of the common life.'

What may be called the General Awakenings began in the second quarter of the eighteenth century, among settlers in New Jersey and refugees from Moravia about the same time. The First Awakening ran its course in fifty years, and was followed by the Second Awakening in 1792, the Third in 1830, the Fourth in 1858-59, the Fifth in 1905.

1

AWAKENINGS AND PIONEERS, 19th Century

Gautama Buddha first proclaimed his eightfold way in India, whose peoples later deserted his teachings. The lovely island of Ceylon, Sri Lanka, offered a more lasting hospitality; but it was east of the sub-continent of India that Buddhism rooted itself and sheltered nations in its shade.

The lands of the Buddha stretch from the Bay of Bengal through the Indo-Chinese countries of Burma, Thailand, Laos, Cambodia and Vietnam, skipping Muslim Malaya, to the sub-continent of China in all its vastness, Mongolia and Tibet to the north and the northwest, and Korea and Japan to the northeast.[1] In each of these countries, Buddhism laid its veneer over the mass of local animism, and combined in the Far East with Oriental sages to give the people an engaging way of life.

Missionary penetration of this great arc of countries by Evangelical Christianity did not begin until the time of the second worldwide Evangelical Awakening, which followed the turmoil of revolution in the West that separated it from the Evangelical Revival of Whitefield and Wesley's day. In some countries, it did not get under way until the fourth worldwide Evangelical Awakening of the mid-nineteenth century, or even the fifth movement of the early twentieth. The revivals provided men and motivation.

There were four great outpourings of the Holy Spirit in the nineteenth century, resulting in revivals and awakenings in sending churches and communities and their extension by evangelism and social action.[2]

The upheavals of the late eighteenth century, especially the American and French Revolutions, had been followed by a decline in Christian witness so serious that, in the judgment of Kenneth Scott Latourette, it seemed as though Christianity became 'a waning influence, about to be ushered out of the affairs of men.'[3] Even in the dynamic society of the United States, the plight of the churches was desperate, the Episcopal Bishop of New York (for example) considering the situation hopeless and simply ceasing to function.[4]

In despair, Christian leaders began to pray for Divine intervention; the answer came in a series of four great waves of evangelical advance which made the extended nineteenth century—from the French Revolution until the First World War—the 'Great Century' of evangelism and Christian action.

When John Wesley died, Evangelical Christendom was confined to Great Britain, Scandinavia, parts of Germany, Holland and Switzerland, minorities in France and Hungary, and territory east of the Alleghenies in North America, while Latin America was closed by the intransigent governments of Spain and Portugal, Africa was unexplored, Islam was hostile to the Gospel, the East India Company made missionaries unwelcome in India, and none resided in China, Japan or Korea. South Seas islanders lived in savagery.

The awakenings raised up evangelists on the American frontier, sent the Haldanes up and down to revive Scotland, produced Hans Nielsen Hauge to transform Norway and provoked revival and evangelism in England, Germany, Holland and other European countries, directly equipping churches with Sunday Schools, home missions, city missions and the auxiliaries taken for granted today. [5]

The 'turn of the century' awakenings sent off pioneer missionaries to the South Seas, to Latin America, Black Africa, India and China. There rose denominational missionary societies such as the Baptist Missionary Society, the American Board and other national missions in Europe. At the same time, the British and Foreign Bible Society was founded, followed by the American Bible Society and other national Bible Societies, as well as societies for promotion of Christian literature.

In Napoleonic times, the movement of missionaries thus thrust out by the Evangelical Awakenings got under way. From the impulse of the student awakenings of the early nineteenth century, various missionary enterprises started. Adoniram Judson, originally a missionary of the American Board but switched by convictions about baptism to the American Baptists, arrived in Rangoon in Burma in 1813. He and his wife went through many years' privation before baptizing their first convert in 1819.[6]

The outbreak of the Anglo-Burmese War in 1824 caused Judson's imprisonment. In 1834, he finished translating the whole Bible into Burmese, the beginning of mission success, though taking unexpected directions.

George Boardman[7] arrived in Burma to assist Judson, and opened a station south of Moulmein where he baptized Ko Tha Byu, a Karen. Soon the Karen convert became a fiery evangelist and began preaching in the foothills and the mountains near and far to Karen villagers.[8] The Karens were a non-Buddhist people, ready for the gospel, and a mass movement followed the preaching and resulted in an inevitable persecution from the Burmese until the annexation of Lower Burma by the British.

Thailand preserved its independence as much from its being a buffer state between British imperialism on the west and French imperialism on the east as from native efforts. American Presbyterians entered Thailand in 1840 and won only a few converts.[9] The evangelization of Thailand proved to be very slow indeed. And in Indo-China, among the Cambodians, Laos and Vietnamese, Evangelical Christianity found practically no contact on account of the colonial policy of the French.[10]

A major target of the missionary body was the great Empire of China, which dominated all of East Asia. Even William Carey in India sought to translate the Scriptures into Chinese.[11] In 1793, that significant year for missions to India, the Emperor of China forbade any teaching of the 'English religion' throughout his wide domains.[12] In the meantime, as the new century began, several missionary bodies were engaged in translating the Scriptures into Chinese.

Then in 1807, a convert of the Scottish Awakening, Robert Morrison of the London Missionary Society,[13] arrived in Canton to begin a very restricted residence as an interpreter. Within a year and a half of his arrival, he had mastered so much of the local Cantonese, the national Mandarin and the literary language of the Empire that he was appointed as official translator for the East India Company. His first assistant, William Milne, like himself a convert of the turn-of-the-century Revival in Britain, arrived in 1813, and in 1814, their first convert was baptized, the forerunner of the Chinese Evangelical movement.

Karl Gützlaff, a convert of the Awakening in Germany and a graduate of Jänicke's missionary school in Berlin, toured the coasts of China in the 1830s, distributing literature.[14] In the 1830s also, the American Board sent its first missionaries to China, as did the American Baptists, who were followed by American Anglicans and Presbyterians, using the port of Canton as a base of operations.

The second wave of the Awakening of the early nineteenth century produced increasing missionary interest, and at the same time, the Anglo-Chinese War of 1839-42 opened up other ports of China to the residence of foreigners. Out of the evil of opium importation came opportunities for the preaching of the gospel. Hong Kong was ceded to Britain, missionaries living there, at Shanghai, and other ports.

Gützlaff gathered about him a staff of Chinese preachers and colporteurs who reported distributing Scriptures and gathering converts in most of the Chinese provinces. He was very discouraged to find that many of his agents were thoroughly dishonest double-crossers.[15]

Society after society entered the Treaty ports of China, Shanghai becoming a strategic point. In 1847, W. C. Burns, whose revival ministry in Scotland had affected not only the Scottish kirks but many who were to become missionaries, came himself out to China, but for more than six years, he worked without a convert in Amoy. As soon as accessions to the church were made, he moved on as an evangelist to other Treaty ports. He impressed many, both missionary and national, by his transparent saintliness.[16]

At the middle of the nineteenth century, the missionary enterprise was confined to Hong Kong and the five Treaty ports around the coast. The Chinese maintained an almost unbroken front of resistance to penetration of the hinterland.

A Hakka villager in South China named Hung Hsiu-Chuan came into touch with Christianity in the 1830s. He caught strange visions of power, and out of his preaching came a new movement in the mountains of Kwangsi. In the 1840s, Hung renewed his contacts with Protestant missionaries, but, in unknown ways, Hung converted his movement into an army which overran China from the south to the middle Yangtze, setting up a capital in Nanking.[17]

From 1856 to 1860, a second Anglo-Chinese War was raging, one in which France joined in. The terms of peace opened China further to trade and missionary penetration followed. It had been suggested that the Chinese guarantee protection for Chinese Christians as well as missionaries in the exercise of their religion. Shortly after, with foreign help, the Imperial Chinese armies were able to crush the Taiping Rebellion under Hung. Although these political upheavals gave many missionary societies freedom to expand, they did not break the uniform Chinese resistance to the Christian missions, and converts were few in number.

Meanwhile, the first and second waves of revival in the early nineteenth century had run their course in the West. Inevitably, there came about a decline in the spirituality of the churches affected by the post-1800 Awakenings. Not only was the attack of unbelievers renewed, but anti-evangelical notions claimed a following in the Anglican, Lutheran, and Reformed constituencies, and even among Baptists, taking the form of non-cooperation with other Christians.

In the autumn of 1857, there were signs of an awakening— success in revival and evangelism in Canada, and an extraordinary movement of men to prayer in New York City which spread from city to city throughout the United States and over the world.[18] Churches, halls and theatres were filled at noon for prayer, and the overflow filled churches of all denominations at night in a truly remarkable turning of a whole nation toward God.

The same movement also affected the United Kingdom, beginning in 1859 in Ulster, the most northerly province in Ireland; approximately ten percent of the population professed conversion in Wales and Scotland as well, and a great awakening continued in England for years. Repercussions were felt in many other European countries.

The phenomena of revival were reported in countries all around the world, including South Africa and India, during the decade that followed the awakening in the sending countries: wherever an Evangelical cause existed, a revival resulted; and the effects were felt for a lifetime.

Out of the 1859 Awakening in Britain arose a phalanx of famous evangelists—aristocrats and working men. Spurgeon built his Tabernacle on the crest of the movement. The War between the States (in which there was extraordinary revival and evangelism) delayed the emergence of great American evangelists from the 1858 Awakening, though Moody himself served his apprenticeship in that movement in Chicago.

The 1858-59 Awakenings extended the working forces of of Evangelical Christendom. Not only were a million converted in both the United States and the United Kingdom, but existing evangelistic and philanthropic organizations were revived and new vehicles of enterprise created. The Bible Societies flourished as never before, Home Missions and the Salvation Army were founded to extend the evangelistic-social ministry of the Revival in a worldwide mission. The impact on the Y. M. C. A. organization was noteworthy, and a remarkable recruitment of university students followed.

The mid-Century Awakenings revived all the existing missionary societies and enabled them to enter other fields. The practical evangelical ecumenism of the Revival was embodied in interdenominational faith missions, as well as a renewed cooperation between denominational organizations. The first permanent missionary enterprises of Protestants in Brazilian territory, for example, began in 1859——which also brought Protestant pioneers to Japan.

In 1860, religious revival broke out among missionaries in Shanghai.[19] China, at that time, constituted the greatest missionary challenge and opportunity in the world. There were only 115 Protestant missionaries in the whole country, concentrated in coastal cities and river ports, thus revived. They reported a remarkable work of grace at Lauling, near Tientsin in the 1860s,[20] described as 'wholly a work of God,' in which seventy men, fifty women and twenty young people requested baptism—a number unheard of in those days.

Many new missionaries came to China in the wake of the Revival, among them Timothy Richard, who had been converted as a youth in the Welsh Revival of 1859. Joining the Baptist Missionary Society, he became the best-known of its missionaries, famed for his educational ministry.[21]

In 1866, the missionary forces in China were increased by 15 per cent through the landing of the Lammermuir party of the newly-formed China Inland Mission under the direction of Dr. J. Hudson Taylor, justly described as one of the greatest missionaries of all time, whose objectives in China were unprecedented.[22]

The founding of the China Inland Mission was epoch-making in a world sense as well as in its relation to China. The story of the call of James Hudson Taylor is well-known but his relation to the 1859 Revival and its relationship to the new Mission has only recently been stressed by a historian. This first organization of its type in missions was begotten in the 1859 Revival, both its founder's vision and its earliest candidates.

While serving as a missionary of the Chinese Evangelization Society, Hudson Taylor had come under the influence of the revivalist, W. C. Burns. A letter (1860) from George Pearse:[23] "You will be glad to know that the Revival has reached London and hundreds are being converted," thrilled him. In need of physical, mental and spiritual recuperation, Hudson Taylor then returned to London. There he trained in medical school.

Hudson Taylor devoted all his spare time, especially his Sundays, to revival ministry in a fruitful training ground, the East End of London. In particular, he helped in the Twig Folly Mission in Bethnal Green which carried on daily prayer meetings and preaching services. A noted infidel was converted there and many converts of the Revival were baptized as believers.[24]

The Revival then in progress (said Marshall Broomhall) was a revelation in the homeland of God's power to bless, while a million a month dying in China without God made its appalling contrast in the mind of the burdened missionary.

While visiting George Pearse in Brighton in the afterglow of the wonderful Brighton Revival, Hudson Taylor faced his life's greatest crisis. On Sunday, 25th June 1865, unable to bear the sight of a thousand Christians rejoicing in their own security while multitudes perished for lack of knowledge, he walked along the beach and made a great decision.

The prayer life of British Christians had risen to record heights. George Müller's example in launching out by faith was being followed elsewhere. The need of China was appreciated by Hudson Taylor as by few others. So he applied the prayer and faith and action as exemplified by the 1859 Awakening to China's need, and the China Inland Mission became its dynamic extension to China's millions.

This newest venture was not denominationally indifferent. The China Inland Mission as envisioned by Hudson Taylor was interdenominational rather than undenominational. Its missionaries were sent to interior provinces of China where others of the same denomination served—Szechwan, for example, was an Anglican diocese. In due course, the China Inland Mission became the largest of all the missionary bodies, Protestant or Roman.

The 1860s were years of expansion for all the missions in China.[25] Under Griffith John, the London Missionary Society reached out into the midlands and north of China. James Gilmour, a convert of the 1859 Revival, ventured north into Mongolia, suffering privation and hardship. In the 1860s, the American Board opened stations in the north. In the same decade, the American Baptists entered the Swatow area. Southern Baptists maintained themselves in Shantung, in spite of the raging Civil War. The American Episcopal Church moved up river. The Church Missionary Society expanded its mid-China work. American Presbyterians spread from Canton southward. Around Amoy, the English

Presbyterians and the Reformed Church of the United States organized a presbytery, and the former opened a work in Formosa among the Chinese. The Methodists of the United States spread from Foochow, opened a work up river on the Yangtze, and entered the north. And Josiah Cox brought the British Methodist enterprise up river also. On all this, Kenneth Scott Latourette made the comment:[26]

> Whatever the denomination, the large majority of the supporting constituencies and the missionaries were from those elements which had been affected by the Evangelical Awakening and kindred revivals . . .

In 1865, R. J. Thomas, a London missionary serving in China, went to Korea as an agent of the National Bible Society of Scotland. He lost his life in a fracas on the beach on landing.[27] Twenty years elapsed before any Protestant missionaries were permitted to reside in the country.

In the 1860s came a development of Protestant missions in Japan, drawn chiefly from American denominations. The American Episcopal Church, the American Presbyterians and the Reformed Church of America were first in the field. The Japanese were still prejudiced against Christian teaching, but there was a desire to learn English and this provided evangelistic contacts.[28]

Until 1872, only ten Japanese had been baptized by Protestant ministers. Neesima, an unusual man, smuggled himself out of Japan and was able to obtain a good education in Christian schools in United States, returning as a missionary to found the Doshisha University.[29] In 1872, the American Baptists sent in two missionaries, one of them a marine (Jonathan Goble) who had been with Commodore Perry in the opening up of Japan by treaty.[30] The Canadian Methodists followed in 1873.[31] Then came the Bible Societies. By 1882, there were five thousand adult church members in Japanese Protestant churches and a beginning had been made.

As in China, the majority of these Christians were under the tutelage of evangelical teachers. Evangelicalism was the dynamic of the societies raised up in the denominations, for neo-Protestantism was still in its incubation stage. Apart from zealous Roman Catholic missionaries, the missionary thrust in the Orient was overwhelmingly evangelical.

Meanwhile, in the 1880s, thousands of university students in the West began to volunteer for missionary service as a result of a revival among students influenced by the ministry of D. L. Moody. They served on every continent.

The Student Volunteers made a contribution to China too. At the time of the 1858-59 Revival, China had been scarcely opened to the Gospel. The China Inland Mission was organized to carry the Word to inland China, and to begin this work the first party had sailed for Shanghai in 1866. In 1875, Hudson Taylor prayed for eighteen missionary reinforcements to raise the mission strength to about fifty; in 1881, he prayed for seventy; and in 1886, he prayed for one hundred more.[32]

Where did Hudson Taylor find his men? As in the Cambridge Seven, he reached for the best and often found them in the universities. W. W. Cassels became a missionary bishop. Within thirty years, the China Inland Mission counted more than six hundred missionaries in two hundred and sixty stations, with nearly five hundred national workers and more than five thousand communicants, though the mission did not set out to build churches. [33]

In the 1880s, the older missionary societies also moved into new territories — the Baptists, Congregationalists, Lutherans, Methodists and Presbyterians. Also, in 1888 the Christian and Missionary Alliance began its operations that were to extend all over China. As yet, there was nothing resembling a China-wide awakening.

As in India and elsewhere, the Young Men's Christian Association organized in China in the middle 1880s. The Y.M.C.A.s were evangelistic, hence enjoyed a rapid growth, stressing Chinese leadership which was immediately forthcoming.[34] H. H. Kung, later Prime Minister of China, in his early days served as a Y.M.C.A. officer—one among many professing Christians (such as Sun Yat-sen or Chiang Kai-shek) in the government of the Republic of China, one full generation afterwards. Christians were being prepared in China for a generation of leadership.

The practical ecumenism of the 1858-59 Revival was felt; the fact that almost all the missionaries in China were of revival-evangelistic background made it very easy to convene them in missionary conference to establish cooperation and comity. In 1890, the second such conference sent out an appeal to the Protestant homelands to equip and send to China a thousand missionaries within five years. The numbers of Chinese communicants were about 50,000; they doubled in ten years, to increase five-fold within twenty-five years.

Japan was the first of the countries of the Orient to experience a revival which touched all of its evangelical folk.

Evangelization had been proceeding slowly in Japan in the 1860s. In 1872, a Week of Prayer sponsored by the World's Evangelical Alliance was held in Yokohama, and there was an encouraging local revival. In 1883, James Ballagh recalled the encouragement of the prayer times of the decade previous, and such was the effect on hearers that an intense revival ensued in all Japanese evangelical circles. Within a short time, the missionaries reported: 'A spirit of religious revival bringing times of refreshing from the presence of the Lord is spreading in Japan.'[35]

The awakening spread to the Aoyama Gakuin in Tokyo, whose staff and students were deeply moved. In 1884, the Week of Prayer at Doshisha University could not be stopped but ran on until March, two hundred students being baptized. The revival spread to Sendai in 1886. 'There were intense emotional upheavals, much confession and restitution, and many testimonies to the joy of new life in Christ.'[36]

Otis Cary has titled the sixth chapter of his history of Christianity in Japan 'Rapid Growth 1883-1888,' when the Protestant enterprise in Japan experienced remarkable growth through 'the beginning of a series of remarkable revivals that exerted a powerful influence upon Christians and through them upon the unbelievers.'[37] Churches became crowded with eager listeners. The word 'rebaiburu' gained a place in the Japanese Christian vocabulary. There were 'tears, sobbings and broken confessions of sin' among these supposed Oriental stoics. The Japanese showed themselves susceptible to the same religious feelings as Westerners.

Concurrently with revival, a dozen societies entered the country. Japanese denominational organizations were then taking shape, such as Nippon Sei Ko Kwai, the Anglican Church of Japan. In 1890, foreign missionary personnel numbered more than five hundred, with about three hundred organized churches and thirty thousand members.[38]

In seven years, adult membership increased from four to thirty thousand, evangelists from a hundred to four hundred, and self-support gained ground among virile Japanese congregations,[39] 'the springtime of Japan and the Church.'

Both Otis Cary (1909) and Iglehart (1959) in turn designated the decade following the period of rapid growth, a period of 'Retarded Growth,' and both attributed the decline to the theological speculations that chilled the faith of the pastors.[40] In the 1890s, a wave of liberalism in theology caused some pastors to leave the ministry, and within ten years, theological students declined in numbers from three hundred to less than one hundred. The optimistic predictions of the full conversion of the Empire to Christianity were not being fulfilled. The Christian faith was less influential in Japan than in China, yet Christianity had ceased to be an alien way of life in the sunrise kingdom.

The pattern was different in nearby Korea. It was in the 1880s that the Evangelicals made an entrance to Korea. American Presbyterians and Methodists bore the brunt of the invasion, though other nationalities and communions participated.[41] Not only was the background of the missionaries largely evangelical but the methods advocated by them were evangelistic, encouraging the Koreans to evangelize the country themselves. In Korea, the ground was being prepared for an evangelical revival on a national scale.

In the 1890s, the Christian and Missionary Alliance tried to enter Indo-China, but failed to win a foothold. In northern Thailand, between 1884 and 1894, membership in the Lao churches increased from 152 to 1841.[42] In southern Thailand, converts were fewer, loyalty to Buddhism being the mark of patriotism. Likewise, in Burma, it was among the Karens rather than the Burmese that an ingathering occurred. Success was also registered among the Kachins, the Shans, and the Chins. Across the Gulf of Bengal, the Anglicans, the Baptists, and the Methodists took up the work begun by the Dutch Reformed, and won thousands of converts from Buddhism and Hinduism in Ceylon.

In all these Buddhist lands, where the Eightfold Way was followed by the few rather than the many who still sought to appease the spirits of animism, the evangelical churches grew slowly. It was not until the twentieth century that the great outpourings of the Spirit descended upon them.

2

THE FIFTH GENERAL AWAKENING

The worldwide Awakening of the early twentieth century came at the end of fifty years of evangelical advance, following the outpouring of the Spirit far and wide in 1858-59 and the 'sixties. Thus it did not represent a recovery from a long night of despair caused by rampant infidelity, as was the case in the days of Wesley. It seemed, rather, a blaze of evening glory at the end of 'the Great Century.'

It was the most extensive Evangelical Awakening of all time, reviving Anglican, Baptist, Congregational, Disciple, Lutheran, Methodist, Presbyterian and Reformed churches and other evangelical bodies throughout Europe and North America, Australasia and South Africa, and their daughter churches and missionary causes throughout Asia, Africa, and Latin America, winning more than five million folk to an evangelical faith in the two years of greatest impact in each country. Indirectly it produced Pentecostalism.

Why did it occur at the time it did? The ways of God are past finding out. One can only surmise. A subtler form of infidelity had arisen, a compromise between Christianity and humanism. A more sophisticated interpretation of human conduct, inspired by Freud, spoke of God as an Illusion.[1]

The prescient widsom of its Author may also account for the sudden spread of the Revival of 1900-1910. Within ten years, the awful slaughter of World War I had begun, and a gentler way of life passed into the twilight of history.

Arnold Toynbee, reminiscing, recalled the trauma of the time, when half his classmates perished in battle. Oneself was a child when the news of the Battle of the Somme threw every family in his native city into mourning for the finest of their fathers and sons and brothers killed in action.[2]

The Awakening was a kind of harvest before the devastation of Christendom. It was Sir Edward Grey who lamented in 1914 that the lights of civilization were going out one by one, not to be lit again in his lifetime. The upheavals of war unloosed the times of revolution on mankind. A biographer of Wilbur Chapman observed:[3]

> As we look back over these extraordinary religious awakenings which . . . so quickened the churches and so effectively pressed the claims of God upon the consciences of multitudes, we cannot escape the conviction that God in gracious providence was reaping a spiritual harvest before He permitted the outburst of revolutionary forces that have overwhelmed the world, impoverished almost every nation, produced economic and social chaos, and stained with dishonor the pride of Christian civilization.
>
> In the history of revivals, it has often been noted that such restoral periods are a warning of, and synchronize with, impending judgment. The harvest is gathered before the field is doomed to death.

The early twentieth century Evangelical Awakening was a worldwide movement. It did not begin with the phenomenal Welsh Revival of 1904-05. Rather its sources were in the springs of little prayer meetings which seemed to arise spontaneously all over the world, combining into the streams of expectation which became a river of blessing in which the Welsh Revival became the greatest cataract.

Meetings for prayer for revival in evangelical gatherings such as Moody Bible Institute and the Keswick Convention greeted the new century—not surprisingly. What was remarkable was that missionaries and national believers in obscure places in India, the Far East, Africa and Latin America seemed moved at the same time to pray for phenomenal revival in their fields and world wide. Most of them had never seen or heard of phenomenal revival occurring on missionfields, and few of them had witnessed it at home. Their experience was limited to reading of past revivals.

The first manifestation of phenomenal revival occurred simultaneously among Boer prisoners of war in places ten thousand miles apart, as far away as Bermuda and Ceylon. The work was marked by extraordinary praying, by faithful preaching, conviction of sin, confession and repentance with lasting conversions and hundreds of enlistments for missionary service. The spirit of Revival spread to South Africa in the throes of economic depression.

Not without significance, an Awakening began in 1900 in the churches of Japan, which had long suffered from a period of retarded growth. It started in an unusually effective movement to prayer, followed by an unusually intensive effort of evangelism, matched by an awakening of Japanese urban masses to the claims of Christ, and such an ingathering that the total membership of the churches almost doubled within the decade. Why did the Japanese Awakening occur in 1900? It would have been impossible four years later when Japan became involved in momentous war with Russia.

Significantly also for the evangelistic follow-up of the general Awakening, the Torrey and Alexander team found that unusual praying had prepared a way for the most fruitful evangelistic ministry ever known in New Zealand and Australia, and the unprecedented success of the campaigns launched Torrey and Alexander (and later Chapman and Alexander) on their worldwide evangelistic crusades,[4] conventionally run but accompanied by revival of the churches.

Gipsy Smith experienced much the same kind of response in his Mission of Peace in war-weary South Africa, successful evangelism provoking an awakening of the population to Christian faith. Gipsy Smith extended his ministry.

Meanwhile worldwide prayer meetings were intensifying. Undoubtedly, the farthest-felt happening of the decade was the Welsh Revival, which began as a local revival in early 1904, moved the whole of Wales by the end of the year, produced the mystic figure of Evan Roberts as leader yet filled simultaneously almost every church in the principality.

The Welsh Revival was the farthest-reaching of the movements of the general Awakening, for it affected the whole of the Evangelical cause in India, Korea and China, renewed revival in Japan and South Africa, and sent a wave of awakening over Africa, Latin America, and the South Seas.

The story of the Welsh Revival is astounding. Begun with prayer meetings of less than a score of intercessors, when it burst its bounds the churches of Wales were crowded for more than two years. A hundred thousand outsiders were converted and added to the churches, the vast majority remaining true to the end. Drunkenness was immediately cut in half, and many taverns went bankrupt. Crime was so diminished that judges were presented with white gloves signifying that there were no cases of murder, assault, rape or robbery or the like to consider. The police became 'unemployed' in many districts. Stoppages occurred in coalmines, not due to unpleasantness between management and workers, but because so many foul-mouthed miners became converted and stopped using foul language that the horses which hauled the coal trucks in the mines could no longer understand what was being said to them, and transportation ground to a halt.

Time and again, the writer has been asked why the Welsh Revival did not last. It did last. The most exciting phase lasted two years. There was an inevitable drifting away of some whose interest was superficial, perhaps one person in forty of the total membership of the Churches. Even critics of the movement conceded that eighty percent of the converts remained in the Churches after five years.

But there was a falling away in Wales. Why? It did not occur among the converts of the 1904 Revival, other than the minority noted. Converts of the Revival continued to be the choicest segment of church life, even in the 1930s, when the writer studied the spiritual life of Wales closely.[5] Two disasters overtook Wales. The first World War slaughtered a high proportion of the generation revived, or converted, or only influenced by the Revival, leaving a dearth of men in the churches; the coal mines of Wales were hit in the 1920s by tragic unemployment, which continued into the thirties in the Depression; and the class under military age during the war, infants during the Revival, espoused the gospel of Marxism. The Aneurin Bevans replaced the Keir Hardies in the party[6].

There was yet another reason. The Welsh Revival took scripture knowledge for granted, and preaching thus deemed superfluous was at a minimum. The Welsh revival constituency was ill-prepared for a new onslaught of anti-evangelicalism which captured a generation of otherwise disillusioned Welshmen. The province of Ulster moved into the place held by the principality of Wales as a land of evangelistic activities.

The story of the Welsh Revival has often been told. Most Christian people, including scholars, have been unaware of the extent of the Awakening which followed in the English-speaking world—in the United Kingdom, the United States, Canada, South Africa, Australia and faraway New Zealand.

The Archbishop of Canterbury called for a nationwide day of prayer. Thirty English bishops declared for the Revival after one of their number, deeply moved, told of confirming 950 new converts in a country parish church. The Revival swept Scotland and Ireland. Under Albert Lunde, also a friend of the researcher in later years, a movement began in Norway described by Bishop Berggrav as the greatest revival of his experience. It affected Sweden, Finland, and Denmark, Lutherans there saying that it was the greatest movement of the Spirit since the Vikings were evangelized. It broke out in Germany, France and other countries of Europe, marked by prayer and confession.

It is difficult to count converts in the Church of England, but, in the years 1903-1906, the other Protestant denominations gained ten percent, or 300,000.[7]

When news of the Awakening reached the United States, huge conferences of ministers gathered in New York and Chicago and other cities to discuss what to do when the Awakening began. Soon the Methodists in Philadelphia had 6101 new converts in trial membership; the ministers of Atlantic City claimed that only fifty adults remained professedly unconverted in a population of 60,000. Churches in New York City took in hundreds on a single Sunday— in one instance, 364 were received into membership, 286 new converts, 217 adults, 134 men, 60 heads of families.

The 1905 Awakening rolled through the South like a tidal wave, packing churches for prayer and confession, adding hundreds to membership rolls—First Baptist in Paducah added a thousand in a couple of months and the old pastor died of overwork. Believers' baptisms among the Southern Baptists rose twenty-five per cent in one year. Other denominations shared equally in the Awakening.

In the Middle West, churches were suddenly inundated by great crowds of seekers. The 'greatest revivals in their history' were reported by Methodists in town after town; the Baptists and others gained likewise. Everyone was so busy in Chicago that the pastors decided to hold their own meetings and help one another deal with the influx. Every store and factory closed in Burlington, Iowa, to permit employees to attend services of intercession and dedication. The mayor of Denver declared a day of prayer: by 10 a.m., churches were filled; at 11.30, almost every store closed; 12,000 attended prayer meetings in downtown theatres and halls; every school closed; the Colorado Legislature closed. The impact was felt for a year.

In the West, great demonstrations marched through the streets of Los Angeles. United meetings attracted attendance of 180,000. The Grand Opera House was filled at midnight as drunks and prostitutes were seeking salvation. For three hours a day, business was practically suspended in Portland, Oregon, bank presidents and bootblacks attending prayer meetings while two hundred department stores in agreement closed from 11 till 2.

Churches of the various denominations, town or country, were moved from Newfoundland to British Columbia across Canada, in spontaneous prayer or ardent evangelism.

Church membership in the United States in seven major Protestant denominations increased by more than two million in five years (870,389 new communicants in 1906) and continued rising.[8] This did not include the gains of the younger denominations of Pentecostal or Holiness dynamic whose rate of increase was considerably greater.

It is naturally difficult to estimate the gains in the Dutch Reformed Church in South Africa, for most converts therein already possessed family affiliation. The Methodist Church increased by thirty percent in the three years of revival.[9] No doubt, the same patterns applied in New Zealand, Australia and South Africa, all stirred by the Welsh Revival.

The writer has visited all the States of India, has addressed more than a million people there, and has lectured in twenty of their theological colleges, and to hundreds of missionaries and national pastors. And yet he encountered only one who knew of the extent of the Indian Revival of 1905-1906, a retired professor of theology. Yet the Awakening in India moved every province and the Christian population increased by seventy percent, sixteen times as fast as the Hindu, the Protestant rate of increase being almost double that of the Roman Catholic.[10] In many places, meetings went on for five to ten hours.

In Burma, 1905 'brought ingathering quite surpassing anything known in the history of the mission.' The A.B.M.U. baptized 2000 Karens that year, 200 being the average. In a single church, 1340 Shans were baptized in December, 3113 in all being added in the 'marvelous ingathering.'[11]

The story of the Korean Revival of 1907 has been told and retold. It is less well-known that the Revival came in three waves, 1903, 1905 and 1907—the membership of the Churches quadrupling within a decade, the national Church being created from almost nothing by the movement. Since then, the Korean Churches have maintained the impetus.[12]

The revival campaigns of Jonathan Goforth in Manchuria have been recorded and published, but the extent of the Awakening in China between the Boxer Uprising and the 1911 Revolution has not been apprehended. China's greatest living evangelist, survivor of the China-wide Awakening of 1927-1939, told the writer that he had not even heard of the Awakening (in every province in the 1900s) apart from the post-Boxer revulsion. Yet the number of Protestant communicants doubled in a decade to quarter of a million, twice that figure for the total Evangelical community.[13]

In Indonesia,[14] the numbers of Evangelicals, 100,000 in 1903, trebled in the decade of general Awakening to 300,000, and in subsequent movements of phenomenal power, the number of believers on one little island (Nias) surpassed the latter figure, winning two-thirds the population. Protestant membership in Malagasia increased sixty-six percent in the years of Revival, 1905-1915. And pioneering success was achieved in the newly-opened Philippines.

The Awakening had limited effect in the Latin American countries: unusual revival in Brazil, phenomenal awakening in Chile, with Evangelical membership in both countries starting to climb—until in our times it passed the number of practising Roman Catholics; pioneering continued in other republics with sparse results but promise of future harvest, since realised.

The Edinburgh World Missionary Conference recognized that more progress had been made in all Africa in the first decade of the twentieth century than experienced hitherto. Protestant communicants in the African mission fields increased in 1903-1910 from 300,000 to 500,000, there having been many awakenings in various parts in those years.[15] But the full impact of the Welsh Revival was not felt until the war years, when phenomenal revival occurred among the Africans. In the next half century, the increase was double that of the general population.

It was most significant that the Awakening of the 1900s was ecumenical, in the best senses of the word.[16] It was thoroughly interdenominational. The foregoing narratives have provided instances of Anglican, Baptist, Brethren, Congregational, Disciple, Lutheran, Methodist, Presbyterian and Reformed congregations sharing in the Revival. There is a total lack of evidence of any response on the part of Roman Catholic or Greek Orthodox communities, but this is not surprising, for it was so in the days of the Puritans, of Wesley, of Finney, and of Moody. Only in the mid-twentieth century, when their changing attitude to Scripture has accompanied a changing attitude to dissent, have heretofore non-evangelical church bodies been affected by evangelical movements.

During the Welsh Revival, there occurred charismatic phenomena—uncanny discernment, visions, trances—but no glossolalia.[17] There was an outbreak of speaking in tongues in India in the aftermath of the Awakening. In 1907, there was speaking in tongues among converts of the Revival in Los Angeles, from which Pentecostalism spread widely.

There is no telling what might have happened in society had not the First World War absorbed the energies of the nations in the aftermath of this Edwardian Awakening. The time, talent, and treasure of the people were pre empted in any struggle for national existence, and what little is over is devoted to the welfare of the fighting men and the victims of war. This was the case in World War I.

Even so, no one could possibly say that the Awakenings of the 1900s in Great Britain or the United States were without social impact. In Britain, there was utter unanimity on the part of observers regarding 'the high ethical character' of the movement. The renewed obedience to the four great social commandments reduced crime, promoted honesty, inculcated truthfulness and produced chastity. Drunkenness and gambling were sharply curtailed. It was the same in the United States, for a wave of morality went over the country, producing a revival of righteousness. Corruption in state and civic government encountered a setback which was attributed by observers in church and state to the Great Awakening. For a dozen years, the country was committed in degree to civic and national integrity, until new forces of corruption triumphed again in the 1920s.[18]

In such awakenings, it seems that the individual response is much more immediate than the social response. British church leaders acclaimed 'the high ethical character of the movement.' The then largest denomination in the United States declared in review that the public conscience had been revived, overthrowing corrupt officials, crossing the party lines, electing Governors, Senators, Assemblymen, Mayors and District Attorneys of recognized honesty. The people of Philadelphia 'threw the rascals out' and put in a dedicated mayor. Washington Gladden, the 'father of the social gospel,' was assured that the general awakening was creating a moral revolution in the lives of the people. In other countries, profound impressions were made.

What was the social effect outside Western Protestantism? On mission fields, the missionaries multiplied their schools and hospitals. In twenty years, pupils in Christian schools in India doubled to 595,725; 90% of all nurses were Christian, mostly trained at mission hospitals. In China, missionaries pioneered secondary and higher education and laid the foundations of the medical service; the beginnings of the African educational systems and medical service were due likewise to the missionary impulse.[19]

The scholarly Prof. Paul Ramsey, in introducing Gabriel Vahanian's treatise on the fatuous 'Death of God' debate, asserted: '. . . every revival of Christianity in the past three hundred years has revived less of it, and each was less and less an enduring revival.'[20]

It is not easy to imagine what criteria were used on which to base such a remarkable opinion. If Christendom were meant by Christianity, it is easy to scan the scope of a given revival and to gauge the number of people influenced thereby. The Puritan Revival influenced fewer people in a smaller territory than were influenced by the Revival of Whitefield and Wesley's days in the British Isles and American Colonies, while the Awakenings of 1792 and 1830 in the same English-speaking territories were even more extensive.

Again, if the number of converts is the test, it is certain that the number of converts added to Methodist churches alone in seven fruitful years in the Revival of 1858-59 far exceeded the total won in Wesley's lifetime, without calculating numbers added to membership of other Churches; the same could be said of the Revivals of 1792 and 1830.

Again, the 1858-59 Revival moved the United States and United Kingdom, affected Scandinavia and other parts of Europe as well as the churches of South Africa, Australasia and parts of India.[21] It was as worldwide as Evangelicalism. But this present treatise has shown that the extent of the Awakening of 1900-1910 far exceeded that of the 1858-1859 Revival. The numbers converted certainly matched those of the mid-nineteenth century in Britain and United States —not to mention unprecedented ingatherings overseas.

It would be wearisome to extend the argument further to show that the growth of the Church in Brazil or Indonesia or Korea or Congo exceeds anything experienced three hundred years ago. True, Christianity is in decline in certain countries, but it is not because of Evangelical Revival— rather the neglect and lack of it.

If Christian faith were meant by Christianity, it can be stated boldly that successive Evangelical Awakenings are each more radically proto-New Testament in emphasis— the Reformers more evangelical than the Lollards, and the Puritans more evangelical than the Reformers, eighteenth century Revivalists more evangelistic than the Puritans and nineteenth century Evangelists more enterprising than their predecessors; while twentieth century ecumenists sincerely credit twentieth century Pentecostals with abounding zeal.

3

TAIKYO DENDO IN JAPAN

In early 1900, a call went out for a General Conference of Protestant missionaries in Japan, the first since the historic year of awakening in 1883, when, following an extended week of prayer, an extraordinary work of revival and evangelism spread throughout Japan, a seven year period of rapid growth when church membership rose from 5,000 to 30,000 and the springtime of the Church was acclaimed.[1]

This period of rapid growth had been followed by one of retarded growth, the last decade of the nineteenth century, in which the Evangelicals increased by only six thousand to a total of thirty-seven thousand.[2] There were at least two reasons for this—a political reaction against westernization and a spiritual sabotage of evangelical theology.[3]

There came a recovery at the beginning of the twentieth century, leading to great conferences of prayer in Tokyo in October 1900. A spirit of ardent prayer fell on the Churches. With the summoning of the General Conference went a call to prayer that 'the Spirit of the Lord prepare the way for a meeting of Pentecostal power.' The Japanese Evangelical Alliance met in the spring of 1900, and proposed a united evangelistic campaign.[4] The Missionary Conference agreed both to mobilizing prayer and to organizing evangelism. So the early months of 1901 were spent in meetings to revive the spiritual life of the believers.[5]

The 1900 movement of prayer was followed by a united evangelistic campaign in May-June of 1901. It was undergirded by faithful prayer and armed by scriptural preaching. Called Taikyo Dendo, literally 'Aggressive Evangelism,' it was translated 'Forward Movement' in English.[6] Tokyo was divided into five districts, and more than fifty churches, sixty pastors and a dozen missionaries participated, aided by twenty seven bands of witnessing lay people, 360 persons in all, marching through the streets singing and engaging in a house-to-house visitation. Three hundred thousand tracts were distributed, along with half a million handbills describing the meetings and giving directions.

Prayer meetings were held in the afternoons, as many as eight hundred intercessors gathering at one time. In the evenings were held the public evangelistic meetings in which a simple Gospel message was preached. Cards were handed out to inquirers, and the contacts were followed up by pastors and people. Professed converts were enrolled in catechetical classes for two years.

It was reported that 11,626 had attended local prayer meetings to intercede for blessing, while 84,247 had attended the preaching of the Gospel in Tokyo, of whom 5,307 made a profession of faith.[7]

By mid-1901,[8] missionaries in Japan did not hesitate to describe the movement as 'Pentecost in Japan.' Anglican, Baptist, Methodist, Presbyterian and other denominations cooperated very freely in Tokyo.[9] In the Kyobashi district alone more than a thousand people 'repented of their sins,' and turned to God.

Japanese took the initiative in the preaching of the Good News of Jesus Christ, the workers participating being of the best classes, including members of the Imperial Diet. Usually meetings were held in churches, but there were many street rallies, and in all of them excellent order prevailed, without a trace of fanaticism.

The greatest benefits were reaped by little suburban churches, which received more eager inquirers than they could handle. Some pastors came to the committee to say: 'We have enough, so please don't help us any more. Our houses will not hold the people.'

In little over five weeks, five thousand were enrolled, and during 1901, there were 15,000 inquirers in all Japan, besides countless thousands who were influenced in ideals. The Taikyo Dendo spread from Tokyo to Yokohama, Sendai, Matsuyama, Nagasaki, Osaka, and other cities as the prayer meetings multiplied and preaching increased. In Yokohama, for example, in June 1901, a great spiritual awakening began, with two thousand inquirers instructed. Other cities saw the same results.[10] It was a time of great challenge to the workers, and of overwhelming joy to the intercessors.

Indeed they were overwhelmed, for no less than 17,939 converts were added in a short time to their churches. The Protestant forces, which had numbered less than 40,000, added a full 25,000 in twelve months, according to reliable missionary opinion.[11] None could say that a great spiritual awakening ill-suited the Japanese.

In the far north of Japan, Christians in Sapporo reported sixty-five inquirers, of whom sixteen were baptized shortly afterward. The attendances at the churches quadrupled and a new Y.M.C.A. was built as a result. It was said that before the Taikyo Dendo, a union meeting of the three Sapporo churches attracted two people—while during and after there was extraordinary attendance at the union prayer meeting in the city.[12]

Taikyo Dendo was extended beyond a year.[13] It continued operative until the outbreak of war between Russia and Japan in 1904, and even a great war did not noticeably slow down its drive. Another awakening followed the news of the Welsh Revival, the news reaching Japan during the war fever.

In 1906, the Taikyo Dendo was still making great progress. Evangelist Taniguchi and Pastor Kaneko held united meetings in Shinshu, 200 inquirers being registered, and like work was performed in other districts by other agents.[14] In October, a stirring revival was reported at Takasaki, and one in November at Maebashi in Joshu Province. This continued into 1907, when a similar work was reported in Miyazaki.[15]

Most of the preaching of the Good News during Taikyo Dendo was accomplished by Japanese.[16] A graduate of Moody Bible Institute, one Seimatsu Kimura, appeared as a full-time evangelist—an unconventional preacher who conducted his mass meetings in vigorous style, a thousand inquirers enrolled in his two-week series of tent meetings in Tokyo. Another dynamic graduate of Moody Bible Institute was Juji Nakada, who stressed a Wesleyan view of holiness.[17]

Serious controversy arose between two men of outstanding native abilities.[18] Masahisa Uemura rose to challenge Danjo Ebina, a liberal Congregational pastor, to debate essential doctrines. As a result, the Japanese Evangelical Alliance excluded Ebina—who was reconciled again in 1906.

Y.M.C.A. workers rendered selfless service to Japanese soldiers during the war, and an unprecedented gift of ten thousand yen was made to this work by the Emperor.[19] After the war, missionaries worked among discharged soldiers, one in Tokyo corresponding with a hundred inquirers.

Following the war, a famine hit northeastern Japan in 1905 and 1906. Christians moved quickly to help.[20] Okayama Christian Orphanage, founded by Juji Ishi, took 1200 children of impoverished parents, a similar number being helped in Sendai. Hundreds of Japanese impressed by such selfless service were received into the faith.

During and after the Taikyo Dendo, outstanding American and British churchmen visited Japan and preached in the mass evangelistic meetings arranged by the Japanese local churches. Among them were John R. Mott, William Booth, Reuben Torrey and Wilbur Chapman. In October of 1901, fifteen hundred young men (a thousand students) were won to Christ in John R. Mott's meetings.[21] Subsequently, Japanese Student Volunteer teams conducted an effective evangelistic 'drive.' General Booth held only nine services in a 1907 Japanese series, but 969 inquirers were helped.[22]

To the influence of the Welsh Revival upon missionaries was added the direct influence of the Korean Revival on the Japanese. Not only evangelism, but local quickenings of the churches continued. In 1907, there were local awakenings throughout Japan, including one at Hiroshima among soldiers in camp.[23] One of the most striking evidences of the great work of the Holy Spirit was witnessed in Hokkaido, the northerly island of Japan.[24] A 'wonderful revival' was reported having started in January 1907 in the Tokachi Prison and swept through that institution until nearly every prisoner, as well as officer and guard, had made public confession of faith in Jesus Christ. From there, it was carried to other parts of the island, accompanied by many remarkable healings of bodily sickness.

By 1909, there were approximately 600 organized churches in Japan,[25] a quarter of which were self-supporting. The membership exceeded 70,000, served by 500 ordained and 600 unordained men, and 200 Bible women. A hundred thousand pupils were taught in a thousand Sunday Schools. There were 4000 students in boarding schools, 8000 in day schools, 400 in theological colleges and 250 in women's Bible schools, plus a leavening of secular higher education.

Much of this progress was attributable to Taikyo Dendo, in which the Christians were never more united, and to an awakening renewed by news from Wales and Korea. A local missionary authority assessed the movement thus:
1. Christianity again secured the attention of the Japanese population. 2. Many people were brought into personal relationship with Jesus Christ. 3. New life and courage were injected into the Church in Japan. 4. It was an ecumenical movement in the best sense of that word. 5. Christians were made aware that the Gospel alone is the power of God to salvation. 6. The movement proved that when the Church is revived, the money for its work is available locally.[26]

Taikyo Dendo was more than a well-planned evangelistic campaign.[27] It was a movement of a spontaneous nature— prayer, followed by mass evangelism well-presented by the whole Church. The Edinburgh Missionary Conference noted that 'in Japan, notwithstanding many difficulties and discouragements, the past ten years have without doubt been the most fruitful in spiritual results ever known in the field.'

The number of Evangelical Christians in Japan in 1900 doubled to become seventy-five thousand in 1910. Their influence was out of all proportion to their numbers, tenfold in Parliament, threefold among army officers, and an overwhelming proportion in social welfare work,[28] in which the Salvation Army entering Japan had performed notable service during the Russo-Japanese War.

It is significant that Taikyo Dendo anticipated a Latin American movement of fifty years later, Evangelism-in-Depth, in emphasizing the role of every Christian in witness rather than that of an evangelist and his team; in preparing all believers as soul-winners instead of training an elite group to counsel inquirers; in multiplying the number of active evangelists rather than multiplying the number of hearers for the evangelist; in urging 'go and preach' instead of 'come and hear'; and in mobilizing the Church instead of doing the work for its members. This was true also of a wider campaign held 1914-1917.[29]

One outcome of the period of revival in Japan was the founding of the Oriental Missionary Society and the growth of the Japanese Holiness Church.[30] Charles Cowman and his wife came to Japan in 1901, and worked with Juji Nakada. Tetsusaburo Sasao, a talented evangelist and teacher, one of the men trained by Barclay Buxton of the Japan Evangelistic Band, joined forces with them.

Japanese Christians were numerically weak, but an ardent spirit of nationalism moved them. In 1879, Masahisa Uemura had been ordained in Presbyterian fellowship. He was convinced that the evangelization of Japan should be done by an indigenous body of believers.[31] Uemura founded a theological seminary in Tokyo in 1904, a spiritual expression of rising nationalism. Secular nationalism was being expressed also. Reaction was already setting in, for in 1911, the Government declared that school children must participate in the national Shinto shrine worship. Some refused the explanation that only the veneration of ancestors was involved; many did not, and a problem rose to vex their conscience.

4

THE KOREAN PENTECOST

The awakenings of the 1900s in Korea were indigenous, of missionary derivation and part of a worldwide movement.

The Reverend R. A. Hardie (a Canadian Colleges medical missionary) arrived in 1890 in Korea. He became associated with Southern Methodists in their mission in 1898,[1] at a time when a noticeable turning to Christian profession occurred.

In August 1903, a group of seven missionaries engaged in a week of study and prayer at Wonsan, including Hardie who had for years been yearning to see Koreans convicted of sin and led to repentance and faith evidencing the fruits thereof, but up to that time in his work 'had not seen any examples of plain, unmistakable, and lasting conversion.'[2]

It thus appeared that accessions between 1895 and 1903 included numbers of people entering the Church as interested disciples rather than regenerate members.

In view of the great need, Dr. Hardie confessed his faults before the missionary body and before the Korean church, leading to confessions of failure by other Christians.[3] Soon after, in October of 1903, the missionary advocate, Fredrik Franson, arrived in Korea.[4] Hardie at once began to prepare for Franson's ministry. When he arrived, a week of meetings was held in which the confession of sins continued to be an outstanding feature of the meetings, yet without abuse. During this awakening, many confessed the theft of goods but offered restitution to the Lord and not to church members (at their request), thus providing the funds for employing a full-time colporteur in the district.[5]

The results of this earliest movement were seen in the transformation of the lives of church members, whose morality was lifted to a high plane of sincerity and purity never before attained. Their brotherhood in this common religious experience led to immediate acceleration of growth in church membership.[6] There were other benefits gained, for in this first wave of revival, Franson taught Hardie and his friends the value of prevailing prayer, for he would cry 'O Father, Thou canst do it; Thou wilt do it; Thou shalt do it.'[7]

The Wonsan Conference was repeated in 1904. In 1905, the armies of Japan defeated Russia and gained control of Korea as spoils of war. A national indignation affected the Christians, and many looked to the churches to provide an organized resistance. Many missionary and church leaders preached forbearance and forgiveness, hence the angrier agitators tried to undermine their work.[8]

The second wave of revival swept Korea in 1905-1906. Spiritual awakenings began in North Korea in 1905. There were remarkable meetings in the city of Pyongyang, both Central and South Gate churches crowded out, seven hundred converts enrolled in two weeks.[9] It was then described as a spreading fire, a continuing religious awakening, the hundreds of conversions not being due to any sudden impulse. More conversions than in any previous year were reported from all over Korea.

In 1906, Dr. Howard Agnew Johnston brought news of the awakenings in Wales and in India.[10] Half the missionaries in Korea were Presbyterian, from the United States, Australia and Canada, deeply moved by the accounts of revival among the Welsh Presbyterians and on their Asian mission fields.

In South Korea, the awakening that began at Mokpo early in 1906 grew steadily until not one square foot in the local building remained unoccupied by the packed congregation, the church being enlarged to double its size.[11] Men stood six deep eagerly waiting their turn to testify of sins forgiven, differences reconciled, and power received.[12]

Dr. S. A. Moffett reported from Pyongyang in 1906:[13] 'We are having another great movement this year, not only in the north but also in the south.' At the New Year, four thousand attended evangelistic services in Pyongyang out of 20,000 population. In North Pyongyang Province, 6507 adherents increased to 11,943, an 83% increase.[14]

In the capital, Seoul, various denominations in 1906 united in the work for the first time and a thousand converts were enrolled.[15] John R. Mott addressed 6000 men in a three-and-a-half hour meeting, 200 inquirers awaiting instruction.[16]

George Heber Jones,[17] a devout Methodist, had worked in Chemulpo without a convert for his travail, but in 1906 he was preaching to as many as 900 in a service, and there were ten thousand Christians in the area. On the island of Kangwha, he reported a turning to Christ with hundreds of converts in the autumn of 1906, and twenty-seven churches catered for the 2500 Christians.[18]

All these were the fruit of the second wave. The coming of the third wave of Revival was imminent. It commenced in North Korea[19] During August of 1906, various missionaries had met at Pyongyang for a week of prayer and of Bible study, led by Dr. R A. Hardie, the Canadian who had already experienced personal reviving[20] All of them shared a deep concern for the need of the country in its time of humiliation. They studied the First Epistle of John, which afterwards became their text-book in revival work. Refreshed themselves, they planned intensive Bible study for the Korean churches. They gave themselves so much to their task that, during the wintertime, social and recreational affairs lost all of their appeal for them.[21]

It was customary for representatives of area churches to come from far and wide at the New Year[22] for Bible study. In spite of tensions, a strange new spirit entered the meeting of fifteen hundred men. So many men wanted to pray that the leader told the whole audience: 'If you want to pray like that, all pray.' The effect was beyond description—not confusion, but a vast harmony of sound and spirit, like the noise of the surf in an ocean of prayer[23] As the prayer continued, an intense conviction of sin settled on the meeting, giving way to bitter weeping over their misdeeds.

As Lord William Cecil told a London newspaper, an elder arose and confessed a grudge against a missionary colleague and asked for forgiveness.[24] The missionary stood to pray but reached only the address to Deity: 'Aboji!' 'Father!' when, with a rush, a power from without seemed to take hold of the meeting. The Europeans described its manifestations as terrifying. Nearly everyone present was seized with the most poignant sense of mental anguish; before each one, his sins seemed to be rising in condemnation of his life. Some were springing to their feet, and pleading for an opportunity to relieve their consciences by making their abasement known; and others were silent, but rent with agony, clenching their fists and striking their heads against the ground in the struggle to resist the Power that was forcing them painfully and agonizingly to confess their misdeeds.[25]

From eight in the evening until two in the morning, it went on, until the missionaries—horror-struck at some of the sins confessed, frightened by the presence of a Power which could work such wonders, reduced to tears by sympathy with the mental agony of their Korean disciples whom they loved so dearly—stopped the meeting.[26]

Some went home to sleep, but many of the Koreans spent the night awake, some in prayer, others in terrible spiritual conflict. Next day, the missionaries hoped that the storm was over and that the comforting teaching of the Holy Word would bind up the wounds of yesternight, but again the same anguish, the same confession—and so it went on for days.

In meetings following, conviction of sin and reconciliation of enemies continued. The heathen Koreans were astounded and a powerful impulse of evangelism was felt. Not only was there deep confession, but much restitution.[27] The movement achieved lasting results. After fifteen years in Pyongyang, one church had a thousand members and the others shared as many, while between 1700 and 2000 attended the Wednesday prayer meetings regularly.[28]

Nine-tenths of the students in Union Christian College in Pyongyang professed conversion in February 1907.[29] A large number of the converts became evangelists with a zeal for the Cross, carrying the fires of revival not only to the city, and nearby country churches, but also as far as Chemulpo and Kongju.[30] The revival did for the characters of some what two years of training could not have done.

The delegates to the Winter Bible Class went back to their homes and carried the revival to their various churches. Everywhere phenomena were the same. There was deep conviction of sin, followed by confession and restitution, a notable feature of all gatherings being the audible prayer en masse —a mode of intercession entirely new.[31]

After the severe judgment, benefit followed. Practically every evangelical church in all of Korea received blessing. Missionaries claimed that the effects were uniformly wholesome, save where believers resisted the Spirit or deceived the brethren. An elder, for example, struggled with his conviction night after night, but received no peace. Then gradually he lost interest and was removed from office; the confession of a woman exposed his immorality. As he sank lower and lower, he became a brothel owner, commercializing his interest in vice.[32] Yet good news predominated.[33]

In five years of rapid growth, 1906-1910, the net gain for all the churches of Korea was 79,221, which was more than the total of members in Japan after half a century of Protestant effort, or twice the number of the Protestants in China in the first eighty years of mission work. By 1912, there were approximately 300,000 Korean church members in a total population of twelve millions.[34]

The Student Volunteer Movement in 1910 cited evidences of 'the present day work of the Holy Spirit in Korea,' noting (first) the unity and the cooperation which prevailed among Christians; (second) the remarkable numerical growth of the Churches; (third) the wonderful religious awakening of 1907 which affected 50,000 converts; (fourth) the noteworthy interest in the Word of God; (fifth) the dedication of national Christians to service, including generous giving; and (sixth) the wonderful prayer life of the Korean Church.[35]

Regarding quality of results, Bishop C. M. Harris of the Methodist Church averred that general effects following the movement were wholly good.[36] The whole church was raised to a higher spiritual level. There had been an almost entire absence of fanaticism because of previous careful instruction in the Bible. There were found greater congregations searching out the Word of God. Drunkards, gamblers, adulterers, murderers, thieves, self-righteous Confucianists and others had been made into new men in Christ, he said.[37]

There was a curious evaluation of the Korean Revival given by Prof. George T. Ladd of Yale University, a strange amalgam of his enthusiasm for all things Japanese, distaste for all things Korean, acceptance of Freudian values and rejection of Christian views.[38] He was the guest in Korea of Prince Ito, Japanese Governor-General, and he had been received by the Emperor Meiji, who granted him the highest orders of chivalry ever given to a foreigner.[39]

Prof. Ladd visited a missionary family in Pyongyang in April 1907, after the excitement of the meetings had died down and the churches were occupied in regular worship. His information was received second-hand—missionaries' accounts interpreted from the official government position, and his conclusions were governed by his attitudes:[40]

> The 'Great Revival' of 1906-07, which added so much to the encouragement of the missionaries and to the number of their converts, can best be understood in its most characteristic features when viewed in the light of what has been said about the nature of the Koreans themselves

Prof. Ladd assumed that the confessions of the Korean penitents under the compulsion of the Revival were more a proof of the corruption of the Korean character than of the power of Truth. The incidents of extreme agitation he set as the norm instead of the unusual. He deemed the attitude of the missionaries too indulgent of the Koreans, and not sufficiently generous towards the Japanese.

It could have been said that a number of the missionaries were inclined to regard Japanese rule as one way of bringing Korea into the twentieth century; nevertheless, they were profoundly sympathetic with the sufferings of their Korean friends during the worst times of national suppression. The American Academy reviewed Ladd's book:[41]

> Too much of this book is a narrative of personal experiences of no interest to the general reader, and at times it must be doubted whether the close connection of the writer with the Japanese authorities may not account for his not seeing many things that have been only too evident to most observers. The general attitude in all the chapters is decidedly pro-Japanese.

Following the great Awakening of the year 1907, it became the normal and accepted practice to hold an evangelistic campaign in each church or circuit at least once a year. The greater part of the responsibility fell upon the Koreans, many of whom developed unusual ability in this line of operation, so indigenous evangelism increased.[42]

The Korean Presbyterian Church was set up in the post-Revival period, a Board of Foreign Missions organized also. Intense efforts were made to evangelize not only the people of Korea but also the Koreans living in Russian Siberia and Chinese Manchuria and overseas.[43]

Illiterate adults as they became Christian were required to learn to read Korean in a simple phonetic alphabet for admission to membership.[44] A further inducement arose when Christians in the country, close-cropped rather than top-knotted, were challenged by Korean patriots to prove that they were Korean Christians rather than Japanese collaborators by reciting the Scriptures! These factors accomplished an almost 100% actual literacy among the Christians in a short space of time. Christians took the lead in Korean life.

An intensive, country-wide effort to win new believers was put forth by all churches in 1909-1910. It began with a small group of missionaries in Songdo, in July of 1909. The American Methodists in 1900 had mounted a campaign to win a million souls in the United States by an organized crusade, but without much success. One of the Methodist missionaries toured the circuit churches, asking the newly revived people to pray for 50,000 converts in that district during the coming year. The Mission Board decided on 200,000 for Christ as a worthy target for the Methodists. In October 1909, the General Council of Evangelical Missions met in Seoul and decided upon a million converts. So far it was a missionary scheme, full of genuine zeal, but marked with the characteristics of its origin in American promotion. The Council had thus adopted Finney's principle that 'Revival is nothing more than the right use of the appropriate means.' The world evangelists, Chapman and Alexander, arrived the first day to launch the great crusade.[45] All that human zeal could do was done, and all was set to win the million, as decided by the praying committee.

It proved to be very different to the Awakening of 1907. The Rev. James E. Adams made a report of the evangelistic campaign held in Taegu during the Million Souls Movement which followed the decline of the Revival proper. Every night the church building was well-filled by a thousand or so, and between 400 and 500 professed conversion and gave their names and addresses. Only one tenth of the inquirers were successfully reached and not all of them were added to the local church or any other congregation.[46]

Statistically, the outcome was cruelly disappointing. Instead of the 200,000 converts, the Southern Methodists won 2,122. Instead of the 1,000,000 converts, the whole Council together won 15,805—for other times, a goodly accession. Clark described the Million Souls Movement as a worked-up campaign with too little antecedent preparation.[47] That it was a worked-up campaign seems certain, but not to say that there was no prayer, no powerful preaching, no preparation. It seemed just that the Holy Spirit would not surrender His prerogatives for a Pentecost to anyone. In the next decade occurred nine lean years. It was obvious that the Revival was over, the Awakening ended.

The Korean Revival of 1903-1908 had its full effect upon church growth in Korea. From 1895 onwards, there was a significant ingathering in both Methodist and Presbyterian fields of a folk who were to become the subjects of reviving. In 1903, not only were some congregations revived but an acceleration of church growth occurred—seen clearly in any graph.[48] This continued steadily through the second phase of revival in 1905-1906, then sharply accelerated again in 1907 as a result of the third phase of revival, which continued till the programmed Million Souls Movement, after which growth of the Christian community declined and that of communicants decelerated for a few years. In some areas and in certain periods, the movement into the churches resembled a folk movement.

Sixty years afterward, the Korean Revival was still recognized as the spiritual birth of the Korean Church. At the Berlin Congress on Evangelism, one of the most stirring addresses reverted to the Revival.[49] It is a mistake however to speak only of the Revival of 1907, in view of the ingathering of 1895, the limited revival of 1903, the more general revivals of 1905, and then the explosive awakening of 1907. And it seems necessary to separate the evangelistic campaign of 1910-1911 (which neither revived the Church nor yet produced significant church growth) from the three-fold Awakening which followed the seven years of providential ingathering between 1895 and 1902.

It is significant that the evangelists raised up by the early twentieth century awakenings became outstanding leaders in Korean Christianity. A prime example may be found in Keil Sun-ju, a leader in the Revival in Pyungyang, famed afterwards as an evangelist and a Korean patriot, his name a household word in church and state. Evangelists and ardent pastors espoused the cause of self-determination.

At the Edinburgh Conference of 1910,[50] it was declared: 'the Korean Revival . . . has been a genuine Pentecost,' for Korean church membership quadrupled in a decade,[51] and it continued to rise, giving to the one per cent Christians in the population an influence far beyond their numbers. Within thirty years, Protestants in Korea numbered three hundred thousand. This nation moved by revival rapidly became the most evangelized part of the Orient.

William N. Blair has speculated upon what might have happened in Korea had the Christian Church yielded to the temptation of resisting the Japanese by carnal rather than by spiritual methods.[52] The country wanted a leader and the Christian Church was the most influential single organization in Korea. The Koreans would have flocked behind the banner of the Cross, and some Constantine might have arisen to use such a banner. But the result would have been a worldly Church, not a spiritual one.

Instead, the Korean Church retained its zeal for God while maintaining its loyalty to country. The Korean Church became self-supporting in a way unknown in the Orient.[53] The Korean church members became enthusiastic in witnessing and generous in giving. More than thirty years went by with Japanese military power in control of their country, but their faith never dimmed. In Korea, a persecuted Church provided the spiritual backbone for a nation.

5

THE CHINESE QUICKENING

In the last decade of the nineteenth century, the Empire of China suffered humiliation after humiliation at the hands of foreign powers.[1] The rising anti-foreign feeling became directed against missionaries as well as other foreigners.

In 1900 came the Boxer movement. It cannot be described as a Rebellion, seeing that it was encouraged by the Imperial Government of China. On the last day of 1899, the Boxers killed a British missionary.[2] The Empress gave an order to execute all foreigners. A blood bath ensued, in which one hundred or more missionaries were done to death along with thousands of their Chinese Christian converts.[3]

The Western Powers intervened with strong military forces and captured Peking. The old order was doomed. The Chinese Christians had acquitted themselves bravely in their hour of martyrdom and persecution, so much curiosity and interest was aroused in the hearts of acquaintances. An itinerating bishop reported that all the churches were crowded to capacity,[4] with increased opportunities of preaching.

The twentieth century Awakening in China, it seems, occurred in three phases: there was a prayer movement between 1900 and 1905; there was a widespread awakening in 1906 and 1907; and there was extraordinary revival throughout 1908 and 1909, continuing until the Revolution in 1911.

In the spring of 1900, a revival of great power swept the North China College and a nearby church at Tungchow. It proved to be a baptism for future suffering. The meetings progressed from times of confession to times of consecration, awakened joy continuing for three weeks or more. Regular work in the College was stopped while students toured the surrounding countryside with an impact that was felt in Peking, Paoting and Tientsin. In the Boxer Uprising, forty of these young men were done to death.[5]

In early 1900, an awakening occurred in the Anglo-Chinese College in Foochow, described by the Reverend Llewellyn Lloyd of the C.M.S. as without parallel in China.[6] A high proportion of the students (about 70) professed conversion.

Manchuria[7] was already being moved by revival in 1903. The awakening 'spread simultaneously through almost every district, humbling, gladdening, and establishing churches, remote and near.'

Early in 1903 in the far South, there was a great ingathering at Canton, 747 being added to the little churches upon examination in the faith.[8] In 1903, the Fukien Prayer Union was formed to enlist both missionaries and nationals to pray for the manifestation of the Spirit's power.[9] The effects were seen at the next August Convention at Kuliang, where unusual blessing ensued.[10] The churches in the districts around Amoy were also moved by a spirit of revival in 1905. It was the same in the West, and missionary writers were commenting upon the 'general spirit of prayer in Central China.' [11]

Throughout 1904 the movement continued. In many places there were results in changed lives. The missionaries and nationals alike were 'praying that China might experience a similarly gracious visitation of the Holy Spirit as has recently been seen in Wales.' [12] The answer came in 1906,[13] when [14]

> China also ... had its revivals this year, especially in the north. It is significant that here and in Shanghai and Canton, the initiative has been so often and so largely Chinese. These revivals have been marked by a wholly unusual conviction of sin and by great anxiety for the conversion of friends and neighbours ... Five denominations united in holding the meetings under the leadership of a Chinese evangelist who had left a lucrative government position to take up this work.

Again the reports showed that the awakening was north, south, east and west. In four years prior to 1906, Chinese communicants jumped from a total of 113,900 to 178,000, an increase of approximately 57%.[15]

A 'gracious movement of the Spirit' in Chihli Province brought a widespread conviction of sin, a spirit of prayer and an eagerness to witness for Christ in the churches.[16] It was most marked at Tsangchow where the London Mission had been stirred by news of the Welsh Revival.[17] Students responded most eagerly to the ministry.

Prayer meetings at sunrise in Tsingtao in 1906 attracted six hundred praying people, one lasting from 6.30 a.m. until the afternoon. Soon the Shantung believers experienced an awakening 'resembling the day of Pentecost,' marked by confessions, apologies, and reconciliations occurring in the prayer meetings that went on long after midnight.[18]

At the Union College in Weihsien in Shantung, 196 students out of 200 publicly professed faith. Near Tsingtao, the people of a place distressed by open quarrels were greatly convicted by the Spirit of God, falling on their faces and crying to God for mercy. In another place, dawn prayer meetings began the movement, and in another a prayer meeting lasting nearly six hours resulted in abandoning of law suits in the fellowship.[19] Other communities in northern provinces saw a similar demonstration of spiritual catharsis.

On the east coast of China, revivals occurred. The redoubtable Fredrik Franson, of the Scandinavian Alliance Mission,[20] visited Foochow in the autumn of 1904 and stirred college students.[21] Through the ministry of a Chinese evangelist, the work spread through all the churches of Foochow district. There was similar revival in Soochow. A spiritual awakening began in 1906 in churches in the city of Yanchow in Kiangsu, north of the Yangtse River.[22] The spirit of revival affected churches in Shanghai and upriver also.

In 1907, an evangelical awakening occurred in Japanese colleges among Chinese students,[23] who were streaming to Japan to learn Western ideas and techniques after the Russo-Japanese War. Among them was Chiang Kai-shek. Of the work, a China expert, Arthur Smith, declared that there was an opportunity of 'doing more for China today in one year in Tokyo' than all the missionaries had done in China in a century. A new church was formed to accommodate the 250 Chinese students who had professed conversion.

In the South, an awakening began at Macao in the Portuguese enclave in Kwangtung and others occurred in Wuchow and Hokow in Kiangsi.[24] As Alliance missionaries assessed the Awakening, they noted an intense conviction of believers, a work of cleansing and of spiritual anointing, followed by evidence of demonic attack against believers; they stressed the preponderating results in the salvation of souls.

In the far southwest of China, in the provinces of Kweichow and Yunnan, there was a different manifestation of the power of God in a widespread folk movement among Miao aboriginals in 1906.[25] Protestant work had begun among the Miao in 1895. The second missionary and the first convert were murdered, and persecution raged for years.

In 1902, twenty Miao were baptized at Anshun. The tribes became intrigued. Increasing numbers 'turned to God from idols,' abandoning drunkenness and immorality.[26] A chapel was built at Kopu. Huge congregations gathered, from 2000 to

3000, and as many as 500 came forward as candidates.[27] So great was the work of examining and baptizing Miao candidates that the time and strength of the missionaries was taxed to the utmost. From the Miao converts went forth evangelists to win their own countrymen. One of the most hopeful signs of the movement was 'the wonderful way the converts told others of the Saviour.'[28]

Lengthy itinerations were made by workers. The awakening took the form of a folk movement, spreading by 'let-me-tell-my-kinfolk' methods.[29] It spread across the border into Yunnan, whose Miao were soon seeking out the missionary. And yet there were evidences of pentecostal power, as there were early morning prayer meetings in which simultaneous prayer occurred. The Miao were very musical, and took to singing songs in great choirs with fervent enthusiasm.

In 1908, a third wave of revival swept Chinese churches, north, south, east, west—every province. The most unusual movement undoubtedly was that which began in the north in the Manchurian provinces bordering Korea.

From the 1887 awakenings in the colleges of Canada, there issued a remarkable missionary,[30] Jonathan Goforth, who proceeded to China with the Canadian Presbyterians. Jonathan Goforth had been deeply moved by news of the Welsh Revival of 1904.[31] A few years later, he heard of the 1907 Korean Revival, and immediately visited the nearby kingdom to observe for himself. There he was impressed first-hand with the boundless possibilities of Revival.

Goforth himself became the prophet and the evangelist of the movement that followed. A sweeping Manchurian Revival began in 1908, and demonstrated its power at Changte.[32] The meetings were often marked by public confession of sins and extremes of emotional conduct.[33] Yet it was conceded by critics that permanent moral and spiritual transformations resulted. Some of the converts relapsed, observers claiming that the most lasting results stemmed from the least demonstrative manifestations of conviction. Presbyterians alone reported about 13,000 baptisms in five years of awakening, not counting the multiplied thousands in China proper.[34]

When the movement began in Manchuria, there was opposition from missionaries and nationals. However, an elder was convicted of misuse of church funds and his confession brought others, including the pastor, to their knees. Simultaneous prayer broke out, followed by confession and restitution. Sometimes half a dozen people would commence praying, and on occasion more than seven hundred people prayed together, without any sense of confusion.[35] Rosalind Goforth was impressed by great silences:[36]

> Again and again during these days when dozens were praying at once and when everyone seemed to be weeping, there came a wonderful sense of quiet. For at such times no one spoke or prayed or cried aloud. The presence of God never seemed more real.

Goforth explained that he never asked anyone to confess publicly. He simply told his hearers: 'You people have an opportunity to pray.' There followed in Mukden confession of sins. An elder confessed that he had thrice tried to poison his wife: an awful conviction of sin was manifested: all around people were crying and confessing 'but the noise was so great that it was impossible to hear a word of it.'

Manchuria had been moved by the first and second waves of revival, and now the movement of 1908 in Manchuria sent the third wave over all of China. The effects were the most striking of all, in thrust and phenomena.

Goforth helped spread the revival in China's provinces outside Manchuria.[37] He reported that in two years he had conducted thirty 'missions' in six provinces, seeing God's power manifest in greater or lesser degree, the sense of God's presence being 'overwhelming ... unbearable.'

In Peiping, the university students had decided that the revival was a work of man and not of God. 'When he comes among us and tries to work on our emotions,' they said before Goforth's arrival, 'we won't shed any tears nor confess any sins.' Upon leaving, Jonathan Goforth said: 'Continue the meetings. There is something hindering.' A week after he arrived in London, a letter reached him, saying: 'The meetings went on until Thursday after you left, and then God broke down all those students. We never witnessed such a scene of judgment.'

Qualified observers noted that the 'remarkable movement' that had spread through the churches of Manchuria was passing into Shansi and Honan.[38] A deep and coercive conviction of sin was one of the chief features of the 'wonderful revival.'

The movement traversed Hopeh, Shansi and Shensi to faraway Kansu, Honan and Shantung—in the north; Kiangsu, Anhwei and Chekiang—in the east; Hupeh, Szechwan and Kweichow—in the west; and Fukien, Kiangsi, Hunan, Kwangtung, Kwangsi and Yunnan in the south. Congregations in all of China were affected by the Awakening.

Jonathan Goforth, often the initiator of the work, was preaching three times a day.[39] But Chinese Christians were active in every place. The Revival caused the emergence of Chinese evangelists of great power, including Wang Chang-tai, Ting Li-mei and Drs. Y. S. Lee and S. S. Yao, the last named receiving his call through having 'read of Evan Roberts.'

There was a moving of the Spirit in the faraway Kansu province to the northwest, breaking out at Minchow, served by the Alliance.[40] In Szechwan, evangelist Wang, missionary Arthur Lutley and others participated in a movement which Bishop W. W. Cassels described as 'a terrible time, like the Judgment Day.' It was followed by a harvest.[41]

A godly missionary, F. S. Joyce, reported a stirring awakening at Siangcheng in Honan in 1909.[42] At Taiyuanfu in Shansi, the American Board, Baptist Missionary Society and China Inland Mission shared in the blessing in October 1908.

In 1909, an extraordinary movement stirred the city of of Kiating in West China.[43] Some people left the city in fear of the power of the Spirit. Others stayed away from meetings in fear of the inward compulsion to confess.

In each place the results were the same, the intense conviction of sin, the open confessions: idolatry, theft, murder, adultery, gambling, opium smoking, disobedience to parents and hatred of employers, quarrelsomeness, lying, cheating, and the like were confessed for forgiveness.[44]

The public confession of sin seemed to be an outstanding feature of the whole movement, which was full of surprises for the missionary leaders. Of positive effects, a British missionary, after careful consideration, expressed his own opinion in writing:

> We know now that Chinese are emotionally susceptible in matters of religion: we know now that 'instantaneous conversion' may be seen in China as in Chicago or London. We know that the longing for the fullness of the Spirit, with accompanying willingness to sacrifice all for its attainment, may be felt in Shensi as in Keswick.[45]

Nanking, southern capital, experienced a great awakening in 1909.[46] Attendances in the meetings averaged 1500. Confession of sins were made by professing Christians of all ranks—pastors, elders, deacons, evangelists, and Bible women, church members and inquirers of both sexes; while adultery, gambling, fraud, hatred, division, misappropriation of funds, idolatry and the like were renounced, even petty school quarrels between children being settled.

The Christian and Missionary Alliance noted that 1908 was 'a year of glorious revival' in South China, following the movements reported there.[47] The China Inland Mission reported that, in all, its stations and outstations had increased from 394 to 1001 in the decade 1900-1910, chapels from 387 to 995, communicants from 8557 to 23,000.[48] Hudson Taylor's Mission reported 2720 baptisms in 1907, and twenty thousand regular communicants.

Into the year 1911 the Revival seethed. Prayer meetings in Honan Province drew great crowds to pray together as 'a mighty wave of prayer'[49] seemed to sweep over the place. In central China at Hankow, 60,000 people heard the Word in six days' preaching sponsored by an Evangelistic Association of concerned Chinese Christians.[50]

It was declared at the Edinburgh Conference that the ethical and social changes and transformations were a work of God.[51] The Revival in China in these years proved to be the beginning of an indigenous spirit in the Chinese churches. In spite of opposition, a way was being prepared for the coming of greater awakenings among the Chinese Christians, who had come of age at last.

One of the most significant local awakenings was the Hinghwa Pentecost, in which a young man named John Sung was converted, afterward to become an American Ph.D. and then one of China's greatest evangelists of all time, a link between the Awakenings of the first decade and the third decade of the twentieth century. [52]

The Pentecostal movement, which expanded in the wake of the 1905 Revival in California, developed an immediate missionary impulse, from which Mr. and Mrs. A. G. Garr of Azusa Street went directly to Canton in 1907, reporting a couple of hundred national workers and foreign missionaries with glossolalic experience within six months. There was an outbreak of glossolalia in Wuchow, in the Alliance schools, in 1908.[53] American and Canadian Pentecostals settled in Hong Kong and the South. In 1910, a team of Pentecostal missionaries arrived in China from Britain, establishing themselves as far apart as Kunming in Yunnan in the southwest and Kalgan in Chahar in the northeast. At the same time, Scandinavian Pentecostals sent missionaries to China. Soon there were Pentecostal missions operating throughout China, even in Kansu, in the northwest. Some of their personnel were recruited from other missions which would not tolerate their particular gifts.

In 1909, Chang Ling-sheng, a Presbyterian elder active in the Shantung Revival, sought a glossolalic experience in Shanghai, but returned disappointed to his native province, where he was satisfied.[54] He teamed up with two other men who had experienced the same phenomenon in Peking, and so was founded the True Jesus Church, pentecostal and sabbatical, spreading as an indigenous fellowship in China. Like the Brethren-influenced Little Flock, the True Jesus Church outgrew in numbers most of the foreign missionary sponsored fellowships in China.

In Foochow, Fukien, lived a godly missionary lady, Miss Margaret E. Barber, who had come out to China an Anglican but had returned from furlough in 1909 an independent 'faith' worker, the result of her baptism as a believer.[55] In 1921, Wang Tsai, a young Chinese naval officer of Foochow birth, converted in 1918 in Nanking, received a call to ministry through Margaret Barber, of whose saintliness he spoke with gratitude to the writer fifty years later. So also did Simon Meek, whose main ministry was exercised in Manila.

Wang Tsai, known as Leland Wang, Nee To-sheng, known as Watchman Nee, and Miao Shou-hsun, known as Simon Meek, a famous trio, were among a team of young men in Foochow revived or converted through Margaret Barber's influence who engaged in ardent evangelism in Chien Shan, a suburb of Foochow on Nantai island. There, in the style of the Christian Brethren, they met for the breaking of bread. Leland Wang became a China-wide, then a worldwide evangelist. Watchman Nee became the organiser of the Little Flock, an indigenous Chinese fellowship of churches.[56]

Along with extraordinary growth came intensified reaction. The Revolution of 1911, although directed by a professed Christian, Dr Sun Yat-sen, marked the beginning of a reaction against Christianity. The popularity of the Church decreased as the strength of nationalism developed. The churches also became less evangelistic as education took the place of a vigorous evangelism, until more than half the missionary force was engaged in teaching.[57]

Fortunately, another evangelical awakening occurred before China's second revolution, beginning in the latter half of the 1920s and continuing throughout the 1930s. This wide movement was even more indigenous in its personnel than the awakening of the 1900s.

6

SOUTHEAST ASIAN REVIVALS, 1900—

Between the sub-continents of China and India lies the great peninsular tract of Indo-China, at the beginning of the twentieth century divided between the British domains of Burma and Malaya and the French possessions of Tonkin, Annam, Cochin China, Cambodia and Laos, with the ancient kingdom of Siam maintaining its position as a buffer state between the colonial territories. The indigenous peoples of this vast area were largely of the same great branch of the human family called Mongoloid, but of a bewildering variety. In each country there was a dominant culture, as well as a number of hill-tribes and distinct populations, and the presence of Indians and Chinese as settlers and traders and businessmen was in evidence.

On the west, Burma had been entered early in the nineteenth century by Adoniram Judson and the American Baptist missionaries. The Burmese people were ardent Buddhists and proved resisant to the message as compared with the Karens and other minority peoples. The Karens and other tribal people were animistic, with the exception of the Shan or Tais, who were strongly Buddhist. Consequently, work had progressed chiefly among Karens, a larger group.

The year of worldwide revival, 1905, was described as a 'notable year' by the missionaries in Burma, one of far-reaching spiritual awakenings.[1] Where 793 churches of the Baptist persuasion with 46,762 members had baptized 3,667 believers in 1904, 814 churches with 53,078 members were baptizing 8,825 in 1905. It was said that the ingathering quite surpassed anything known in the history of the mission, three years of increase producing 73 churches and 11,748 members, of whom the vast majority were Karens.[2]

Revival was reported among the Pwo Karens at Maubin, signs of awakening among the Kachins, a movement among the Chins, and a phenomenal awakening at Kentung in Shan territory among the Lahu tribespeople.[3] It is of significance that 'accounts of the great revivals in Wales stirred the pastors deeply' and produced a new spirit of prayer.[4]

In 1905, a remarkable movement of indigenous leadership
with both religious and social implications affected the work
in Burma. A talented Karen, Ko San Ye, able but untutored,
promoted schemes for the well-being of the people and drew
much support, many of his followers entering the churches
as members.[5] At first, the missionaries seemed to support
the movement, despite extravagant teaching by some of Ko
San Ye's followers.   In 1906, it was reported at Henzada
that nearly all the Karen accessions were the fruit of the
Ko San Ye movement.[6] In 1907, unique but erratic interest
was reported, some moved by excitement only.[7] In 1908,
problems were multiplying, some being attracted to the
movement by hope of material gain, others distracted by
'pretenders' teaching fantastic ideas, while a great number
of genuine converts were enrolled.[8] At Henzada, the gain to
the churches through the Ko San Ye movement had not been
equalled.   By 1909, the schemes were proving unproductive,
and by 1910 the opposition of the missionaries was general.
Many Karens withdrew from the Baptist fellowship and set
up an independent church in Rangoon, perhaps 1700 or so
defecting.[9] Yet much good came from the movement.

In all of Burma, the extraordinary growth of the work in
Kengtung among the Lahu tribes was the most sensational.
It is interesting to note that the Lahu prophets had taught the
people that, when the time was fulfilled, God would search
for them as a people, and that the sign of His mission would
be that white people on white horses would bring to them
the Scriptures.[10] They saw the fulfillment of the prophecy in
the coming of the Rev. William M. Young in the early 1900s
to preach in the bazaar of the city of Kengtung.   Lahu tribesmen flocked in to hear him, some walking for several days.
In December 1905, thirteen hundred believers were baptized
to bring the total for the year to twenty-eight hundred which
surpassed the annual rate of baptisms in the whole country,
which rose to 8500 in the year of revival.[11] In 1906, interest
among the gospel-resistant Burmese themselves was 'quite
unprecededented.'[12] The extraordinary ingatherings among
the Lahu and Wa tribesmen continued all year, more than
three thousand baptized. The movements among the Karens
and the Lahus were extended into 1907 and 1908, converts
at Kengtung then totalling more than nine thousand, effects
being felt across the border in Yunnan in China.[13] There
were movements felt in the other tribes of Burma in the
years that followed.

In 1910, the Baptists were reporting an unusual opportunity among the Burmese-speaking people, while on the
Bassein field there was a substantial increase of converts
among the Sgaw Karens, and a real if gradual awakening
among the Pwo Karens.[14] Missionaries reported a forty per
cent increase of baptisms among the Kachins, with unusually
successful evangelism among the Chins.[15] While the folk
movement among the Lahu continued, there was no great
ingathering among the intensely Buddhist Shans.   Growth
was occurring mostly among the animistic tribes.

Baptist growth in Burma in the decade of world war may
be seen by comparing the statistics of 1910 with those of
1920.[16] In 1910, 43 Burmese-speaking Baptist churches with
3843 members baptized 432 believers; 794 Karen-speaking
churches with 45,623 members baptized 2,213 believers;
but in the Shan States an awakening among the Lahu and Wa
tribespeople rather than in the few Shan-speaking churches
added nearly a thousand to the 10,187 believers there, most
of them the fruit of a general movement. In 1910, in all of
Burma, 898 churches with a membership of 62,496 added
3893 believers by baptism.   Ten years later, 56 Burmese-
speaking churches with 5,176 members baptized 625—a
slight increase; 871 Karen-speaking churches with 55,713
members baptized 2850; and 90 churches in the Shan States
with 12,036 members were incompletely reported as having
baptized 37.   In 1920, in all of Burma, 1097 churches with
80,764 members baptized 3919 believers.

The Methodists and the Anglicans shared in the general
prosperity of the revival years in Burma, but by far the
greatest advances were made by the Baptists.   Education
as well as evangelism received attention from missionaries,
Rangoon Baptist College becoming a fully-fledged degree-
granting institution in 1909,[17] ten years later changing its
name to Judson College and affiliating with the University
of Rangoon.   Most encouraging in Burma was the readiness
with which evangelized peoples undertook the evangelizing
of other tribes.[18] The Karens were most zealous in this
respect.   Self-supporting in their home churches, they set
aside men and money to reach the unreached peoples, only
the Burmese encountering a measure of hereditary antipathy.
Meanwhile, Burma was separated politically from the Indian
Empire, and nationalist aspirations were growing.   The
Burmese-speaking majority tended to identify Buddhism
with patriotism, but not so the other peoples.

The rivalry of Britain and France enabled Thailand—or Siam, as it was then called— to maintain its independence but numbers of its people and sections of its territory were under British, French and Chinese control.[19] The leading missionary enterprise was that of the American Presbyterian Mission, but progress among the Siamese in the south was slow. Following the 1858-59 Awakening, Daniel McGilvary established a mission to the Lao in the north, and among this kindred people there was successful evangelism.[20] At the end of the nineteenth century, there were a couple of thousand believers gathered in churches around Chiengmai in the north, but much less membership in the populous and more developed south around Bangkok.[21]

In the period of worldwide revival, the Bible colporteurs distributed tens of thousands of portions of Scripture in the various parts of Thailand. It was said that there were 'unmistakable signs that the Holy Spirit is working mightily' in Thailand, but most of the activity reported by missionaries and visiting observers seemed to be social amelioration in education, medicine, and the like.[22] However, by 1912 there was a movement under way in northern Thailand among the Laos, American Presbyterians reporting the most successful year in their history, more than six hundred being added to the Lao Church, a thousand or more the following year in unusual encouragement. In 1914, there were sixteen hundred more converts added, bringing the membership of the twenty-six churches to 6299, the fruit of fifty years which contrasted with thirteen churches and 662 communicants won in nearly a century in the south.[23] However, Christianity was respected in the capital, and was granted equal rights with Buddhism.

In French Indo-China, the Khmer people in Cambodia, the Lao in interior Laos and the Annamese in Cochin China, Annam and Tonking remained untouched by Evangelicals—apart from a few French Protestant pastors whose concern was with the settlers of French nationality. In 1911, the Christian and Missionary Alliance secured a foothold on the coast, four years later building a chapel in Tourane (Danang) to accommodate six Annamese communicants.[24] This compared with nearly a million Roman Catholics, the fruit of an ardent missionary effort and unrelenting military, political and economic domination by the French, whose missionaries successfully developed schools, hospitals and orphanages as well as promoting projects to alleviate poverty. The great majority of the people still professed Buddhism.

7

YEARS OF WAR IN JAPAN

At the Edinburgh Missionary Conference in 1910, the Rev. Yugoro Chiba reported that the great majority of the 80,000 Protestant Christians in Japan resided in the larger cities, and that the smaller towns had been barely touched by the gospel; farmers and factory workers were neglected. He added that Buddhism was corrupt, Shintoism political, and Confucianism merely ethical.[1]

John R. Mott revisited Japan in 1913, when the population was 51,287,091, of whom 96% were unevangelized.[2] He felt sure that they were ready for an ingathering, and the need and opportunity so impressed the Church that the first day of March in 1914 was set aside as a national day of prayer.

Thus began another movement of evangelism in depth, officially named 'Zenkoku Kyodo Dendo,' but, coinciding with the accession of a new emperor, popularly called the Taisho Evangelistic Campaign. Its motto was 'Christ for the citizens of Japan, and the citizens of Japan for Christ.' It proved to be the most determined and comprehensive of all efforts ever made in the Empire, for it lasted for three years, and enjoyed the participation of 90% of Protestant members and adherents.[3]

During the course of the campaign, all of Japan was covered, though not in simultaneous meetings. Millions of tracts were distributed. An aggregate of 777,119 attended 4788 meetings, and 27,350 registered their names as inquirers.[4] The Taisho Campaign did not produce as much church growth as did its predecessor in the previous decade, but its impact upon the non-Christian world was striking.

At Takahashi, in the Okayama prefecture, the meeting house of the pioneers had been stoned and demolished, but now, in the 1914 campaign, the church building was packed, seventy-five boys sitting in front on the floor, every seat in the gallery and main floor occupied, with men standing at the back and outside every window. When the second message was completed, it was nearly 11 p.m., yet all remained unwearied.[5]

It was much the same in Kasaoka, where the Methodists, Congregationalists and Salvation Army united, and not only townspeople but Buddhist priests attended. In town after town, the people rallied to the meetings, so much so that the anger of the Buddhists was incurred, and a Buddhist campaign with tents and special speakers was undertaken. The outbreak of the First World War caused little slow-down of the evangelistic campaign. The cities of Moji and Shimonoseki 'were moved en masse by religious feeling'— according to one report,[6] which told of the largest public halls being rented and crowded out, with hundreds turned away. Churches gained a host of inquirers.

On 13th April 1915, the Tokyo committee invited 250 of the city's high ranking officials and prominent citizens to a banquet to hear the Word. The guests invited the banquet speakers to address school assemblies, factory staffs, businessmen's meetings, postal workers, soldiers and railway workers.[7]

Dr. Robert E. Speer visited Japan in August of 1915 and contrasted the small audiences, shabby churches, closed schools and anti-Christian feeling of two decades before with the great congregations coming to hear the message and the fervent worship of 1915.[8]

During the year 1915, Osaka was campaigned for five months, meetings being held in theatres, schools, hotels and banks as well as churches. Nineteen hundred decision cards were signed, and many of the seekers were baptized. At the imperial coronation, prominent Christians were honored by awards for significant services rendered.[9]

Count Okuma, the prime minister of Japan, declared publicly that, although Christianity had enrolled less than 200,000 believers, yet the indirect influence of Christianity had poured into every realm of Japanese life, adding that 'concerning the future, it is my own conviction that no prac-tical solution of any pressing problems is in sight apart from Christianity.' [10] Those were the days of goodwill.

The Taisho Evangelistic Campaign ended officially in July 1917, with a five-day prayer meeting attended by the 250 active workers, nine-tenths national. The work of God continued, and by 1920 the active membership of evangelical churches numbered 133,794.[11] Revived churches and much encouraged pastors catered for the influx of inquirers, and evangelists continued to travel the countryside with the Christian message.

All through the first four decades of the twentieth century, an extraordinary influence for good was exercised by an English missionary, Barclay Buxton, of the family of the Emancipator of the slaves. An Anglican of evangelical and 'Keswick' loyalty, he founded the Japan Evangelistic Band which stressed both conversion and commitment. A modest missionary, he attracted some of the best national Christian leaders, and trained them for their lifetime of service. He was ably assisted by Paget Wilkes. [12]

Although almost every Japanese pastor operated as an evangelist, and a majority of the laymen as workers, there were several outstanding evangelists of national reputation operating during the Awakening.

Seimatsu Kimura had emerged to usefulness during the Taikyo Dendo of 1901 onwards. When plans were announced for the three-year campaign, he proceeded to the United States and studied popular evangelism there. He became the 'Billy Sunday of Japan,' thousands flocking to his tent. [13]

Paul Kanamori became known in Japan as the 'preacher with only one sermon,'—literally so, for wherever he went, he preached the same sermon, taking three hours so to do, dealing with 'God, sin, and salvation.' From September 1916 until June 1919, he preached in 204 cities and towns, often renting the largest theatres and halls, with an aggregate or total attendance of 270,000 and 43,370 professed seekers. [14]

Colonel Yamamuro of the Salvation Army became known as 'the prophet of the poor.' His messages had great appeal for the common man. [15] He began his ministry when William Booth stood in high esteem in Japanese governing circles, but he lived to see the Salvation Army persecuted thereby.

Juji Nakada had founded an indigenous movement in 1905, designated 'the Holiness Church.' In 1919, at Yodobashi Holiness Church in Tokyo, a revival of Christian commitment occurred, deepening the dedication of the members, increasing the giving, promoting spiritual unity with other believers, and increasing evangelism. [16]

Ten years later, on 19th May 1930, a phenomenal outbreak of revival was experienced at Tokyo Bible Seminary, Prayer meetings multiplied in the Holiness churches, this time accompanied by a general ingathering of converts. By the end of 1930, 4311 had been added to the eight thousand or so members, and the following year another 3487 were converted, the membership rising to nearly twenty thousand by the end of 1932, when the denomination suffered a split.

In 1927, a student awakening occurred at Aoyama Gakuin in Tokyo and Doshisha University in Kyoto. It spread to other schools, three hundred and fifty girls at Baika Girls School in Osaka asking for baptism, for instance.[17]

In the mid-twenties also, Toyohiko Kagawa was engaged in social work but concentrated for a few years until 1929 on preaching missions.[18] More than 27,000 came to hear him in the island of Hokkaido, and fourteen hundred decisions were made. But Kagawa's emphasis was liberal, and his evangelistic appeal occasionally vague.

By 1930, this effort became the 'Kingdom of God' movement, with Kagawa and his friends striving for a million membership in all Christian churches in Japan. During four years, 1859 meetings were held, reaching 799,037 people, of whom 62,460 professed faith. Then enthusiasm began to flag as nationalism intensified.

As the military clique gained more and more control of national life, with some bright exceptions, the witness of the Church declined. Christians were forced to consider the claim of the Government that shrine worship was not a religious, but a patriotic act. In 1930, the National Christian Council of Japan pronounced obeisance at Shinto shrines as religious acts; in 1936, they reversed themselves and fully accepted the government's definition as 'non-religious.'[19]

In 1940, a law governing religious bodies, Christian as well as Buddhist and Shintoist, went into effect. As a result, the various Protestant bodies were fused into a single organization, the United Church of Christ in Japan, 'Nihon Kirisuto Kyodan.'[20] War in mainland China had become by 1941 worldwide war, and a majority of professed Christians (but not all) came to support their government's military aims. Even Dr. Kagawa cooperated with the government in promoting the Greater East Asia project.[21]

After brilliant military successes, the Japanese forces began to suffer attrition and defeat. As the ring of fire about Japan came closer, the Christians could only long and pray for peace. They needed all the fortitude of faith to suffer the destruction which rained upon the home country in the concluding months of the war.[22]

The destruction of Tokyo and other great cities by fire preceded the tragic annihilation of Hiroshima and Nagasaki. The coming of peace brought about an influx of missionary enterprise, chiefly of an evangelical variety, and a brave resurgence of Japanese Christian activity.

8

LIGHT IN KOREA'S DARKEST DAYS

Korea was profoundly affected by World War I, 1914-1919, and World War II, 1939-1945. The 1920s and 1930s between these global conflicts were considered 'the darkest days' by Korean Christians who suffered repression which was both religious and political in its motivation and in its effects. Yet the Christian cause advanced.

President Wilson's plea for national self-determination fanned the fire of Korean aspirations for independence. Thirty-three Korean patriots signed a declaration of Korean independence in Seoul, and invited the imperial authorities to arrest them. Although no missionary seemed aware of the movement, fifteen of the signers were active Christians concerned for the national cause.[1]

On 1st March 1919, Koreans demonstrated throughout Korea for the independence of their country. Upon the insistence of the Christians, the demonstrations were wholly peaceful. Korean flags appeared from nowhere and crowds shouted for freedom in the streets. The authorities were taken by surprise and reacted with brutality, filling prisons to overflowing. In the 1919 demonstrations for freedom, Christians played a leading part. Hence, police action was severe, churches were raided, and, in the sorriest instance, a church was set afire while filled with people, who were shot down as they tried to escape. In the repression that followed, the heavy hand of the imperialists fell upon the Korean Church in a systematic persecution.[2]

The independence movement failed, but Koreans were filled with self-respect. The military government was exchanged for a civilian regime, and reforms were instituted. More Korean schools were built in five years than during the previous fifteen. The impact upon the Christian Church was forceful. Koreans recognized the Christians as ardent patriots, and the churches enjoyed a period of popularity. This coincided with an aggressive project of evangelism, and the churches reaped a harvest, though (it was said) only one in four registering decision persevered in the faith.

At the end of the First World War, the General Assembly of the Korean Presbyterian Church inaugurated a three-years Forward Movement, to secure a 25% increase of attendance at church and Sunday School, a 50% increase at mid-week prayer meetings, and a 100% increase in family worship. A 25% increase in attendance at the annual Bible Conference and local Bible institutes was also coveted, together with 50% increased giving to local causes, 100% to evangelism elsewhere.[3]   A nation-wide evangelistic campaign was planned for the autumn of 1920.

In the north, William Newton Blair visited a congregation where the attendance had increased from 150 to 375, and the offerings for the support of local workers had also more than doubled in 1920. There were great evangelistic series in the northern towns, and a fruitful campaign in Pyongyang. The north there was much encouragement. The membership of the Presbyterian Church increased from 69,025 in 1920 to 72,138 in 1921.[4] The Methodists also experienced rapid growth following 1920.

In the southern parts of Korea, a general movement of people to Christ was reported in 1920. An evangelistic team of college students from Pyongyang visited Pusan and Chengju, and held meetings that were crowded to the doors. One meeting drew 1250 adults admitted by ticket. Churches united to organize evangelistic campaigns throughout the district, and workers were trained in special sessions for the task of witnessing and counseling. Groups of converts met weekly in various villages, asking admission to church membership.[5]

Missionaries in the south reported great encouragement in their work:[6]

> Last summer reports of great meetings in Pyongyang, with something like one thousand decisions, sounded like a dream or fairy tale to those in the extreme south of the peninsula. But last fall we went from church to church and gathered crowds numbering from a third to four and five times the usual congregation; and noted representatives of the best classes—the wealthy, the old Chinese scholar or the modern school teacher, substantial citizens or progressive young men and school boys. In Pulky—a large and important center where we have never been able to get a foothold—a nearby church rented a large tile-roofed building and packed it to overflowing three or four nights—in fact, almost half the crowd could not get in, and the leading

citizens of the community were there long before time
to begin. On the third night, when decisions were called
for by passing slips of paper, thirty men, thirty school-
boys and thirty women, a total of ninety, gave in their
names as wanting to 'believe.'

The greatest progress of Evangelical Christianity had
been made in the northern provinces of Pyongan, Ham-
kyung, and Whanghai, where the people were less conservative and tradition-bound.[7] Class distinctions prevalent
in other parts of Korea were almost unknown in the north.
Most belonged to the independent middle class, and many
cultivated their own land; and a majority of the men were
literate. Consequently, all unordained workers in charge of
churches or circuits were supported by local congregations.

The churches had also grown in the southern provinces
of Chulla and Kyungsang, in which the bulk of the rice crop
of Korea was grown. In the south were wealthy landowners
and poor tenants, the latter generally illiterate and lacking
in political, social, economic and religious progress.[8]

The old aristocracy were entrenched in the more central
provinces, where the people had suffered the oppression of
absentee landlords and the discouragement of Confucianist
traditionalism.[9] Illiteracy was greater in the middle belt
of Korea than elsewhere. Except in Songdo and Seoul, the
ancient and modern capitals of the country, the churches
had made the least headway in numbers and self-support.

In the late 1920s, four out of every five Koreans were
engaged in agriculture and forestry, and thus suffered from
the worldwide depression in farming. Many of the people
were unable to purchase meat more than a couple of times
each year. There was a severe drought in southern Korea
in 1928 and 1929, adding to the general misery.[10] But in
1930, the rice crop in Japan and Korea broke records, and
the price of rice dropped to 50% of its 1929 price, actually
making things worse for farmers unable to pay off their
debts. About a quarter of tillable land passed into the hands
of Japanese settlers.[11] Poverty was all-prevailing, one in
ten suffering dire poverty, one in fifty being beggars.

Imperialist oppression slackened in 1921, but the foreign
presence still irritated the Koreans, many of whom escaped
to Manchuria, including teachers in Christian day and Sunday
schools. But the awakening continued in Korea, impelled by
sacrificial giving by Korean Christians who sold houses or
fields or cattle or clothes or jewelry to help the work.[12]

About a million Koreans settled in Manchuria. Before
very long, there were four hundred churches in the northeastern provinces of China.[13] The work was initiated and
maintained by Korean Christians themselves, with some
secondary assistance from the missionaries.

In 1921, Pastor Kim Ik-Tu conducted evangelistic series
of meetings in Seoul, resulting in numerous conversions,
increased attendance at Bible classes, and generous offerings for the work of God—including gold and silver rings,
hairpins, watches, bridal ornaments and the like.[14]

In Pyongyang, Christian working men formed a band
of evangelists, themselves preaching and themselves providing the funds. This preaching band promoted a church
among the poverty-stricken people squatting on the banks
of the Potong river, gathering 150 inquirers and setting up
a Sunday School which attracted 350 people.[15]

About the same time as the outbreak of revival in the
city of Shanghai in China, a revival began in 1927 in Seoul,
through the zeal of a young national minister, Lee Yong-Do,
a Methodist. He was sick with tuberculosis, and began to pray
much concerning his illness. It was an even greater answer
to his prayer when he was filled with the Holy Spirit, and
became an evangelist in Korea when only thirty years old.[16]

The revival broke out in Seoul City, and spread like fire
all over Korea. When the revival broke out among the body
of students in the Methodist Theological Seminary, the faculty
of the Seminary tried to close the entrance and exit of the
dormitory every evening, thinking the students spent too many
hours in the chapel and the garden of the campus in prayer.
The students crept out through the windows.

When the Rev. Lee Yong-Do was delivering the Word of
God in the Central Methodist Church in Pyongyang, he was
compelled to suspend preaching, because the congregation
had stopped listening to him, but were repenting and confessing their sins before God.[17] This interruption often thus
occurred. One day, as he was about to preach the Word in
an evangelistic meeting, he felt guided to read only certain
chapters of Scripture, the Gospel of John, chapters 14 to 18;
while he read, the congregation broke into prayer.

In the autumn of 1928, yet another awakening occurred
in North Korea, as a result of which two thousand professed
faith in three weeks.[18] Two hundred students bound themselves in a covenant of prayer, Bible reading and witness,
their numbers soon doubling. They met in fifteen groups

on each Sunday except the first in the month, when they gathered unitedly. Attendance at their evening meetings for students reached a thousand, many becoming Christians, others already converted committing lives in service.

A revival began in the Presbyterian Theological Seminary among the students, who were convicted of their lack of earnestness in preaching the Good News. For two days, all classes were abandoned. The revived students conducted meetings in three of Pyongyang's city churches, resulting in many conversions and much blessing for the people of God in the northern capital.[19]

In 1928, a spirit of revival was reported from various parts of Korea. Prayer and intercession abounded, in one place (Yundukwon) the Christians fasting and praying for seven weeks before beginning evangelistic services. An all-night of prayer provoked heart-searching among believers, who later spent three hours confessing their faults and asking mutual forgiveness before being moved collectively to witness to every household in town.[20]

Then, in 1929, a Forward Movement of the Presbyterian Church of Korea was begun with three days of 'meetings of consecration' in each of twenty-two presbyteries—daybreak meetings for prayer, and other gatherings at 10 a.m. and 3 p.m., and rallies in the evening. The missionaries reported extraordinary blessing. The leaders scattered to their churches and repeated the three days of consecration in every one of the twenty-six hundred churches in Korea, and nearly every church then promoted at least one week of evangelistic meetings, great numbers of Christians being revived and new converts won. The churches were crowded and new churches were built. A thousand men attended the annual Bible School in Pyongyang in January, and fifteen hundred women enrolled in March.[21]

More than twelve hundred people attended the daybreak prayer meetings in Pyongyang in November 1929. There were morning Bible classes, afternoon house meetings and evening services led by Pastor Kim Ik-Tu, who was becoming the national evangelist of Korea. The largest church in Pyongyang was unable to accommodate the crowds, hence a gymnasium-auditorium was built to seat 5000 on the floor.[22]

These times of refreshing fortified Korean Christians before a storm of persecution broke upon the churches of the country, when faith was tested to breaking point. So often, revival is sent before tribulation.

Using every possible device and exercising pressure this way and that, the imperial authorities sought to make the Korean Christians conform. As part of their military plans for East Asia, they had decided to use Shinto as a unifying force throughout the Empire. The authorities pressurized single churches at first, and following capitulation tackled presbyteries and larger groupings.[23] Finally, the General Assembly of the Presbyterian Church in 1938 was forced by police action to capitulate on the shrine issue. Worship services were limited in the churches, and their doors were closed against the missionaries, except in large city churches.[24] Missionary evangelists attempted to keep up evangelism by tent campaigns, but reported a drop in tent attendance and in decisions for Christ. While the Methodist Missions kept their schools open, accepting the claim of the authorities that there was no religious significance in the act of obeisance, Methodist communicant membership— which had been in decline since 1925—benefitted nothing.[25]

In 1930, the imperial government pressed Shinto worship upon the Korean churches and Christian schools. Students and teachers alike were required to bow before the state Shinto shrines. The administration insisted that this was not a religious but a patriotic act. Many Korean Christians could not accept this explanation, nor could Presbyterian missionaries, who closed their schools rather than comply. The Methodists accepted the official explanation.

Many faithful pastors and laymen were thrown into prison for their resistance to shrine worship, and some suffered torture. With the outbreak of World War II, missionaries were forced to leave the country.[26] More than one hundred churches were closed, and two thousand Christians were imprisoned, of whom fifty suffered martyrdom.[27] In 1942, the churches were forbidden to use their denominational names, the Korean equivalent of the Japanese Kyodan being forced upon them.[28] In 1945, they were forced into union, those protesting being driven from their pulpits and either imprisoned or placed under house arrest. Many Christians went underground, and the total membership of 700,000 was reduced to half that figure.[29]

The imperial authorities prohibited the reading or the exposition of the biblical books of Daniel and Revelation and any Scriptures dealing with the Second Coming of Christ or eschatology, even the singing of hymns about the Second Coming being prohibited by edict.

The missionary body in Korea was prepared for the evil days of World War II by a revival among themselves in the year 1939.   Miss Aletta Jacobsz, who had been a teacher in the Dutch Reformed Missionary Training School in South Africa, was visiting a lady missionary to the Orient whom she had won to Christian faith and commitment. Her methods bore a striking resemblance to those of Marie Monsen in China—a direct questioning of all whom she encountered regarding spiritual things.[30]

Cottage prayer meetings were held daily at Whajinpo by missionaries, and Aletta Jacobsz was asked to lead on one occasion.   Her ministry was so powerful that she was requested to conduct a week of meetings.   This led to another series at Kwangju.   The effect was impressive.   She asked penitents to sit down with a pencil and notebook and Bible, and write down what clearly was sin in God's sight.   She referred them to the First Epistle of John, chapter one.   A uniform result was the confession of wrongdoing to fellow-missionaries, and the seeking out of national pastors and leaders to put things right.

In November 1939, Miss Jacobsz arrived in Andong for yet another series.   Again the missionary body was moved, including Harold Voelkel, who began listening with the air of a theological connoisseur but who soon became so burdened about his failures that he could not eat.   Voelkel became a very effective missionary in Korea in later years.   And so it went on, missionaries in station after station quickened until a hundred had entered into 'a life more abundant.'   Korean helpers associated with the missionaries were also moved, but there was no widespread awakening in those days of the great political repression.

Some of the missionaries in Korea were deported by the military late in 1941 for promoting prayers for peace, a few of whom were interned for the duration of the war in Manila, where a number died from starvation—the writer was one of the first military chaplains to arrive with rescue funds.[31]   A number of others were repatriated from Japan in 1942.   On a North Atlantic voyage, Aletta Jacobz died of exposure in 1942 also after her ship was torpedoed.   She was buried at sea, a choice memory in the minds of many.[32]

Many of the revived missionaries returned to Korea and witnessed after Liberation another great spiritual movement. The fires of revival had burned low, but never really went out in the Korean churches.

9

DESPAIR AND RECOVERY IN CHINA

The revolution of 1911 which overthrew the feeble Manchu dynasty proved to be a serious setback for Christianity in China. The new regime was so weak that it could not enforce its authority against the regional tyrannies of war lords who struggled for power; and, within a decade, Communism rose in China and took advantage of the confusion.

In the 1910s and 1920s, the missionaries and local pastors encountered two major obstacles to their work. The widespread operations of bandits and outlaws made travel in the country extremely hazardous, especially for foreigners who were often held to ransom; and the spontaneous demonstrations of frustrated patriots, cleverly manipulated by anti-Christian agitators and Communists, provoked riots and looting that hampered the preaching of the Good News in most of the provinces.

Anti-foreign feeling in China included a strong antipathy against Japan, whose growing imperialism was beginning to surpass that of the Western Powers throughout the country. On 15th May of 1925, Ku Cheng-hung, a Chinese worker, was killed by the Japanese staff of the Naigai cotton mill in Shanghai.[1] This provoked student rioting throughout the city, and on 30th May, the British police opened fire upon a mob of protesters. The uproar that followed shook all of China. The national situation became critical, forcing the foreign missionaries to evacuate their stations and shelter in the International Settlement at Shanghai, many thousands leaving China. Some indication of the extent of the evacuation of the missionaries from inland China may be gained from the statistics of the China Inland Mission. Of twelve hundred missionaries, four hundred were on regular or emergency furlough in the homelands, four hundred were relocated in Shanghai, Chefoo or Tientsin, and only 213 were carrying on in the interior.[2]

At the end of 1926, it was a common missionary opinion that there was 'a sense of discouragement in the Church amounting almost to despair.'[3] National leaders shared the pessimism, and no solution to the difficulties suggested itself to either the missionaries or the Chinese leaders. Chinese churches were unable to concentrate on much more than mere survival.

In 1925, the more evangelistic and optimistic missionaries at Shanghai decided to hold a conference for the deepening of the spiritual life.[4] Their Chinese friends thought their choice of a speaker most unfortunate, if not the height of madness—Paget Wilkes, an Englishman serving in the Japan Evangelistic Band—and it was predicted that the militant students would seize on the obvious opportunity of rioting against both Britain and Japan. Yet it proved otherwise, and the three weeks of meetings were extended for another six. Paget Wilkes revived the flagging spirits of the missionaries and exercised an electrifying effect upon Chinese hearers, for he insisted again and again that China must be evangelized by Christian Chinese. This was far in advance of missionary practice, most of the work done by American and European personnel. Shanghai's Chinese, the most enterprising and sophisticated in the country, provided some of the volunteers who responded.

Politically also, the tide was turning. Chiang Kai-shek, graduate of the Paoting and first principal of the Whampoa Military Academy, marched north from Canton to unify the country, at first cooperating with the Communists and their Russian mentors—his troops destroying churches and persecuting Christians—but afterward turning against the Reds. By 1927, his objectives were rapidly being realized. For the ten years following, China enjoyed a comparatively peaceful period of reconstruction, interrupted by Japan's seizure of the Manchurian provinces in 1931 and a clash in Shanghai the following year.

Natural disasters added to the woes of the Chinese people. In 1928 and 1929, famine affected all the provinces of China, and there were at least fifty million people seeking relief. In 1931, the great flood of the Yellow river drowned half-a-million, and rendered thirty million people homeless; sixteen of China's eighteen provinces were adversely affected. The cup of misery overflowed.[5]

Among Protestants, there were two constituencies in all China—those who considered the Scriptures the revelation of God and those who appreciated them as literature; those who believed in prayer and those who taught that prayer had only a subjective value. The latter had no message.

Early in 1927, a Day of Prayer was arranged in Nanking, the sessions being largely attended, almost every church and school in the area being represented. In their calamity, there was a unanimity of turning to God.[6] This gathering of intercessors in the capital was repeated elsewhere. Contributing to the movement of prayer were: the internal weakness of China, with the oppression of the people by the militarists and unjust officials, the civil wars with soldiers everywhere killing people and burning property, with robbers and Communists swarming over the country, despoiling the fields and homes, burning, killing, raping, stealing, and kidnaping; the external aggression on the part of foreign powers; natural calamities, floods and drought, famine; student agitations, nationalist uprising, anti-Christian propaganda, the evacuation of the missionaries, lack of funds, gross sins among church members—all these contributed.[7]

Soon missionary journals were noting 'Signs of Spiritual Revival in China,' G. T. B. Davis of Philadelphia—who had observed the Welsh Revival and concurrent movements—predicting that the Chinese Church was 'on the eve of an era of unparalleled spiritual progress,' reporting that the sale of Bibles and Testaments was increasing rapidly, and that already remarkable revivals had occurred in certain places 'along the lines of the Welsh Revival.'[8]

The coming revival in China was preceded by a vast increase in Christian publication, in part made possible by a switch from classic Wenli to popular Kuoyu script.[9]

In the New Year of 1931, a Five-Year Forward Movement proposed by an inter-Church conference and sponsored by the National Christian Council of China was commenced, to revitalize the life of the churches of China and to carry out a vigorous evangelism aimed at doubling the number of Christians.[10] A slogan adopted by the movement revealed its philosophy: 'Lord, revive Thy Church, beginning with me!'

In 1932, 'a spiritual awakening' was being reported in China, affecting the churches everywhere, some as by a rising tide, others with floods of blessing.[11] There was no doubt that China's Christians were enjoying a visitation.

In early 1933, an interdenominational periodical published in Shanghai gave expression to a general conviction held by missionaries and nationals alike in China: 'Revival is in the air . . . In numerous places, there are spiritual awakenings.' The tide of revival was coming to the full in the country, all eighteen provinces being affected.[12]

A leading figure in the decades of revival in China was Dr. Marcus Cheng, professor in the Hunan Bible Institute in Changsha, an international Christian. Marcus Cheng experienced revival and a filling of the Holy Spirit in the earlier movement of 1906. He served as chaplain in the army of the 'Christian General,' Feng Yu-hsiang, and also intinerated as an evangelist.[13]

Wang Ming-tao was a native of Peking. His father, a doctor of medicine, was killed during the Boxer uprising in 1900.[14] Wang was converted at the age of 20, sought as a believer baptism by immersion, began to evangelize his pupils in school. He became a vigorous independent, making his appeal to the will rather than the emotions. His service was much in demand during the revival period.

Another of the evangelists of the Awakening was Pastor Hsieh Meng-tse, born in Anhwei, converted at thirty years of age, influenced by Jonathan Goforth to enter the ministry, busy throughout the 1910s and 1920s, evangelizing in North China, Central China and West China, particularly after 1931 in Szechwan and Kweichow.[15]

Pastor Liu Tao-sheng, a native of Honan, was converted to God in the city of Lushan. In 1910, he became a full-time evangelist, and in 1927 he was ordained to the ministry. In the stirrings of 1929, Liu received a special blessing and became a revivalist.[16]

Leland Wang enrolled in the Naval Academy at Yentai in Shantung in 1912, and after his graduation and commission as an officer, he married a Christian girl. From there he went to Nanking Military Academy, where he began daily scripture reading—for which he became noted till old age— and was converted. He was assigned to a naval vessel, but felt the call of God to the ministry, choosing to live by faith in itinerant evangelism.[17]

During a typical spring in the 1930s, Leland Wang toured a dozen provinces, from Hangchow and Shanghai on the east up the Yangtse valley through Hankow and Wuchang, north to Kaifeng and Loyang in Honan, west again through Sian and Lanchow, the capitals of Shensi and Kansu, making his way by rail and plane, and after reaching the borders of Tibet, he turned east across the northern parts of China to Peking, thence south through Tientsin and Tsinan to Shanghai and to Hong Kong.[18] This was a formidable itinerary in those days of slower travel, uncertain timings, and interminable delay on roads and railways.

Marie Monsen was confirmed as a believer in the church at Sandviken, on the outskirts of Bergen.[19] The Norwegian Lutheran China Mission sent her to a hospital and training school in Oslo. In her preparatory ministry, she lived by faith, often in a venturesome way. She arrived in China in the autumn of 1901, when the memory of the Boxer uprising was fresh in missionary minds. She suffered many handicaps —falling down a stairway in Shanghai and suffering a concussion of the brain, arriving on the field only to come down with a bad attack of malaria. In 1906, she testified of healing through prayer.[20] Marie Monsen was always an early riser, dedicating the first couple of hours of the day to devotion.

Another missionary with noteworthy service in the revival movement was Anna Christensen, a Danish member of the China Inland Mission.[21] Her ministry was also one of exhortation, and in her visits to various mission stations she helped pastors and congregations find blessing. The writer met Frøken Christensen in the 1930s.

Andrew Gih was born in Shanghai on 10th January 1901. His father was a Confucian scholar, and under him his son studied for five years until his death in 1913. Of four boys and three girls, only Andrew and two sisters survived the years of hardship. To learn English, Andrew enrolled in the Bethel High School in Shanghai, and studied the Bible as English Literature. The message of a C.I.M. missionary, Miss C. F. Tippet, led to his conversion. Shortly thereafter, Andrew obtained a Post Office appointment by competitive examination.[22] Dorcas, his wife, was an ardent Christian.

Andrew Gih was thoroughly challenged by the ministry of Paget Wilkes in Shanghai.[23] Thereafter he became the founder of the Bethel Bands, which did more to extend the revival in China than any other agency.

Andrew Gih contracted tuberculosis, but persisted in his evangelistic ministry, sometimes spitting blood between addresses.[24] He seemed to outgrow the consumption, though in the severest hardships of World War II he suffered a relapse. Unlike his former colleague, who wore himself out, Andrew Gih organized his time and maintained health to manage a missionary society of three hundred workers.

After the summer conference of 1931, Andrew Gih asked John Sung to join the Bethel Worldwide Evangelistic Band, even though, as Leslie Lyall observed, it meant that Gih as leader of the Band would be less prominent than Dr. Sung. The association lasted thirty fruitful months.[25]

John Sung was the son of a pastor, and his first youthful impression of the Christian faith came through the revival at Hinghwa in 1907, 'the Hinghwa Pentecost.'[26]   His home church seated 3000.   Upon graduation from high school, he was offered a scholarship at a college in the United States. Instead of studying theology, he majored in science, with highest honors. With success, his spiritual life declined. His bachelor of science degree at Ohio Wesleyan University was followed by a master of science and doctor of philosophy at Ohio State University. He was offered a scholarship at Union Theological Seminary in New York.[27]

At Union Seminary, John Sung found the approach to the Christian faith largely philosophical, to Scripture rather sceptical, and to Christ one of human imitation rather than divine worship.[28] He was rapidly losing his faith; but he happened to attend a 'real' evangelistic service at Calvary Baptist Church and went back four times consecutively to hear the young evangelist. Shortly afterward—on the 10th February of 1927, a year of revival in China—he was truly converted, or re-converted.[29] So great was his joy of forgiveness and concern to witness that he forgot that it was midnight, and wakened his classmates with his vocal praise. The seminary authorities decided he was unbalanced,[30] and President Henry Sloan Coffin insisted upon his going to 'a quiet place to rest'—which turned out to be an insane asylum. Alone with his Bible for more than six months, Sung claimed that he learned more of true theology than all he had heard in the lecture halls. He read the Bible through forty times.

A friend from abroad, with the help of the Chinese consul, secured his release. He returned to China by ship, throwing overboard all his diplomas except his doctoral certificate which he kept for his father. At Hinghwa, Sung's parents were satisfied that his 'mental unbalance' had been an exuberant new birth.[31] After the Bethel Band had stirred up Hinghwa, John Sung formed a gospel team and began evangelizing the country villages. Then he joined the Bethel Worldwide Evangelistic Band.

From 1934 until his death in 1944, John Sung ministered alone.[32] His parting from his Bethel colleagues was sad rather than bitter.[33] He readily acknowledged his debt to Andrew Gih, and the Bethel evangelists spoke highly of his faithfulness and effectiveness, though privately wondering at his idiosyncrasies. His fatal cancer, no doubt, caused much of his irritability and rudeness.

It is not known whether John Sung ever heard Billy Sunday in the United States, but his platform manner resembled somewhat the corybantic American evangelist. Sung often pantomimed his messages, jumping from the platform into the assembly, rooting up plants—a modern version of the Hebrew prophet.[34] In his later years, his fearlessness of utterance became a severity in denunciation of persons— several of his closest friends of revival times assured the writer that he was the rudest Chinese known to them.

The other four members of the Bethel Worldwide Evangelistic Band were Philip Lee, son of a Cantonese evangelist, who was expelled from school as an agitator, sent to Bethel in Shanghai;[35] became involved with a band as a pianist at Ichang, and was finally converted, becoming the pianist of the Worldwide Band; Frank Lin, born in Foochow, educated in a Christian school, but not truly converted until his years of teaching in the Bethel High School;[36] Lincoln Nieh, who was a member of the propaganda corps of the Communist Party, had enjoyed a Christian education, but lived a wild life until his conversion to God in 1929;[37] John Shih, who was a Buddhist,[38] professed faith in Christ in spite of parental opposition, but was not converted until the revival of 1927. In the 1930s, the writer itinerated and preached with three of the members of the original worldwide band in China.

It can be seen in the perspective of history that the full twelve years following the New Year of 1927 constituted a major awakening of New Testament Christianity in China. It continued through the undeclared war between Japan and China, and was ended at the outbreak of World War II in 1939 which had far-reaching effects upon the lands of the Pacific. The indigenous movement was helped by the friendly attitude of the Kuomintang Government of China, and was paralleled by successful missionary outreach. It prepared the Chinese churches for self-support and self-propagation in wartime, but it was followed by one of the most severe and rigorous anti-Christian dictatorships in the history of the world, one which adapted many of its techniques to win the masses.

10

AWAKENING BEYOND THE WALL

Tungpei, in Chinese 'the Northeast,' has been known to Europeans as Manchuria, a name never used by its citizens, though not as objectionable as the term Manchukuo foisted on it by Japanese militarists. The Northeast included the provinces of Liaoning, Kirin, and Heilungkiang, with a total population of some forty million, the great majority Chinese. There were also two million Korean settlers. Manchuria thus was the great frontier area of China, the people of the Northeast being uprooted, less bound by tradition, and more susceptible to change. It is significant that many sweeping revival movements affecting all of China originated in the Manchurian provinces, generally in the industrial cities.

The rule of Marshal Chang Tso-lin, the war lord of the Manchurian provinces, was succeeded by a weaker administration under Chang Hsueh-liang, who failed in an attempt to oust the Russian presence; and his government collapsed before the invasion of the Japanese Army at midnight, 18th September 1931. A puppet regime was set up.

No doubt, the political turmoil accelerated the evangelical revival in Manchuria, but the fact remains that the movement had begun long before—in anticipation of it, Evangelicals would say. The earliest manifestations followed the uproar of 1927 far to the south in China proper.

Among the many foreign missionaries who had been forced to retreat to Shanghai in 1927 was Marie Monsen, then a middle-aged Norwegian lady.[1] Since hearing in 1907 of the revival in Korea, she had been praying for a similar awakening in China. Even though the Lord had blessed her through the years among women at her own station in bringing about conviction of sin resulting in changed lives, she had little realized what lay in store for her as a pioneer of another such revival movement of vaster proportions.

After a brief stay in Shanghai, she went to Manchuria to visit the work of Emil Jensen, a Danish missionary living at Dalny.[2] She was asked to substitute for another speaker at the annual conference for Chinese workers and Christians.

A movement of the Spirit began in their midst and not only were her listeners touched, but she herself felt the impact in a special way. At this conference she experienced her first taste of the revival for which she had prayed so long. An extraordinary revival began in Dairen, in eastern Manchuria, in September 1929.[3] The movement was wholly indigenous. Most provocative was the ministry of a young candidate for the ministry, Pastor Hsieh. Another useful evangelist was Wang Ming-tao, who not only attracted great crowds but held them spellbound for great lengths of time by simple Bible teaching. On one occasion, Wang Ming-tao preached for seven hours without apparent fatigue.

The awakening spread like wildfire over Manchuria, the Chinese evangelists rather than the missionaries being the major instruments.[4] Great meetings were held in Dairen, Port Arthur, Chingchow, Newchang, Takushan, Antung, Mukden, and other great cities of the industrial northeast. The missionaries in Newchang, as a result of the revival, announced the best year ever,[5] with the highest number of baptisms in ten years, indicating that the awakening, though emotional outwardly, was not all froth and bubble.

In 1931, the Bethel Band tackled the cities of Manchuria. They were invited to minister at a triennial conference of Lutheran church leaders at Fenghwangchen. Those in charge proved unsympathetic and suspicious, objecting to the free-style preaching and the praying in unison, threatening to withdraw missionary funds from the church if the invitation to the Bethel evangelists were not withdrawn.[6] The young evangelists packed up and left by the night train, followed to the station by some believers who had been moved.

Ahead of schedule, the Bethel Band arrived in Mukden. Meetings were called hastily, three hundred attending the first night, soon becoming fifteen hundred, overflowing the place, people standing outside in bitter cold. Converts were numbered in the hundreds.[7]

Conditions among the churches in Harbin matched the disorganized state of Manchuria at the time. Andrew Gih preached from seven until nine each morning, John Sung from five until seven in the evenings. Congregations of Koreans, Russians and Germans cooperated, only one church in the city refusing.[8] A great revival began, with results among the Christians — reconciliation of pastors, workers and missionaries, restitution of wrongs, and total commitment—and hundreds of lasting conversions.

After Harbin, John Sung, Frank Lin, and Philip Lee temporarily separated from Andrew Gih and Lincoln Nieh in ministering to smaller cities.[9] In every place there was unusual response to the message, and in some places the people were electrified by the miraculous. For instance, a man whose arm had been paralysed since he murdered a missionary in the Boxer uprising suddenly realised that God had forgiven him, and recovered the use of his arm.

The seizure of the Manchurian provinces by Japanese militarists trapped the Bethel Band near the Siberian border. They worked for six weeks in the towns around, often having four meetings a day. Sometimes, people would rush forward confessing their sins before the sermon was preached.[10]

On the way south, the Bethel Band again visited Mukden, where the response had been so great that the missionaries were sceptical of its lasting value.[11] But the converts had persevered through the troublous times of occupation, and the missionaries now admitted that the work was of God, a nurse who had called the evangelists 'five crazy Chinese from Shanghai' testifying of a wonderful change in hospital.

During the autumn months of 1931, the Bethel Band in Manchuria witnessed the conversion of more than three thousand people, yet the major achievement had been the revival of the churches.[12]

In 1932, in Taonan, Manchuria, Dr. Jonathan Goforth, a veteran revivalist of the movement of 1908, conducted a series of meetings crowded to capacity and marked by the same kind of revival.[13] It is noteworthy that Goforth had a profound effect and marked influence upon the lives of the Chinese evangelists of the 1930s.

In 1933, Irish and Scottish Presbyterians in Manchuria reviewed the situation following the Revival.[14] In Kirin, the Rev. James McWhirter reported flood-tides of spiritual power sweeping people out of their complacency into church membership, often through agonizing prayer and emotional confession. Wang Ming-tao, the Bethel Band, and Pastors Han and Chia of Manchuria were the chief evangelists. The Rev. L. D. M. Wedderburn, in Hailung, returned from 1932 furlough to find the churches crowded, thanks to the political situation and the visit of the Bethel Band. In Mukden, Miss Dorothy Rutherford testified of renewed church life everywhere, accompanied by ardent Bible study. In Hsinmin, the Rev. Ralph Morton reported greater attendance, giving and understanding, and ardent inquiry by newcomers.

A discordant note was struck by the Rev. D. T. Robertson, who deplored a fanatical addiction to revivalism in Harbin, with little welcome to any other kind of constructive effort. He was also dismayed by conservative theology and emotional appeal manifested in the movement.[15]

But, on the other hand, the Lutherans in Harbin rejoiced in the Revival, citing Pastor Han of Newchang and Marie Monsen as factors, most of all the visit of the Bethel Band. In union prayer meetings, the whole company often burst into simultaneous prayer, and the big Lutheran church was over-crowded daily. One night, all the pastors spent a full night of prayer around the altar of the Lutheran church.[16]

The years went by without much diminishing of the work. In 1935, 'standing room only' was reported in the churches of Manchuria, the various missions in all three northeastern provinces sharing in the blessing, despite the difficulties of the political situation.[17]

Although the invasion and occupation of Manchuria was condemned by the League of Nations, from which the government of Japan withdrew, the imperial authorities strove for some kind of legitimacy in their state of Manchukuo, using local Chinese leaders for administration and elevating the ex-emperor of China, Pu-Yi, to the throne.

The effect of the Japanese occupation of Manchuria was felt in different ways. In some areas, partisans and bandits caused much unrest, and forced the closing of the Christian schools and churches. The imperial forces viewed Chinese churches with suspicion. But the movement towards the churches continued, uneasy people finding stability in the Christian faith. Church membership rapidly increased.[18]

On 10th October 1935, the Chinese national day, police arrested sixty leading Chinese Christians among others, cracking down on Chinese Christianity. Pressure was then brought on church members to make obeisance in ancient Confucian temples—as in Shinto in Korea and Japan. The Christians in the main remained faithful.[19]

The annexation of the Inner Mongolian province of Jehol to Manchukuo convinced many patriots that 'Manchu' rule was to be re-established in all China by Japan. Declaration of war between the United States and Great Britain and the Empire of Japan on 8th December 1941 brought about the internment of missionaries and their repatriation. As in Korea and Japan, the Manchurian Churches were forced into an unwilling union, and days of persecution ensued.

The Inner Mongolian provinces of China, integrated into the Republic—unlike Outer Mongolia, which became the Republic of Mongolia under Russian tutelage—were Jehol, Chahar, Suiyuan, and Ninghsia.

During the autumn of 1932, there was a movement of the Spirit in Ninghsia province in the northwest beyond the wall. The work was a pioneer one, but there were responses to preaching in the streets as well as revival in the little chapel. That meant only that fourteen believers suddenly became twenty-five, but as the weeks went by, progress was noted in the life of each believer.[20]

The Bethel Band decided to visit Inner Mongolia.[21] It was a long and arduous journey north from Shanghai. In Kalgan, they stayed with devoted missionaries whose support had not come from home, who trusted God for daily necessities. Unknowingly, Chinese friends brought them foodstuffs. When revival came, a great stir was created in the city, preaching bands going out to the streets with drums, songs and tracts. Among the converts was a man who confessed that he had killed seven babies by stuffing their mouths with cotton and throwing them to the dogs. Female infanticide was all too prevalent, few homes having more than two girls.

Thus in the autumn of 1933, John Sung and Andrew Gih held meetings in Kalgan, capital of Chahar; then Kweihwa, Paochow, and Saratsi in Suiyuan; then to Paoting in Hopei, where great crowds attended the meetings.[22]

The China Inland Mission reported that a great revival had broken out in both church and orphanage in Saratsi in Suiyuan, resulting immediately in more than sixty baptisms. These were encouraging results in Inner Mongolia, where conditions were altogether different from Manchuria, there being distressing moral degradation.[23]

As the months went by in various parts of greater China, a strain developed between John Sung and other members of the team, attributed by most observers to the former's eccentricities.[24] Even critics of Andrew Gih have readily conceded (to the present writer) John Sung's awkwardness. It has been suggested that John Sung objected to a doctrine of 'eradication' supposedly held by the Bethel Band. None of the other members of the Bands claimed such a degree of sanctity, and their very human failings contradicted the idea as they also insisted verbally. Although Bethel Mission was of Wesleyan affiliation, its practice was that of 'Keswick.'

11

AWAKENINGS IN NORTH CHINA

The northern tier of Chinese provinces included Shantung, Hopei, Shansi, and Shensi, with the metropolis of Peking, sometimes called Peiping, one of the great population concentrations, the northern capital of China, Nanking being in fact the capital chosen by the Kuomintang as central.

In summer 1927, Marie Monsen visited the beach resort of Chefoo in Shantung Province, where she met many of the missionaries forced to leave the interior of China.[1] All of them shared the same burden for spiritual renewal, and a spirit of prayer fell on them in their ardent prayer meetings. Confession of sins followed conviction, and a quickening came. They went back to their stations thoroughly revived, and the same sort of prayer meetings were experienced there.

In the missionary prayer meetings, Mrs. C. L. Culpepper was anointed with oil in prayer for her failing eyesight. The same Scripture used suggested the confession of faults . . . and this was followed by an immediate healing.[2]

Missionaries of the Southern Baptist North China Mission were particularly challenged by Marie Monsen's ministry. Seventy of their churches had died away,[3] and their best Chinese evangelist, on the verge of despair, insisted that a thousand of their members had not been truly converted. A series of meetings led by Miss Monsen stirred believers, a definite expectation of blessing being created.

Late in 1931, some stirrings were felt. By mid-1932, a score of missionaries and many national leaders had entered into a new experience with God. This infilling of the Holy Spirit was thought by some to be alien to Southern Baptist doctrine and practice. Everyone on the faculty of the North China Baptist Theological Seminary experienced an infilling, as did the staff of the Warren Hospital. Then conversions began to occur in the churches.[4]

A factor in the unusual stirring of the churches, pastors, and ministerial students was the visit of the Bethel Band to Shantung. Andrew Gih and his colleagues came north in 1931, before Dr. John Sung joined their ranks.[5]

Most noteworthy was the movement of the Spirit in the peninsular province of Shantung in 1931-32. At Hwanghsien, the base of the Southern Baptist mission, a 'deep, genuine' work of God stirred the Chinese congregation through and through.[6] In Pingtu, 'the Holy Spirit came in power' and a large number of outsiders professed faith besides many in the church fellowship being revived. A godly missionary, C. L. Culpepper, reported 'wonderful things,' with hundreds being converted in the villages round about. There was a sweeping revival in Laiyang and Laichow.[7]

In Taian, Shantung, the Bethel Band found that anti-Christian action had wrecked churches and closed schools and looted buildings. In Andrew Gih's absence in Shanghai, John Sung preached powerfully, and more than a hundred outsiders professed faith, to the great encouragment of the local Christians.[8] At Tenghsien,[9] the Band experienced a surge of revival in the churches, high schools and seminary, the largest building in the city being filled to overflowing. Often sermons were cut short by people anxious to make restitution in the meetings, services continuing until twelve midnight, students marching to their dormitories singing. In Tsinan, two hundred soldiers professed Christ in three days. Among other converts was a banker from Shanghai.

In 1934, it was reported that a thousand believers had been baptized in Pingtu as a result of the Shantung Revival, and a new church had been organized there and at Tsinan; while forty bands were evangelizing around Hwanghsien.[10]

The Presbyterians also reported a great revival throughout Shantung, beginning in 1931 and continuing through 1933. Thrilling reports were received from the churches, and the city of Weihsien was particularly moved.[11] In two years, the number of Christians in Weihsien increased 25%, a total of 1500 being received into the Presbyterian congregations. In Weihsien, between 1930 and 1935, total church membership increased from over three thousand to over eight thousand in the American Presbyterian mission.[12] The American Lutherans in Shantung also reported revival, accompanied by excrescences of irregular response.[13]

Presbyterian observers in Shantung attributed much of the impulse for revival to an indigenous movement, Ling Eng Hui, or Spiritual Gifts movement. They conceded that there had been some excesses manifest, but insisted that on the whole the movement demonstrated 'marvelous evidence of the power of the Holy Spirit.'[14]

It was in Shantung that the communal 'Jesus Family' had its beginnings; likewise the charismatic 'Spiritual Gifts' movement; and earlier the Pentecostal 'True Jesus Church.' The Bethel Band taught the necessity of decisive dedication and the filling of the Holy Spirit for service, without going to any extremes about it.[15] Thus they avoided the pitfalls of those who preferred inner guidance to Scripture.

Dr. Paul Abbott, chairman of the Shantung Mission of the Presbyterian Church in the United States of America, well able to compare the Bethel Band's ministry with those of other Chinese indigenous groups, observed in 1932: [16]

> Their work impresses one as sane and constructive with emotion released in laughter and song, under control and with no excesses or results to undo or live down. Their follow-up work with correspondence, prayer lists and printed material is skillfully carried on as part of their service to the churches.

On his way back from Manchuria, John Sung visited the city of Hwanghsien in Shantung, and exercised a powerful ministry in the churches of the Southern Baptist Mission. In Pingtu, where revival was already underway, a great outpouring of the Spirit followed.[17] In Tsinan, more than forty students enrolled at Cheloo Christian University made profession of faith in the home of Dr. Thornton Stearns.

In 1933, the Bethel Band again visited Shantung province. Meetings were held in Tsinan, Tsining, Hwanghsien, and Tengchow, then Chefoo[18]—where many American and British schoolchildren were converted or helped—then Kaomi and Kiaochow. The sustained invitation of the churches was testimony enough to the effectiveness of their work.

At Tsingtao, John Sung first encountered the 'spiritual Gifts' movement, in which many seeking the filling of the Spirit coveted speaking with tongues, visions, dreams and the like. His reaction was not to seek satisfaction thus, but to become a clean and open channel for the Spirit. He encountered the movement again on his way back from the revival ministry in Manchuria, and still remained convinced that a life of witness was preferable to spiritual experiences of ecstatic or introspective kinds.[19]

In 1934, John Sung alone revisited Shantung, ministering in Tsinan to great crowds including businessmen, officials, professional men, and university students. He preached again in many other Shantung cities. The Awakening was a continuing force in all the churches.

Conditions prevailing at her own mission station did not allow Marie Monsen to return to her regular work there, so she accepted an invitation to hold meetings in Peking in 1927, the power of the Holy Spirit being experienced among Blind School students and among Seminary trainees. [20]

From then on Marie Monsen fulfilled an extensive schedule of speaking in revival meetings at various mission stations throughout the northern half of China during 1928-1932. It was interrupted dangerously when, in April of 1929, she was captured by a band of pirates and held for twenty-three days, en route to meetings in the province of Shantung.[21] Her itinerary took her to the provinces of Shansi, Honan, Hopei, Chahar, Shantung, Suiyuan, Hupeh and Kiangsu. Her work was accompanied by an outpouring of the Spirit everywhere she went, bringing many people to a personal experience of conversion. Outstanding was a work of the Spirit among the students in Hsuchow in Kiangsu Province, still effective in 1934, after two years' observation. Leslie Lyall described her as 'the pioneer of the spiritual new life movement.'[22]

The first campaign of the Bethel Worldwide Evangelistic Band was held in Taiming, in 1931, in the northern province, Hopei. The meetings were difficult from the start, dragging on . . . then a break came, and one who had resisted conviction wholly yielded. Then the whole Christian community shared in the revival.[23]

Andrew Gih and his colleagues often traversed Hopei, in most cases holding campaigns in the strategic province. In Hopei in 1933, the Bethel Band held revival meetings for the Assembly of God at Shihkiachwang, a railway junction.[24] Of those who repented of sin were a number who had relied upon their possession of the gift of tongues. Twenty missionaries from surrounding cities attended the meetings and went back to their charges refreshed.

The China Inland Mission reported extraordinary revival from Shunteh, in Hopei province, due to a movement of the Spirit following the visits of the Bethel Band and of Anna Christensen.[25] The attendance waxed so large that a tabernacle of matting was erected. Anna Christensen's ministry drew quiet and attentive crowds, there being no undue excitement or mere emotionalism, but many hearts were 'broken with grief for sin.' Quarrels were made up and restitutions and confessions followed. A lawsuit involving believers was withdrawn, and the whole congregation was possessed by overflowing joy.

The editor of a worldwide missionary review was so impressed with a Christmas letter sent out by a missionary in Peking in 1933 that he reproduced it in several pages. The Rev. James P. Leynse announced that 'a crowning revival has come to Peiping.' Every night, people slept on benches in the church in order to find a place in the early morning prayer meetings. For a month, crowds of between a thousand and fifteen hundred jammed the auditorium to hear the Good News preached 'in arresting simplicity.' In these main meetings, the great crowd knelt in united prayer —spontaneously praying aloud in a 'sound of many waters.' Hundreds confessed sins and made restitution. The leaders of the movement were Andrew Gih and John Sung, Frank Lin, Philip Lee and Lincoln Nieh, Bethel evangelists.[26]

Among those moved in Peking was the chief of police, who confessed that he had murdered a man to get his money. There was no one to receive the restitution, so he gave it for the relief of the poor. Other converts included bandits, rapacious officials, arrogant soldiers, rebellious college students, and dishonest servants.[27]

The value of the revival movement in Peking was made clear by the fact that a year later the three city churches had become self-supporting. The congregations were all pulsating with new life.[28]

In Paoting, southwest of Peking, the Bethel Band brought a reviving to a needy cause.[29] A local missionary reported:

> We are still filled with amazement at the miracles our
> eyes have seen. For many barren years, we have longed
> and prayed for reviving. Now it has been poured out . . .
> none of us have seen anything like it.

The Paoting church was transformed. Local preaching bands were formed and speedily evangelized in the villages, forming little churches and other preaching bands.

It was Marie Monsen's opinion that the splendid work done in previous decades was like a bundle of brushwood laid and ready for the flame with which the Holy Spirit would set it ablaze. The Norwegian pioneer of revival visited other parts of Hopei besides Peking.[30] Ernest Thompson, of the China Inland Mission, engaged in fruitful tent evangelism.

The churches of Tientsin invited John Sung to hold ten days' meetings, using a large Methodist church building. Despite opposition from worldly Christians, the work was effective, and Sung stayed another eight days on the south side of the city. Fifty witness teams were organized.[31]

In 1934, John Sung returned to the city of Tientsin, but all the churches refused their buildings for special services. Hence, a large hall was rented, and was packed with people. Some churchmen launched a campaign of vilification of John Sung, with the result that three hundred believers left the churches and built their own congregation, which so prospered in evangelism that the preaching bands made it their headquarters.[32] This was the only case of secession known to result from John Sung's ministry. John Sung made not a few enemies by his forthrightness.

To the west of Hopei is the great province of Shansi. Anna Christensen ministered alone in Shansi in 1927 when missionaries of other nationalities had been withdrawn.[33] In her ministry, the presence and power of the Holy Spirit was manifest, despite the turmoil of the times.

Leslie T. Lyall, son of a famed revivalist who had moved many in Australia and New Zealand at the beginning of the century, was a very young missionary in early 1933. He was in Pingyang, Shansi, when the Bethel Band moved the Chinese church and community.[34] While insisting that the messages of the evangelists were completely lacking in excitement, Lyall was amazed that sobbing was heard from all over the hall when the message sank home—'I have never been in meetings like those,' he said.

In Shansi province, in 1933, the Bethel Band commenced revival ministry in Taiyuan, the capital of the province.[35] It was a difficult series, partly due to John Sung's poor health and partly to the lukewarmness of the leadership. Pingting provided much the same response, for the same reasons. In Pingyao, the work was limited by the conservatism of the local Christians, and their limited education. In Hungtung, the base of the China Inland Mission in the province, there were happier results, and although John Sung had behaved very brusquely with both missionaries and national leaders, there was a common response to his challenge to them and a revival began which continued for years.

In mid-1934, the results of the Bethel Band visit to the city of Pingyao in Shansi were still continuing, the local Christians being fired by the warmth of the virile, indigenous evangelistic ministry.[36]

The Bethel Band simply could not accept all the calls by telegram or urgent letter received at Shanghai, hence they encouraged other evangelists to team up to meet the need, and they found many volunteers.

To the northwest, Pastors Liu and Shih conducted revival
meetings in twenty-three major cities, stirring the churches,
and also preached in the open-air to as many as twenty-
thousand at a time.[37] They were followed by bands preaching
in Shansi and Shensi provinces, with as many as forty-five
meetings in a ten-day series. Many were the converts.

During 1934, there was an extensive revival throughout
the churches of Shensi, in one locality seven hundred having
been baptized within twelve months, with six hundred eager
inquirers receiving counsel. It was noted that all the seven
hundred converts were in faithful attendance at worship.[38]

In early 1935, a Bethel Band composed of two minor
prophets, John Shih and James Chang, was ministering in
Shensi. Neither evangelist had a reputation like John Sung
or Andrew Gih, yet men and women were falling under deep
conviction of sin, and a hundred people had been hopefully
converted to God. A watchful missionary commented:[39]

> Messrs. Shih and Chang have been all that could be
> desired as evangelists—faithful in preaching, Christ-
> like in demeanor, earnest in spiritual life. They left
> behind a spirit of unity among believers.

The Shensi meetings were not spectacular, but the given
messages were clear and convincing. In one town, ten local
preaching bands went forth as a result of the meetings.

This Bethel Band found that, in one city, membership of
the church was only fifteen, but the evangelists took to alleys
and streets, Chang playing his trumpet. Eighteen professed
faith in the first chapel service.[40] On occasion, there were
so many inquirers that no message could be given. They
were interrupted in the arduous work. The Red Army units
traversed Shensi on their Long March, and both evangelists
and missionaries were forced to flee.

In 1935, a thousand conversions were reported in the
churches of Shensi, as the work of God went further in that
province.[41] Missionaries and national leaders alike rejoiced
in the good health of the churches.

Leland Wang ministered in crowded revival meetings in
Shensi, Shansi, and Hopei. His mother tongue was a Fukien
dialect, but he settled in Shanghai and itinerated through the
Mandarin-speaking provinces as well as the South.[42] There
were also Chinese evangelists from the churches awakened
in the mission fields of Honan to the southeast—Lutherans
in many instances—who evangelized Shansi and Shensi, and
these provinces were also visited by Shantung evangelists.

12

SHANGHAI AND CENTRAL CHINA

Not only Manchuria but the burgeoning metropolis of Shanghai was the object of intra-provincial migration in the period between World Wars I and II. Shanghai was the most dynamic community in China, matched only by Hong Kong outside the Republic and the Wuhan tri-cities up the Yangtse. And events in Shanghai had the widest reaching effects in the Awakening of 1927-1939 in China.

Leland Wang of Foochow, who had been converted in 1918, had resigned from his promising career to go into full-time service for the Lord in preaching the Gospel. This led to a wider ministry in time, and by 1925 there was spiritual power in his meetings in Shanghai, where people were being converted to God and many Christians dedicating their lives afresh to the Cause. Some of these later became well-known Christian leaders, among them a young post-office clerk— Gih Su-wen, baptized by Leland Wang in Shanghai in 1925, and known throughout the world as Andrew Gih.[1]

As a new convert, Andrew Gih attended the revival series addressed by Paget Wilkes in Shanghai in 1925. He was one of those deeply moved when he heard Wilkes make a special plea for totally dedicated Chinese Christians to evangelize all of China. He decided within the depths of his heart to heed that call, and began to preach, despite severest handicaps. He soon developed into a very powerful evangelist, thanks in part to the training and leadership provided him by Mary Stone, a well-known Chinese lady physician who was the co-founder of the virile Bethel Mission in Shanghai. Gih began evangelistic work out of Bethel Mission and, in 1927, with other young like-minded men formed a Bethel Evangelistic Band, dedicating themselves to take the gospel message into every province of the vast land of China.[2]

Meantime, there was a deep moving of the Spirit at the Bethel Mission in Shanghai, where an eight-day retreat was arranged for church leaders of all denominations.[3] The movement among the leaders spread to the Moore Memorial Church where a thousand attended nightly sessions.

On 1st January 1932, the Bethel Band ministered in the capacious Allen Memorial Church in the Chapei district of Shanghai at the invitation of the Shanghai Ministers. The church was crowded, and the series was extended twice, a densely packed audience overflowing to the streets.[4] There were hundreds professing conversion. Before the end of the month, war broke out between China and Japan, Chapei being bombed and bombarded, the Allen Church coming under fire, some workers therein killed. Bethel Mission was moved to the safety of the International Settlement, its staff working among the multitudes of refugees pouring in.[5]

John Shih operated as an evangelist singly and with his own team as well as with the major Bethel Band.[6] His work in Kiangsu began when he and other student leaders were sent to substitute for Andrew Gih and John Sung, causing an initial disappointment among church members, but enjoying the greatest reviving the place had ever known. Shih also journeyed to the far northwest in Kansu with Pastor Liu Tao-sheng, and evangelized with James Chang.

After leaving Bethel Mission, John Sung ministered in churches in the metropolis of Shanghai, with much success. He preached next in Chinkiang, on the Yangtse river, then at Suchow, in both cities winning numbers to Christ.[7]

At Shanghai Christian University, John Sung encountered Dr. Toyohito Kagawa, who was lecturing along the lines of the 'social gospel.' The Japanese invited his Chinese counterpart to address a prayer meeting, and, with memories of Union Theological Seminary in mind, Sung propounded the doctrines of the Cross, the New Birth, and the filling of the Holy Spirit.[8] It was clear that his message was unwelcome to the sponsors, so he declined a further invitation.

In Nanking, the national capital, huge audiences gathered to hear John Sung in 1934.[9] The ordinary church members responded warmly to him, but harsh criticisms angered the leaders. John Sung was becoming more severe in his pulpit denunciations, no longer having colleagues in the Bethel Band to advise and restrain him.

During 1935, Dr. John Sung conducted a united campaign for the churches of Nanking and its hinterland.[10] A spirit of revival was manifest, and a thousand people attended nightly. Out of the reviving of the churches, fifty evangelistic bands were organized for witness in the churches, in the streets, and in the villages round about. A few years before, anti-Christian forces had looted Christian properties there.

It is not surprising that the Awakening took hold early in the mission field of the Norwegian Lutheran Mission, to which Marie Monsen belonged. The years 1932, 1933 and 1934 were especially fruitful in central China.[11] In 1931, Marie Monsen returned from her special ministry up north, and addressed the workers of the Mission during the middle days of December.[12] Not a few of the converts of the ensuing movement were baptized people, some even evangelists.

In Honan, the Lutherans claimed that the churches of six societies—Norwegian, Swedish, and American—experienced awakenings. Opium sots, adulterers, thieves, hypocrites and idolaters were converted by the hundreds. The chief evangelists were Liu Tao-sheng and Wu Tjen-ming, both ordained Lutherans.

The Lutherans reported preparation for revival as early as 1930 in Honan province. At Hsuchang, the workers were holding noon prayer meetings daily in 1931. In March 1932, Marie Monsen and Pastor Liu Tao-sheng came to minister, bringing a holy hush and eager expectancy never before experienced. Then the Chinese pastors and evangelists began their fearless preaching of the Word, resulting in a deep conviction and contrition designated 'sin-sickness.' The thoroughgoing repentance was followed by joy and zeal for the salvation of others.[13] It was a genuine revival.

In March 1933, the Bethel Band commenced meetings in Kaifeng, capital city of Honan.[14] A deep work of the Spirit was reported by the missionaries. At Changteh, they found the missionaries opposed to the 'out-of-date stuff' that they were preaching, but the Chinese congregation was deeply moved, and their pastor professed conversion.

In 1933, Andrew Gih and John Sung visited Changteh in Honan again.[15] This time, instead of a couple of hundred hearers, a thousand people attended the meetings, the whole situation having changed since the conversion of the pastor.

John Sung stopped off at Hwaiyang in Honan for a series of meetings held in a large tent, there being no churches large enough for united meetings.[16] Those attending were simple country people, but a number responded.

Liu Tao-sheng visited Miyang, Honan, in 1933, bringing the 'most powerful revival' yet experienced. He preached on 'Ye must be born again,' and intense conviction followed. The missionaries had never seen anything like such contrition, Chinese beating their fists against the wall, or on the floor, before pouring out their hearts in confession.[17]

From Hiangcheng, in Honan, the China Inland Mission reported a special work of the Spirit following the visit of Marie Monsen.[18] The Christians there in West Honan were 'smitten by a phenomenal conviction' of sin, driving some out of the meeting to get alone with God to confess the error of their ways, or to seek out other Christians to whom to confess their faults regardless of 'loss of face.'

China Inland missionaries reported revival in Shangtsai, in Honan, beginning with a visit by F. H. Joyce, a British missionary, followed by the preaching of Pastor Liu which was provocative of remarkable repentance.[19]

In mid-1933, a stirring revival was reported from the Hospital in Kaifeng, a C.I.M. institution where Guinness of Honan had ministered. The evangelist was the Danish Anna Christensen.[20] The staff were deeply moved, conscience money being presented, along with the restitution of many things stolen or pilfered. In Chowkiakow and Chenchow, in the same province, Anna Christensen's message was given with searching power. Men and women were gripped by her messages, and many were the results recorded. Powerful in the autumn of 1933, the revival was still continuing in Kaifeng, Chowkiakow, and other Honan cities, the work of grace having been thoroughly effective.[21]

The spiritual awakening continued into 1935 in Honan. Of one town it was said that, during some special meetings, even before they commenced and after they ended, the Holy Spirit mightily convinced men and women of sin, resulting in confessions in spite of the risk of 'loss of face.'[22]

Anhwei province was greatly disturbed by the civil war, but local revivals occurred here and there, one at Suancheng being noteworthy.[23] Again the movements were marked by confession of sin among church members and inquiry after salvation by their friends.

In December of 1934, two young missionaries, John and Betty Stam, were seized by the Communists in Anhwei and a $20,000 ransom was demanded.[24] Not long after, they were murdered, their baby girl escaping miraculously. It was touching that John Stam had sent his father some verses at that time:

> Afraid? Of what?
> A flash—a crash—a pierced heart;
> Darkness—light— O Heaven's art!
> A wound of His a counterpart!
> Afraid? Of that?

Afraid? Of what?
To do by death what life could not—
Baptize with blood a stony plot,
That souls may blossom from the spot?
Afraid? Of that?

There was much prayer for war-torn Anhwei following the murder of John and Betty Stam. In 1936, a 'wonderful work' was reported from Suancheng, visited by John Sung. In summer, Pastor Hsieh Meng-tseh itinerated from station to station.[25] Great crowds attended the meetings of John Sung, and a wave of revival overflowed.

In 1933, the Lutheran United Mission, working in Hupeh and Honan, announced that a spiritual movement had begun in their mission field, filling them with hope.[26] Lutherans of other societies cited as factors in the movement: united and continuous prayer, with noonday prayer meetings at all stations, constant and faithful preaching of the Word and distribution of tracts and scripture portions.[27]

The Bethel Band tackled the industrial Wuhan complex. In Hankow, the Chicago of China, the meetings were over-crowded nightly, and people responded to every invitation. Stolen things were returned, old debts were paid, enemies were reconciled. Visitors came in from a hundred outlying places. Twenty volunteer preaching bands were formed. The warden of the prison invited the Band to conduct an evangelistic service therein, and the convicts responded to the message. An officer, deathly pale, stepped forward and confessed having extorted bribes from their relatives and having dealt crookedly with the prisoners, crying in a loud voice: 'Will you forgive me?'—which they heartily did. [28]

Dr. Marcus Cheng, an internationally known Christian leader, affirmed simply 'I can say definitely that the Day of Pentecost has come to China.'[29] The revival began at the deadest church in the Mission Covenant field, Icheng.[30] Liu Tao-sheng became the John the Baptist of a sweeping move-ment, his words a hammer which smashed resistance. Two Norwegian missionaries, Olaf Lie and Knut Nordhaug, came to help, their speech slow, but with words that cut to the quick. In May 1934,[31] Pentecost in Siangyang was reported, revival beginning in the church body, with quarrels made up and enemies reconciled, and 'all the sins of the calendar' confessed: idolatry, hatred, murder, adultery, theft, lying, gambling, covetousness, and the use of narcotics such as opium and tobacco. The Sunday began with an early morning prayer meeting; morning service went on from 10.30 a.m. until 2.30 p.m. The Rev. D. R. Wahlquist of Sweden wrote:

> We have been permitted to see some of this wonderful glory. The winds of revival which have been blowing over wide areas of China have also come to our field, the martyr district, where the blood of the martyrs now bears its rich harvest.

Many professing Christians experienced the new birth, and entire families were won.[32] Not a few raw heathen were converted. Sins 'as black as night' were confessed, among them fornication and child murder, one woman confessing that she had destroyed six baby girls. At Wuchang, Pastor Wu Tjen-ming preached for two weeks in middle October 1934, leading a morning watch, a class for inquirers, a reading class, a class for voluntary workers, and three public rallies. His quiet ministry was followed by the 'somewhat noisy' exhortation of a Bethel Band, led by Frank Lin.[33] Some who had been unmoved by Pastor Wu were won by the younger men.

In 1933, an awakening began at the Union Seminary in Shekow, where Hunanese students were enrolled.[34] A team of students came south into Hunan, and began ministry in Changsha in June, reaching out into other smaller cities. The Rev. Einar Smebye, superintendent of the Norwegian Missionary Society field, described the results as 'the most glorious experience I have had in China. . . It was revival after the old Hauge pattern . . . deep contrition . . . assurance of forgiveness.'[35] Often there was 'a mighty torrent of prayer.' The Finnish Lutheran fields were likewise visited, the Word sinking into the conscience and breaking down all opposition, provoking confession of sins past and present.[36]

In November 1933, the whole city of Changsha, capital of Hunan, was stirred by the ministry of John Sung and Andrew Gih.[37] Chinese gentlefolk, rough soldiers, peasants, townsfolk, missionaries and others attended the meetings. All three missions operating in Changsha cooperated and all three reaped a harvest.[38] There were more than three hundred students professedly converted the first night that Dr. Sung spoke to gatherings of a thousand students. Hengyang in southern Hunan was the scene of another revival of the churches, John Sung ministering with Frank Lin interpreting. The Rev. J. R. Wilson, of the Church Missionary Society, recalled twenty years later: 'Such was the power of the presentation of the messages that many of them are still vivid in my memory.'[39]

13

REVIVAL IN THE SOUTH AND WEST

The Awakening began in the South China provinces almost as early as in Manchuria. In several of the southern provinces, a language very different to Mandarin Chinese but using the same ideographs was spoken. Members of the Bethel Band, a major factor in spreading revival in the South, shared these various languages, being bi-lingual in speech. In Kwantung and Fukien, for example, Andrew Gih spoke by interpretation into Cantonese or one of the Fukienese dialects. John Sung, who began his ministry in Fukien, sometimes spoke in his Hinghwa dialect in parts of Fukien, but in others used an interpreter, as he did in Cantonese-speaking areas and throughout the rest of China until he became proficient in Mandarin. In some places, the leaders used English and were interpreted into a local language by missionaries.

The Bethel Band received a pathetic call to a church in Hinghwa which had endured persistent persecution from the Communists.[1] A great congregation had been scattered, and, when a faithful few gathered, shouting agitators would interrupt the pastor, seize the pulpit, and blaspheme the Name before an unwilling audience.

The evangelists found a church, seated for 3000, covered with posters denouncing Christianity.[2] The meetings began without interference on weekdays, but by the time a revival had moved two thousand people, the Communists came to break up the meeting. There was such power in the service that they hesitated, interested in spite of themselves, and one of their number went forward with others seeking peace with God.

About the same time in 1928, Dr. George Ridout with the Bethel Band visited Sienyu, Futsing and Foochow in the province of Fukien.[3] Ridout was a Methodist evangelist based at Asbury College in Kentucky, exercising a worldwide ministry. Bethel Mission, which sponsored the Bethel Band, also had its links with Asbury College. In all three cities and districts, extraordinary revival was reported in the churches.

It was at Sienyu, a city near Hinghwa, where the same dialect was spoken, that the revival seemed most remarkable. A Methodist missionary, W. B. Cole, writing from Sienyu in June 1928, reported that 'Many were in tears and sobbing out confessions of sin. The meeting lasted from two o'clock until five. Many came into the joyful experience of salvation.' Christians came into deeper spiritual blessing. Commenting further on the band of young Bethel workers, he likened them to the 'good old-fashioned Methodists of the John Wesley type who believed in conversion and sanctification.' The Revival had just begun, he affirmed.[4]

One of the many Christians in that area to catch the spiritual fire from the Bethel Band was John Sung, a native of Hinghwa.[5] Greatly inspired by the success of the Bethel Band, he likewise formed a local band from the younger converts and went out preaching the gospel in the summer months with remarkable blessing. Of him, W. B. Cole wrote in July 1928, 'He has great power and consecration. He is growing. He got much good from his contact with the Bethel Band . . .'[6] Thus began John Sung's remarkable ministry.

In 1928, the Bethel Band visited the cities of the South, including Canton and Wuchow in Kwangsi where attendances were overflowing, thousands of Christians confessed their faults, and hundreds professed conversion,[7] eight hundred in Wuchow in eight days. In Canton, where an interpreter translated Mandarin into Cantonese, the preaching ceased temporarily when the interpreter began to weep in contrition over his own shortcomings.[8]

In the spring of 1929, Dr. John Sung conducted a lively series of meetings at Changchow, Fukien, for the deepening of the Christian life and the evangelization of the outsiders. The meetings were undergirded by prayer meetings at six o'clock in the morning.[9] The evening meetings in the local chapel attracted never less than five hundred hearers. It was strange to note that John Sung spoke by interpretation in a city within his native province, for there are distinctive dialects in three or more districts of Fukien.

Early in 1929, John Sung visited the cities of Amoy, and Chuanchow, and Changchow in the south of his native Fukien. And during the spring of 1930, he ministered in Shunchang, and Yenping, and Yangkou in the north.[10] The response of the people was encouraging. Sung planned follow-up courses of teaching for both workers and converts. He had learned to be systematic in study, biblical in content.

In June 1932, John Sung and Frank Lin ministered in Foochow, Fukien province, while Andrew Gih and the others visited Hinghwa and Sienyu. The Hinghwa-Sienyu meetings produced a great revival.[11] In Foochow, four hundred local university students were among the thousands attending and a thousand young people professed faith—this in spite of a bitter anti-evangelistic newspaper campaign.[12]

When the Bethel Band visited the port of Foochow, in 1933, a thousand or more people attended the evangelistic meetings twice a day for four weeks, rain or shine.[13] There was a remarkable revival of church life there.

In the autumn of 1934, John Sung revisited Foochow in his native Fukien.[14] It compared with his earlier visit in revival results. In Amoy, the largest church was filled to overflowing, hearers crowding the doors, windows and a platform erected outside. A mat shed was put up for 2500 people, and the final rally attracted 5000 folk. A gambling house in Amoy failed, for lack of patrons. The city council requested the evangelist to leave, complaining of the disruption of communications. There were justified criticisms made of the arbitrary actions of Dr. Sung.

The work of God was flourishing so much in Fukien that a hundred and twenty evangelistic bands were operating in the province, stirring the churches and winning a host of outsiders to the Faith; the year 1935 showed no diminishing of the enterprise.[15]

Civil war was raging in the province of Kiangsi between the Nationalist and Communist armies in 1930 and 1931. A Methodist missionary, W. E. Schubert, with his Chinese colleague in Nanchang, the provincial capital, had prayed for thirty days in 1930 for revival, and in 1931 they had prayed for fifty days when John Sung arrived in February. Sung accepted the invitation against the advice of his Bethel friends in Shanghai, fearful for his safety. Less than ninety people attended the opening meetings, and there appeared to be no results. But when Sung overheard his American host praying: 'Lord, let me see revival in Nanchang or let me go home to America,' his faith was stirred.[16] He received a distinct leading to attack the problems of sin, and as he so preached the attendances grew. A side trip to Kiukiang resulted in a couple of hundred high school students turning to God. In the extended meetings at Nanchang, there was an outbreak of confession of sin, first in the school and then in the church, a genuine revival of Christianity.[17]

The China Inland Mission reported a revival in Nanchang, Kiangsi province, in May 1933. The evangelist was Leland Wang, and a wonderful spirit of expectancy at the united weekly prayer meetings preceded his coming.[18] Four of the largest and most central churches were filled to capacity each afternoon and evening, and 250 inquirers came forward in response to the ministry. Madame Chiang Kai-shek was then in Nanchang, and suggested that meetings be held for the wounded soldiers in nearby military hospitals, thus beginning a fruitful ministry in the Nationalist Army. There were many instances of the friendliness of the Chiangs, and their associates, to missionaries and evangelists. In 1938, the writer had happy fellowship with the H. H. Kungs, first with Madame Kung in Hong Kong, Dr. Kung in Chungking.[19]

In April 1934, the Bethel Band had visited Nanchang, the Kiangsi capital, and ministered for ten days in seven or eight cities where there was a Christian cause. In the New Year of 1935, the missionaries reported that the work was still continuing effectively.[20]

Following a great Bible Conference in Shanghai in 1932, the Bethel Band moved south to Hong Kong, 4th March 1932, a 'lasting spiritual awakening' and many conversions in the Colony following.[21] In one meeting on Hong Kong island, Gih felt impelled to give an invitation—even though the local conservative church leaders were against it, and the Holy Spirit vindicated his leading by sending almost the entire crowd up to the altar. Later, thirteen evangelistic bands were formed among the Christians of this one congregation. The Peniel Mission, seating 500, was packed out by more than a thousand eager hearers. Andrew Gih and John Sung shared the preaching, Philip Lee interpreting into Cantonese. These Kowloon meetings attracted rich and poor, educated and illiterate, and hundreds were converted. Nearly seven years later, the writer preached in the same place, crowded out, the blessing still continuing.[22]

Dr. E. Stanley Jones, noted for his ministry in India, visited China for evangelistic work during the 1930s.[23] He preached in the larger cities from Peking to Canton, his being a genteel, conventional type of evangelism, resulting in the signing of cards by inquirers who were followed up by the sponsors. In Canton, a thousand such cards were received. Jones's work enjoyed the blessing of the rising tide of interest in Christianity in China, though not part of the dynamic indigenous revival movement.

The Bethel Band journeyed up the Pearl river to Wuchow, Kwangsi, for meetings with the Christian and Missionary Alliance.[24] After initial disappointment, a revival swept the students of the Bible School there and overflowed to the city. At Wuchow, a college professor and an American teacher professed conversion while the student body was being swept by revival, yet the movement began in the face of suspicion, theological in nature. Meetings were also held in Yulin and Nanning, Kwangsi cities. Vera Shen, Hong Kong educator, an Anhwei girl, was converted in the Wuchow series.[25]

Next the Band ministered in Canton, the Kwantung provincial metropolis, reaping the harvest.[26] Andrew Gih began a campaign in Swatow, yet another language area, while the others of the Band conducted a second enthusiastic series in Hong Kong.[27]

In summer, 1934, John Sung preached for ten days in the lakeside city of Hangchow in Chekiang.[28] Fifty preaching bands were formed of those converted and revived. He returned to Hangchow, but he angered the leaders (who had withheld their support) by criticizing them publicly.

A Bethel Band was formed to make a run through the Japanese lines in Kwantung, and preach its way up through Kwangsi, Kweichow—where the Bethel Mission maintained a growing orphanage work—to Szechwan.[29] It was composed of Andrew Gih, John Koo, James Chang, John Shih, and Ou I-wen (Edwin Orr), assisted by Nurse S. S. Yao and Hope Chow. Many were the vicissitudes of travel, many the opportunities of ministry; and at last Andrew Gih and Edwin Orr reached Chungking, where they were received by the Prime Minister of China, and where they conducted a series of revival meetings under difficult conditions, air raids.

Back in Hong Kong, Andrew Gih directed the meetings for his Irish friend in the Peniel Mission in Kowloon, the messages being translated into Cantonese. By 7 p.m., the seats were filled up and many stood outside. Andrew Gih dealt with the many inquirers who remained for counsel. Meanwhile, another series was held on the island for those who spoke English. The contrast in atmosphere and response was significant—the Chinese were still enjoying the general revival, whereas the British and Americans in Hong Kong were unaffected, though a number of British military men professed conversion, and an American afterwards noted as a children's evangelist in the United States—the Rev. Willard Grant—was converted also.

There were five million people on the island of Taiwan in the mid-1930s, mainly Chinese of Amoy (Minnan) speech but including aboriginal tribes in the mountains and more than a quarter of a million Japanese. For forty years, the Japanese government had pushed the Nipponization of the island, not discouraging Christianity among the Chinese and Japanese, but firmly forbidding any approach to the tribespeople in the hills.[30]

Until World War II, the evangelization of the island lay in the hands of English and Canadian Presbyterians, and a total of six thousand at the beginning of World War I had grown to approximately fifteen thousand in quarter of a century.[31] The Presbyterian churches were practically self-supporting in the 'thirties, growing more rapidly than the Roman Catholics, of whom there were seven thousand.

In 1938, a three-year movement of evangelization was begun by the Presbyterian leaders. This came in the wake of a series of meetings conducted by Dr. John Sung on the island, thousands attending and hundreds professing personal conversion.[32] As usual, preaching bands were formed—in fact, several hundred evangelistic teams whose members pledged themselves to witness for Christ at least once a week. The whole spiritual life of the island was quickened.

As elsewhere, the 1938 revival came before a period of persecution of the Church in Taiwan. Taiwanese Christians were suspected of disloyalty to the Japanese government. The authorities insisted upon obeisance at the shrines as a means of assimilating the population into the Empire.   On the other hand, the Taiwanese regarded their congregational life as the only fellowship in which they could be themselves. In 1940 and 1941, the missionaries were evacuated from the island, cutting off the believers from association with other Christians.[33]

When the tide began to turn against the Japanese military in World War II, and American troops liberated the islands of the Philippine archipelago to the south, the authorities became alarmed, fearing an American landing.[34]

> The Japanese made no concealment of the fact that they planned to massacre all Christians, men, women, and children, if American troops landed on the island. A death list of all Christians was compiled.

Fortunately, the American forces landed to the north on the Ryukyu chain, on Okinawa, which spared the Christians on Taiwan a bloodbath.

In 1929, a woman of the Sediq tribe, Chi-oang by name, had entered the Bible School in Tansui. She was especially welcomed by the missionaries, who had decided that the only way to reach the mountain tribes was by training tribal people there and sending them back to their own people with the message of salvation.

Chi-oang had married a Taiwanese, who was murdered by the tribesmen.[35] She had played the part of a reconciler between the tribe and the Japanese, who threatened them with extermination. Consequently, she was esteemed both by the Sediq and by the Japanese.

At sixty years of age, Chi-oang returned to the Hualien area to evangelize the Sediq people. She itinerated from village to village, enjoying a sympathetic hearing, working patiently and carefully and secretly because of Japanese restrictions. She preached the holiness of God, the need of repentance, the necessity of prayer, and the virtue of good works and steadfastness in face of persecution.

Two other Sediq evangelists, Dowai and Weilan Tako, became powerful leaders of the movement in the villages. Dowai was brutally beaten by the police and imprisoned for seven years for preaching. At one point, Weilan Tako was beaten and left for dead. But the Japanese authorities were never able to crush the movement.

Japanese Bibles were smuggled into the villages, and Chi-oang secretly taught Bible classes, beginning with the Creation, explaining the Old Testament stories, and finally preaching the Cross. The pioneers of the movement were men and women of prayer, praying with believers as well as unbelievers, the latter greatly impressed when answers to prayer were observed.[36]

Several Taiwanese pastors shared in the evangelization of the mountain tribes. In spite of persecution and rigid repression during the war, the Christ-ward movement in the Sediq and Amis tribes accelerated. Often vivid dreams helped persuade important tribesmen of the truth of the Gospel, even when the Scriptures were unfamiliar to them. The message spread from one to another along the lines of family connections and tribal relations.

When the missionaries returned to Taiwan after the war, four thousand believers asked for baptism. In the decade following, all restrictions having been lifted, four hundred churches came into being in the mountains. Thus a new constituency had been established.

The most backward part of China in the 1930s was the far west, the province of Kansu—with Sinkiang beyond in Central Asia; Szechwan—with its Tibetan borderlands; and Kweichow, a mountainous country also; and Yunnan, far to the southwest. While there were mission stations and city churches in each province, especially in Szechwan, there was a backwardness in the people, isolated from the coast and from international influence.

The missionaries in Kansu province were encouraged by the movement of the Spirit in their faraway towns. In 1932, towards the year's end, a 'great spiritual uplift' was felt in all the meetings at Chenyuan, a C.I.M. station, and there were three-score baptisms, such a response of inquirers that one of the Chinese preachers 'jumped for joy.'[37]

From the Shantung revival, many evangelists went forth to other provinces of China. One such was Evangelist Tuan, who journeyed like the disciples of old, carrying all his earthly belongings in a bundle, together with his Bible. He would accept no money. The missionaries in Kanku, about a thousand miles west in Kansu province, welcomed him. His visit provoked a revival in the church and an awakening in the community, unbelievers seeking salvation.[38]

In the spring of 1934, the revival in C.I.M. stations in Kansu was continuing, the preaching of Evangelist Tuan provoking intense weeping over sin, while demons were cast out of the afflicted, and divisions were healed in the local church.[39]

Leland Wang and other more sophisticated evangelists, from Shanghai and the big cities, also visited Kansu in due course, but did not initiate the revival ministry. Pastors Liu and Shih of Bethel contributed much.

In Pingliang, Kansu, in mid-1935, a revival broke out, the ministry being devoid of sensationalism, still, deep and yet overwhelming.[40] As usual, the preaching services were preceded by early morning prayer meetings.

An old friend of the writer, Raymond Joyce, pioneered in Sinkiang with a party of younger missionaries in those days of revival, but reported no extraordinary movement.

Betty Hu, a graduate of Asbury College, was chosen to lead a band of evangelists to the far west.[41] She took with her Constance Ngo and two inexperienced young men, Koo and Chien. At the same time, Alice Lan, also of Asbury, took Dorcas Gih and two younger men north to Peking where likewise there was an encouraging response.

The major Bethel Band took up the challenge of the West. It took sixteen days of arduous travel for the evangelists to reach Szechwan.[42] A conference of Christians had been convened for Szechwan, but it seemed that the leaders were reluctant, and the people hindered.   Gih preached on the King of Nineveh coming down from his throne . . . and the first to respond was a Chinese bishop, followed by pastors and missionaries.

At Anshun, in Kweichow province, where a great awakening followed by a folk movement had occurred among the Miao tribesmen three decades earlier, there were six weeks of earnest intercession early in 1934.[43] Another startling movement began, one in which the confession of 'most awful sins' preceded the revival of believers and salvation of non-Christian tribespeople.[44]

Late in 1935, the revival was continuing among the Miao tribes of the Southwest, 'a profound work of grace' going on at Anshun, the revived Christians forming many preaching bands which went everywhere preaching the Word.[45]

In 1936, the Bethel Band moved into the mountainous province of Kweichow, reaping a harvest where the seed had been sown, stirring up hitherto unvisited congregations, urging out local preaching bands.

In the New Year of 1935, revival had been reported by missionaries in Kweichow.[46] More than six months later, the missionaries were telling of prayer meetings going on till midnight, with a deep sense of conviction followed by a manifestation of confession and crying for forgiveness.

Frank Lin, with two helpers, Koh and Tien, evangelized in Kweichow province,[47] among the mountains to the west. They began in a church with only a couple of old men and old women and a few children, the most spiritual church in the area, the missionary assured them.   After much hard work and urgent prayer, a break came, and revival began in the congregation.   Scores of students were converted, and four preaching bands were organized.

A call came from faraway Yunnan province, in the southwest, and an elder and younger evangelist Koo (no relations) responded with Pastor Koh—nicknamed by missionaries the Koo-Koo-Koh Band.[48] Revival began on the fifth day of their meetings, with weeping and confession of sin, after which the place was thronged with outsiders, many of whom were converted.   Yunnan was cursed with opium smoking, and the work was very difficult.   In a remote town without resident missionaries, they found a church whose members refused to admit 'unclean heathen' to the 'holy place.' The team struck up an acquaintance with the priests at the local temple, and preached from a high platform amid the hideous idols to great crowds, even school teachers repenting, and— last of all— the pharisees of the local church. Their work was interrupted by an invasion of the Red Army, fleeing out of Szechwan into Yunnan south and Shensi north.

The Bethel workers still found opportunities of service even after the Japanese launched their full-scale offensive in 1937. The huge number of refugees (estimated to number 100,000,000) moving into the interior were also hungry for the gospel. This proved to be a means of penetrating into backward areas that had never before been open to Christian workers, or had been closed to such a work.

The writer visited Szechwan, Kweichow, and Yunnan in the late 1930s with the Bethel Band—but not Kansu.

14

CHINA IN REVIVAL, 1927-1939

The Awakening which began in China in 1927 reached its peak in the early 1930s, but continued on throughout the thirties, inhibited but not extinguished by the massive dislocation of population that followed all-out war with Japan.

An editorial in the organ of the China Inland Mission in early 1935 noted a spiritual awakening or revival in various parts of China.[1] There were several features of the movement which impressed the observers: first, there had been much intercession, and prayer had been answered; second; the instruments in God's hands were chiefly Chinese evangelists and a number of foreigners, men and women; third; the movement was marked by conviction and confession of sin; fourth, the movement had not only revived the Church but had brought accessions in considerable numbers.

Although the Awakening of the late 1920s and the 1930s was primarily provoked by the ministry of Chinese, the missionary contribution was not forgotten. Andrew Gih commented:[2]

> The present reviving in China owes much to the God-fearing missionaries who have faithfully sowed the seed that is now coming to harvest. Through the self-sacrificing labours of those who have penetrated far into the interior, the gospel has been rooted deeply in Chinese soil. How we honour those early missionaries who endured hardship, suffered persecution, and many of them were even martyred.

Gih Tsu-wen regretted the presence of a different type of missionary, but rejoiced that 'some of these modernists' had been converted. Gih was not opposed to social service, saying that the Bethel Band had enjoyed its most wonderful results in mission schools where the students had possessed some background of Christian teaching. The work was slower in non-Christian schools, but most difficult of all in the schools where 'modernism' was taught, the poison to be taken out of their system before students could be converted. About this, he was most dogmatic.

And Gih boasted that he was converted under the ministry of Miss C. F. Tippet, received into the church by Jonathan Goforth, ordained by Alexander Saunders, and taught by Jennie Hughes—all evangelical missionaries.[3]

An editorial in the organ of the China Inland Mission in March 1936 drew attention to a significant development in connection with the Awakening in China.[4] Quoting the editor of a liberal magazine, the observer emphasized that 'available facts show that the Depression has decimated the liberal ranks and left their conservative colleagues stronger.' The percentage of 'sound evangelicals' in China had markedly increased in the 1930s.

Latourette, himself a missionary in China, has noted the sharp drop in Protestant missionary strength between the mid-1920s and mid-1930s.[5] In 1926, there were 8325 in China; in 1933, after the vicissitudes of seven years, only 5743, quite a contrast to the rise in numbers of Roman Catholic missionaries and certain evangelical affiliations. Communicants increased more rapidly than those in Roman Catholic missions during the same period—402,539 in 1924 and 567,390 in 1936, an increase of nearly fourteen thousand a year for twelve years.   It was also remarkable that the Protestant churches attracted more men than women to the membership, reporting a proportion of three to two.

Educational services did not dwindle with liberal causes. Though Christian primary schools declined in numbers—as in India—giving way to a national system, most colleges and universities of Christian foundation increased in their enrollments.[6] There were more than five thousand students in Christian colleges in 1932; in 1937, the figure had become seven thousand; then came the great trek of students and faculties to the West, to 'Free China.'   By 1942, the number of students in Christian colleges passed nine thousand for students trudging west carried their libraries and their laboratory equipment with them.   This migration occurred in non-Christian universities also.

But in evangelism more than education Chinese excelled. So gratifying were the results of the visits of the Bethel Band to Chefoo that Mrs. F. H. Judd, a veteran, wondering that the day of Chinese indigenous ministry had arrived, was moved to say: 'Lord, lettest Thou Thy servant depart in peace . . .'[7] The missionaries felt that the Chinese had come of age in the Gospel.   Little did they know that a mid-century revolution would drive missionaries out of China.

As the demand grew so rapidly for the ministry of the Bethel Band, other bands were formed to meet the need. Ten Bethel Bands were working simultaneously in China. Convinced that the work of the less-known workers was as great as that of the famous ones, a lady missionary wrote from Shansi: 'It certainly gives one great hopes for China when we see how her own sons and daughters are so filled with the Holy Spirit.'[8]

Andrew Gih later published the story of how these 'Bands of Soldiers for War'—including young ladies—were led to preach the gospel and minister revival in all parts of China and to the overseas Chinese during the 1930s.[9] They went all the way through Central China, West China up to the Tibetan border, Shensi and Kansu provinces in the northwest, Kweichow and Yunnan in the southwest, Peking and Inner Mongolia in the north, and Manchuria in the northeast. In 1933, a 'War Zone Band' was formed to minister to the soldiers fighting the Japanese in the north in one of the many theatres of combat.

In one year, from the summer of 1931 to the summer of 1932, the Bethel Band covered 54,823 miles through thirteen provinces, preaching to approximately 400,000 people in 1199 meetings, with 18,000 recorded decisions for Christ— the divine blessing on the work of one team.[10]

The Bethel Bands enjoyed the cooperation of a wide circle of missions. Among these were the China Inland Mission, the Chinese Christian Church, the Christian and Missionary Alliance, the Oriental Missionary Society, and the Peniel Mission, the Baptist, Lutheran, Mennonite, Methodist, National Holiness, Nazarene, and Presbyterian Missions —as well as Church of England and the Y. M. C. A.[11]

The statistics for four years give a valuable impression of the scope of the ministry:[12]

Approximate mileage	50,000
Cities visited	133
Meetings held	3,389
Aggregate attendance	508,600
Professions of faith and reaffirmations	51,659
Volunteers for service	4,834
Evangelistic teams formed	1,863
Letters of testimony received	15,000
Letters requesting prayer	16,000

These statistics referred to evangelistic results only, a measure of the outreach. No statistics revealed the great impact made in reviving the churches.

It was surely a recognized fact—in summing up this great ministry of the two leading Bethel Mission preachers, Andrew Gih and John Sung, that the success was wholly a work of the Holy Spirit. Andrew Gih told of how he had to allow the Spirit to work. 'There was no attempt to work up a revival,' he said.[13] The report of the Paoting Conference also gave the credit for this revival movement—bringing about changed lives and real transformation of hearts—to the Holy Spirit entirely.

Yet the Bethel Bands practised all the best methods of evangelism—personal witness, open-air meetings, gospel rallies, revival meetings, and the like. They used simple but moving music in harmony with the messages to follow. Both Andrew Gih and John Sung were considered outstanding Bible expositors, and they encouraged much prayer. In the Awakening, simultaneous prayer had broken forth, as twenty years earlier, but Andrew Gih introduced the people, in various places, to simultaneous praying for the first time, and even an astonished Presbyterian missionary admitted that it worked.[14]

Confession of sin and restitution of wrongs were marks of true revival in the Bethel Band's ministry. A missionary observed that a famous writer on things Chinese recently had written that the Chinese 'are troubled by a consciousness of sin.' But, in the revival, he added, men and women were terrified and literally watered the altar with their tears as they made confession.[15]

Among evangelists, Andrew Gih also recalled that 'the burning desire to confess sin' was the first indication of an imminent revival.' The convicting power of the Holy Spirit softened many hardened hearts, especially among students and faculty of missionary schools. In Peking, the Band saw members in one church bring $20,000 in 'conscience money.' A preacher returned $300 which he had embezzled from the church fund. An army officer confessed that he had taken a bribe of $5,000. A husband returned to the wife whom he had deserted. Examples could be multiplied from north and south, east and west, in the ministry of various evangelists.[16]

Another outcome of the Awakening that the Band always encouraged was the formation of evangelistic teams of local Christians to evangelize their own districts. In one Peking church alone, seventy-six such teams were formed, becoming a permanent organization with a continuing work. In a Peking missionary nurses school, the Awakening so changed the hearts of the students that the school had no difficulty in recruiting graduates to be nurse-evangelists in the country areas—long a goal of the school founders but never before attained, for lack of dedication.

It should be pointed out that the greatest successes thus enjoyed by the Band were in the geographical or social sectors of China where thousands of foreign missions worked! A missionary wrote from Szechuan to the Bethel Mission: 'At long last, in the providence of God, your devoted workers were sent by Him to gather the harvest for which we have prayed for many years.'[17]

At the same time, there were indigenous movements of evangelical Christianity spreading, unrelated to missionary enterprise. Leland Wang, John Sung, Andrew Gih, and the Bethel evangelists had worked wholeheartedly with mission churches regardless of denomination, but Chang Ling-sheng and the True Jesus Church evangelized or proselytized non-Christians or Christians during the revival period, packing a thousand into its congregation in Changsha in 1934. By the end of World War II, the movement had spread to every province, a total of seven hundred churches registered, more than half of them in Hunan and Honan and in Fukien.[18]

Meanwhile, Watchman Nee moved to Shanghai, and in 1928 rented a modest house in the International Settlement, teaching and preaching, a congregation growing up around him, later given the name Little Flock. Nee was greatly influenced first by the Exclusive Brethren and then by the Honor Oak Fellowship in London.[19]

In the 1930s, Watchman Nee ministered widely in China. In 1934, he met with John Sung and Leland Wang in Shanghai, but nothing came of the conference, the other two going on in cooperative ministry while Nee built up an undenominational denomination, an unsectarian sect. Nee was a prolific and persuasive writer, providing literature for the thousands awakened in the 1927-39 Revival. All the while, the Little Flocks were growing, a restoration movement as much as were the Brethren or Disciples, drawing from dissatisfied members and adherents of other denominations rather than engaging in direct evangelism. However, meetings held in believers' homes flourished, an outreach of the central assembly in each city, 'one-city one-church' being a notion peculiar to Watchman Nee. It was estimated that the whole fellowship had more than seven hundred churches and seventy thousand communicants at the end of World War II.[20]

15

SOUTH-EAST ASIAN REVIVALS, 1920—

The Evangelical Church planted in Danang by the pioneers of the Christian and Missionary Alliance in 1911 grew each year until in 1924 it nurtured sixteen hundred communicants, truly encouraging growth but a tiny minority among the many millions of Annamese-speaking people in Tonkin, Annam, and Cochin China.[1] In 1924, the Rev. and Mrs. R. A. Jaffray and Evangelist Wong of Wuchow arrived from South China for the first conference of the Evangelical Church of French Indo-China, arranged for the latter half of March.

Sixty-five delegates, mostly Annamese but including a few Cambodians and expatriate Chinese, attended the sessions along with local church members.[2] English, French and Chinese addresses were interpreted into Annamese, as was the Cambodian. The cumulative effect of the ministry was conviction of sin, at first resented, but later producing a spirit of repentance, confession, reconciliation, restitution, restoration and conversion—no dry eyes, and no time for the business sessions that were planned. One man tore up his books on hypnotism, later shouting for joy; another paid back money he had stolen; another hired a doctor to remove a couple of gold needles from his arms— Buddhist charms. The local Christians and those from afar were transformed.

The immediate effect of the revival on church membership was an increase of 82% in a year, thirteen hundred converts; and the Annamese Church continued growing for another ten years, when the total number of communicants reached 8384. In the mid-thirties, there came a disquieting change. In 1936, 751 new members were added to the rolls, but nearly four hundred members were lost.[3] In 1937, 779 converts were baptized, but nearly as many were lost to the active membership. Clearly, the upward climb of membership following the 1924 Revival had ended. The missionaries and national pastors began to pray for another outpouring of the Spirit. At that time, there were a million and a half Roman Catholics in the country, with a growth rate between two and three per cent, normal family increase.

John Sung agreed to visit the Evangelical Church rally near Saigon in June 1938, on the occasion of the annual meetings.[4] There came about such a revival, such a great outpouring of the Spirit that its effect was felt for a whole generation throughout the churches of Vietnam. Christians gathered in Saigon from all parts, Annamese-speaking people from the lowlands, mountain tribesmen from the highlands. Dr. Sung preached three times a day, in the morning, afternoon and evening, each service lasting three hours.[5] Thousands attended and hundreds responded. A spontaneous outburst of confession and restitution occurred, some instances being very striking. Sung was his usual, unusual self, startling people with a frankness so strange in an Oriental. His messages were direct, well-illustrated, biblical and topical.[6]

In the style of the Bethel Bands, John Sung organized evangelistic teams, church after church taking up the idea with much success. Delegates to the conference scattered to their home churches, telling the congregations of the revival, whereupon similar revival broke out everywhere. Ordinary pastors suddenly became outstanding evangelists, and adopted evangelistic methods in congregational ministry besides engaging in itinerant evangelism.[7] Laymen, even young people, began to engage in similar ministry, one who lacked formal training becoming an ardent expositor.[8]

Throughout Tonkin, missionaries and national workers and student evangelists increased their activities, church attendance and giving increasing all the while. In Tonkin, two teams of student evangelists held weekly series of evangelistic meetings in twenty-eight chapels, thirty-five thousand attending. Hundreds of streets were canvassed, thousands of houses visited, and thousands of tracts distributed, 392 inquirers being registered—all in a summer.

In Annam, stretching along the coast, evangelistic bands itinerated throughout the cities and towns, 1629 inquirers being registered, hundreds baptized, church membership increasing 14%.[9] The Bible School at Danang was crowded out, with 112 students enrolled. As in Tonkin, many new preaching stations were established.

In Cochin China, southern Vietnam, more than two thousand people professed conversion, and hundreds were soon thereafter baptized. In a single church, a hundred former members returned to the faith. Evangelistic bands went everywhere, preaching the Word.

There was a thriving work at Dalat, in the highlands, among the mountain tribes.[10] When a missionary and a native pastor returned to recount the story of the revival at Vinh-Long, a spirit of prayer fell upon the Koho-speaking students resulting in a seeking for God. Prayer interrupted and replaced the class periods next day. On the day following, the students devoted themselves to prayer followed by confession and the same was intensified the next day. Restitution was evidenced on the day following—thus it went on for a whole week, the students eating little and sleeping little. Then, as forgiveness was appropriated, joy swept the school and the spirit of worship was extraordinary on Sunday. The students asked for a month off, and returned to their villages to tell the Good News, returning to report several hundred professed conversions. The revival spread from the tribal Christians to the Annamese-speaking people round about.

In late 1938, two members of a Bethel Band (Gih Tsu-wen —Andrew Gih—and Ou I-wen—Edwin Orr) crossed from Yunnan to Tonkin, and visited Hanoi and Haiphong.[11] Next July, Andrew Gih addressed the national conference in the city of Saigon, attended by a couple of hundred pastors and evangelists and leaders.[12] While Gih was preaching, the Spirit 'as if suddenly fell from heaven as at Pentecost and people all over the meeting began to cry out.' The president of the Annamese Evangelical Church reported in 1939 'a blessed revival' in the churches and evangelistic bands, accompanied by miraculous healing.

Three years later, when French Indo-China experienced a Japanese occupation, mission subsidies were lacking and churches and preaching stations were closing down, a pastor (Le-van-Thai, who had been revived in 1924) emerged as a revivalist, provoking heart-felt response to the message. The movement spread from the South to Central Vietnam, and reached the North, the offering of jewelry and money for the threatened churches being substantial. Immediately there was an upsurge of consecration and evangelization in all parts of the Annamese-speaking territories.[13]

Meanwhile, Cambodia was first entered by the Christian and Missionary Alliance in 1922, growing in strength in the face of royal and Buddhist opposition. The Alliance opened its work in Luang Prabang in 1929 and in Vientiane in 1931, taking over also the converts of the Presbyterian Mission in Laos. In both Cambodia and Laos, the work was in the pioneering stage. Buddhism seemed entrenched.

In Thailand, in the period of the two world wars and the economic depression, the growth of evangelical churches remained slow, eight thousand or so in the early 1920s gaining four hundred or so in a dozen years.[14] Most of the growth occurred among the Laos of northern Siam, people whose Buddhism was diluted by animism, and some took place among the Chinese in the country.

There was a recurring interest in the subject of revival by the missionaries and national leaders in Thailand.[15] Thus in 1925, before the Awakening had begun in China, there was a quarterly conference of workers in Bangkok to discuss the conditions governing revivals, Thai leaders taking the lead, with a certain measure of quickening in the churches.

In the spring of 1938, a private invitation not officially sponsored by the churches brought Dr. John Sung to Bangkok where he began preaching in the large Baptist Church. His presence was scarcely welcomed by the missionaries, but the Chinese Christians gave him hearty support, the Rev. Boon Mark Getesarn being his host.[16]

For a month, John Sung preached to the Christians in the mornings and to curious inquirers in the evenings, about seven hundred professing conversion in meetings attended by a thousand people. A dozen Christians responded to the devotional ministry by offering for full-time service, and a couple of hundred enrolled in seventy evangelistic bands which continued active for a generation.

The opposition or indifference of most missionaries in southern Thailand being dissolved, Sung returned to Bangkok at the invitation of the Thai churches and ministered widely in Thailand, from Chiengmai and Lampang in the north to Nakorn Pathom and Petchaburi in the south. The missionaries reported unity and cooperation instead of division and such an impact that whole congregations fell to their knees to confess sin and pray for forgiveness.[17] Lives were set right, quarrels settled, debts paid, laymen deeply moved and pastors 'on fire.' The Rev. Sook Pongsanoi of Trang, for instance, was deeply moved by Sung's ministry, his church stirred in turn and packed out Sunday by Sunday.

Pastor Boon Mark reported the phenomenal in the work, the blind seeing, the deaf hearing, the lame walking, the dumb speaking, and many sick people healed permanently. Many evangelistic bands were formed, church attendance increased, spirituality prospered. The work remained more effective among the Chinese than among the Thai churches.

Thailand came under Japanese military occupation in the year 1942.[18] American and British missionaries were interned, and church and school buildings were requisitioned. Many church leaders were imprisoned, and restrictions were placed upon church activities, most of the witness bands of the Thai churches ceasing operation. Buddhism revived, taking advantage of the feelings of nationalism and the sentiment of pan-Asian solidarity then fostered. But the evangelical Christianity of the Thais and Chinese in the kingdom survived, and the revival during and after the visit of John Sung was considered a major factor in its survival. After the war, it quickly recovered.

To the west, in Burma, the 1920s were years of steady growth in almost all the language groups.[19] The 1922 census showed 11,210,943 Buddhists, 702,587 Animists, 500,592 Muslims, 420,782 Hindus, and 257,107 Christians, the last-named including 160,655 Baptists, 72,715 Roman Catholics, 19,636 Anglicans, 1,508 Presbyterians and 1,424 Methodists. The 160,000 Baptists represented a denomination which had grown 25% in ten years; some denominations had not grown at all during the decade.[20]

The Baptists in 1920, however, maintained 1097 churches with 80,764 members, having baptized 3919 the previous year. In 1930, they had 1449 churches with 116,406 members of whom 7933 had been baptized the previous year.[21] By far, the greatest growth was among the tribes in the Shan states where members increased from more than twelve thousand to more than thirty thousand, a 250% gain, 25% annually.

The Baptists in Rangoon were as concerned about schools as their missionary confreres in Bangkok, but it was noted that the educational work was thoroughly evangelistic, and Judson College statistics showed 'that there has never come from a mission high school an unconverted Karen boy or girl' for higher education.[22]

In the mid-1920s, mass evangelism was conducted among Burmese-speaking people by evangelistic teams of college students. During a year and a quarter of effort in a dozen campaigns reaching Burmese high schools and grammar schools, more than five hundred students professed faith, three hundred coming from Burmese Buddhist homes— coming out more or less secretly, one or two at a time.

In 1928, an evangelistic campaign conducted by E. Stanley Jones in Rangoon, Mandalay and Moulmein resulted in much quickening of spiritual life, it was said.[23]

Meanwhile, in other parts of Burma, the continuing folk movements among the tribes were adding members to the churches, 20% of the 2491 Kachin communicants having been baptized in 1924, 23% of the 3064 in 1925. At the end of the decade, a 'steady, quiet revival' was reported in Maymyo among Kachin soldiers, a movement carried on by soldiers themselves, that resulted in baptisms every month.[24] Team evangelism was succeeding in Shwegyin.

In 1931, a Burma for Christ movement was reported. In Mandalay, fifty Buddhist elders professed faith in Christ. A team of five Burmese and four Karens, assisted by two missionaries, crossed the mountains into Thailand and won a couple of scores of Buddhist students to Christ.

In the 1930s, the number of Baptist churches scarcely grew, and membership increased only 15% in ten years, even though baptisms of believers were still in excess of seven thousand annually.[25] Nothing like the movements that occurred in Thailand and Vietnam under John Sung in 1938 was reported from Burma.

There were approximately three hundred missionaries residing in Burma in 1941 when the storm of war burst upon the country; 109 Baptist missionaries were safely evacuated to India, though one died of his hardships later. The believers in Burma were left to face a baptism that exceeded many other great persecutions in scope.

16

POST-WAR EVANGELISM IN JAPAN

In September 1945, the heart of Tokyo was utterly ruined and desolate.[1] With the exception of the Imperial Palace and some modern buildings left standing and now occupied by General MacArthur's staff, there was not a building of any sort intact for miles, the place looking like a bull-dozed graveyard. It was then that I saw the brightest rainbow of all my experience, bathing the buildings and the desolation beyond in an eerie light for twenty minutes.

At that time, in the ruined heart of Tokyo, the present writer talked to Dr. Toyohiko Kagawa, who then announced that, as soon as he was free of emergency relief work, he would devote his time to evangelism.

In June 1946, the Kyodan, the United Church of Japan, decided to inaugurate a movement of reconstruction in the devastated country, presenting Christ to all Japan, exerting Christian influence upon the people, reviving Christian faith and strengthening and extending the Church. Kagawa was chosen as the national evangelist, devoting two weeks out of each month to itinerant ministry.[2]

It was reported that twenty thousand decision cards had been signed in Kagawa's campaigns in 1946. Many of these decisions were registered in school meetings, such as the girls' junior high school in Ikimizu, Nagasaki on December 17, eleven hundred pupils listening and 639 signing cards. In Itanishi, on the island of Shikoku, Kagawa addressed 700 hearers on 9th January 1947, of whom 76 signed decision cards. It was much the same for three years, an attendance of interested people and a polite response, but membership in the churches did not rise proportionately.

Also helping were personnel of the occupying government, both military and civilian, either earnest Christians anxious to assist in evangelism and social uplift, or former missionaries and missionaries' children with a good knowledge of the language and culture. Gradually, missionaries were permitted to enter Japan, those with previous experience of the country given preference.

General Douglas MacArthur, a professing Christian, had concluded the transactions on the deck of the battleship Missouri with the remark, 'The problem now is a theological one.' As executive of the Allied Powers, he made a private plea for ten thousand missionaries and ten million Bibles for Japan.³ Within half a dozen years, two thousand eager missionaries entered Japan, three-quarters of them from new societies representing the upsurge of evangelicalism around the world at the mid-century. While five hundred of the new missionaries were affiliated with the societies historically related to Japanese Christianity, the vast majority of the newcomers were avowedly evangelical.⁴ The composition of the missionary force had changed, and with the change came an evangelistic drive.

Dr. E. Stanley Jones visited Japan every other year in the immediate post-war period. His was a genial evangelism which attracted interested people not only in the larger cities but in smaller places, using the decision card method of follow-up.⁵ In 1951, more than twenty thousand cards were received; in 1953, more than twenty-five thousand. As was the rule, only a small percentage—perhaps ten per cent— resulted in baptism and church membership.

An American navy chaplain, Lawrence Lacour, returned to Japan in mid-summer of 1950.⁶ With his wife and two young ladies, he engaged in a five months' evangelistic tour of Honshu, Kyushu, Shikoku, and Hokkaido, visiting more than a hundred and twenty cities in ten thousand miles of travel, holding nearly two hundred meetings with an aggregate attendance of more than 400,000—averaging 3000 a day! Of the thirty-eight thousand who professed decision, more than three thousand were baptized and added to the churches. Lacour noted, however, that where there had been proper preparation and diligent pastoral follow-up, nearly half of the inquirers were satisfactorily enrolled.

In 1953, there were reports of a striking revival among evangelical missionaries in Japan, one marked by tears and confession, reconciliation and restitution.⁷ High hopes were held that this movement would extend to the Japanese churches, but it did not. Finney had written that, when the people of God exaggerate a movement of the Spirit in their midst, the Spirit of God is grieved. It was a pity that reports in American evangelical periodicals carried headlines: 'Japan Aflame,' 'Revival Sweeps Tokyo,' and the like. The movement touched a few hundred lives for good.

Lawrence Lacour returned to Japan for six years or so of sustained effort between 1954 and 1959.[8] The follow-up was based upon stations staffed by Japanese ministers or seminarians established as outposts of nearby congregations. In six years, thirty-four churches with fourteen hundred members and as many inquirers were planted.

World Vision sponsored an evangelistic crusade in the city of Osaka during the last three weeks of May 1959. The Festival Hall in the Osaka Grand Hotel was the largest hall in the tri-city area of Osaka, Kobe and Kyoto, population seven million, of whom only twenty-five thousand could be considered Christians.[9] The aggregate attendance reached 96,000, and approximately 7500 inquirers were enrolled, all of them visited by national pastors within three weeks. A quarter of these seekers attended services in one of 435 churches by the end of the crusade, the most responsive group being young people in their late teens. The evangelist was Bob Pierce.

Two years later, a thirty-day crusade was held in Tokyo Gymnasium. The aggregate attendance was approximately 225,000, the average evening attendance 7500. As in Osaka, no expense was spared to make the meetings a success. A choir of a thousand voices assisted, together with a splendid orchestra. In the main meetings, there were 7500 decisions and in 140 school meetings another 1400.[10] The evangelist again was Pierce, assisted by many American volunteers.

In the 1960s, Koji Honda emerged to national usefulness as an evangelist, conducting more than a hundred campaigns and enlisting five thousand inquirers.[11] Other very effective Japanese evangelists came to the fore, including Paul Ariga and Philip Tsuchiya.

In 1964, a group of men began to meet and pray and plan for a total mobilization evangelism in Japan. They had been influenced by reports of Evangelism-in-Depth from Latin American countries. It was significant that long and frequent times of prayer were engaged in, and Sodoin Dendo (total mobilization evangelism) was thus initiated.[12]

In September 1967, the leaders of Sodoin Dendo applied their principles of prayer and witness in the Tokyo Crusade of Billy Graham. Four thousand prayer cells were formed in the metropolitan area, while united prayer meetings were begun with 225 people, attendance rising to six thousand. The great hall of the Budokan attracted upwards of two hundred thousand people, almost as many in ten days as in '61.

Of a total of a thousand or more churches in the metropolis, three-quarters cooperated. Five thousand Christians were mobilized and trained, and four million homes in the Tokyo area were visited, tracts for adults and for children being left with the people.

In the Graham Crusade, more than fifteen thousand signed decision cards, and three thousand of these inquirers were baptized within seven months. Five thousand students registered their names in a rally for students. In a baseball stadium, 36,000 attended the closing meeting of the Crusade, the largest Christian gathering in the history of missions in Japan.[13] It was a successful campaign. After six years, there were more churches cooperating than in 1961, and a more thorough follow-up was achieved. Still, the problem in evangelism in Japan was noticed in the poor ratio of baptisms to inquiries.

In February 1968, the leaders of Sodoin Dendo met in a hotel in Hakone for two days of prayer. They were snowed in, and the prayer meeting was extended. Out of the sessions came a plan for total evangelism in Shikoku, an island the size of Wales or New Jersey, with a population of more than five million. An all-Shikoku Christian Conference was held in early 1969, a key speaker being Petrus Octavianus of Indonesia, experienced in the Timor revival. For four days the meetings produced the manifestations of revival, such as confession of sin and reconciliation, followed by great joy.

Prayer cells were formed throughout Shikoku, and fully a million homes were visited.[14] By the New Year of 1970, a majority of the churches in Shikoku were engaged in the movement, special evangelistic meetings being held in every church simultaneously, cooperative campaigns in key cities, radio evangelism and summer projects added. The result was the quadrupling of the number of converts received in a usual year, and the campaign was hailed as a success.

In the quarter of a century from 1947, the Protestant and Roman Catholic Churches in Japan tripled their membership, the latter rising from a hundred thousand to three hundred thousand, the former from two hundred thousand to nearly seven hundred thousand, the more spectacular growth noted in the late 1960s and early 1970s.[15] Nothing that could be called a revival, in the historic sense of that word, was reported, but there were local revivals in the hearts of workers preparing for the harvest. The post-war quarter-century was one of success for evangelical Christianity.

Communism gained a following in Japan, but did not become a serious menace to Christianity, perhaps because of
the success of the Japanese economic recovery, which kept
the people busy and provided them with material wealth and
educational opportunity. Of course, Marxism had its many
advocates in the student world, enough to cause disruption—
in fact, to trigger the worldwide phenomena of uproar.

While Evangelical Christianity progressed in post-war
Japan, it was paralleled and surpassed in years following
the Occupation by a resurgence of non-Christian religion.
The signing of the Peace Treaty in September 1951 heralded
a rise of interest in Shinto, shrines being repaired, attendance on festival days increasing, and government personnel
lending dignity to the ceremonies.[16] A professed Christian,
Secretary-General Matsuda of the Liberal Party, reported
on behalf of the Prime Minister the signing of the Peace
Treaty to the Sun Goddess at the Ise Shrine. A little later,
the Prime Minister and his cabinet attended the fall festival
at the Yasukuni Shrine, saying that it was equivalent to the
attendance of an American official at the tomb of the Unknown
Soldier. However, when it was suggested to Vice-President
Nixon in 1953 that he should lay a wreath at the Yasukuni
Shrine in reciprocal acknowledgment of the Crown Prince
Akihito's laying a wreath at the Unknown Soldier's tomb in
Arlington National Cemetery,[17] it was tactfully disregarded.
So, while precautions were taken to avoid the militaristic
overtones of pre-war shrine worship, attendance at all the
shrines increased. On New Year's Day of 1955, all records
were broken as more than 2,700,000 pilgrims visited the
Meiji Shrine in Tokyo. A year later, three million people
attended. Again there was a confusion of voices regarding
the nature of obeisance at the shrines, some saying that it
was idolatry and others patriotism.

Much more startling was the growth of an organization
renamed Soka Gakkai, a militant Buddhism.[18] Its spiritual
mother was a small sect, Nicheren Shoshu, going back six
hundred years or more.[19] Soka Gakkai had sixty members
in 1937, not very strong, but its leaders refused to participate in national Shinto, and Makiguchi and Toda and a score
of others were imprisoned during World War II. Toda was
released in 1945 and set about extending the movement. In
a quarter of a century, Soka Gakkai gained a following pro-
bably in excess of fifteen million people, converting people
in Buddhism where Christians converted from Buddhism.

Josei Toda possessed an organizing genius and fanatical dedication. Within seven years, Soka Gakkai had enlisted three quarters of a million families. Toda died in 1958, a quarter of a million or more attending his funeral, among them the Prime Minister, Nobusuke Kishi. Daisaku Ikeda became the third president, and within ten years seven million family units were claimed.[20]

In 1964, Soka Gakkai converted its parliamentary strength into a new political party, the Komei-to or Fairness Party. In the elections of 1967, twenty-five of their thirty-two candidates were elected to the Lower House. Within a few years the Soka Gakkai political party held twenty-five seats in the Upper House and forty-seven in the Lower, the third largest party in Japanese politics.[21]

Ikeda also expanded the movement overseas, conducting missions in thirty countries. Chapters of Soka Gakkai were established in the United States and Canada, headquartered in Santa Monica, in the countries of Europe, headquartered in Paris, in Latin America, headquartered in Sao Paulo.[22] Its converts were recruited chiefly from Japanese immigrants.

Soka Gakkai's philosophy is based upon Makiguchi's own theory of value, developed in his posthumously published book, Kachiron.[23] Its premise is that 'the object of human life consists in the pursuit of happiness; it is value, and not truth, that constitutes the substance as well as the element of happiness.' The attainment of happiness is determined by the possession of values.

Of most significance to Christians is the apologetics-evangelism—'Shakubuku'—of Soka Gakkai.[24] It has charged Christianity as over-estimating sin, and puts a higher value upon human goodness. Its subtilty has rested in a double-method of operation, 'shoju' which accommodates the cultic ideas to the religion of the inquirer, and 'shakubuku' which challenges the 'mistakes' of the other religion. Its danger has lain in the simplicity of its slogans, such as 'Any man can attain to happiness now.' It could be said that Soka Gakkai conducted the most extraordinary plan of 'evangelism and indoctrination' in Japan, and in that sense provided the greatest competition to the Christian faith.

What a contrast this provided with Korea, where in the North a militant Communism swept people by the hundred thousand into atheism, and in the South, an evangelistic Christianity won like numbers by persuasion. In Japan, old faiths were not moribund; they were being renovated.

17

THE 1947 QUICKENING IN KOREA

The present writer arrived in Korea in early September 1945. At that time, it was very difficult for anyone to cross from Soviet-occupied North Korea to American-occupied South Korea, or vice versa.[1] One found it impossible to continue on to Manchuria, and instead crossed the Yellow Sea to Shantung, thence to Shanghai.

The arrangements made between Roosevelt and Stalin, with the reluctant consent of Churchill and a disregard of Chinese interests, boded evil for China and Korea. The position of strength held by the Allied Powers at the end of World War II was foolishly squandered.

At the Moscow Conference in December 1945, it was agreed that North and South Korea should be unified, and a provisional Korean government set up in consultation with the several Korean democratic parties. A joint commission met in the spring of 1946, but was stalemated by the refusal of the Soviet authorities to allow certain Korean groups to participate. Negotiations dragged on until November 1947, when the United Nations called for elections throughout the country under United Nations supervision. The Soviet high command refused to permit United Nations commissioners or observers to enter North Korea. This action frustrated unification completely.

In February 1946, the American occupation authorities created a Democratic Representative Council to advise the commanding general, but the Soviet occupation authorities set up a Provisional People's Committee, giving executive power to Kim Il Sung, a Korean Communist.

When it was seen that the Soviet grip on Korea was being tightened, the Presbyterians in the North organized a five-province Joint Presbytery in December 1945.[2] By this time, it was impossible for Koreans to cross the 38th parallel. The Presbyterians decided upon urgent evangelism to redeem the time. They also tried to maintain contact with their brethren south of the dividing line. Christians of all denominations found liberated joy giving way to foreboding.

As thirteen of the thirty-three signers of the 1919 Korean Declaration of Independence were active Christians and so many thousands of Christian folk at that time suffered imprisonment, the Churches North and South were anxious to commemorate Korean Independence Day, 1st March 1946. The relative strengths of opinion were seen in the rallies held in Seoul, where there was no regulation of assembly. Two hundred thousand attended the Christian celebration at the Stadium in Seoul, while forty thousand attended the rally at Namsan Park under Communist auspices.[3] In Pyongyang, the Communist government prohibited any celebration by Christians as such, and arrested sixty leaders the week before. Nevertheless, ten thousand Christians gathered at Chang Tai Hyun (Central Presbyterian) Church, surrounded by armed men. The chief speaker was arrested. Similarly, rallies and arrests occurred in other northern towns.

Various patriotic societies, hopeful of sharing in the life of freedom which liberation promised, recruited members in the Christian churches, earning first the suspicion and then the hostility of the Soviet authorities. A Christian Social Democratic Party proved so successful that Korean Communists incited factory workers to attack a church in Yonampo, beating to death an elder seated in the pews and wrecking the church as well as the homes of its elders. In protest, five thousand students demonstrated, attacking the police station and Communist headquarters. They were mowed down by machine gun fire on the ground and from the air. Repression began in earnest.[4]

In the autumn of 1945, Lee Sung-Bong, a Holiness Church evangelist associated with the Oriental Missionary Society, returned to Korea from Manchuria, and began to preach in the various churches in Pyongyang.[5] The Presbyterians of Sungkang district invited Sung to minister to a conference of four hundred elders, deacons and teachers. On the second night, a revival began, marked by repentance, weeping and confession which went on till midnight. The revival began to spread across the Pyongyang territory, but before the end of 1946 its leaders were being arrested by the Korean Communists. Lee Sung-Bong escaped to South Korea.

Many North Korean pastors fled south to safety, but many others stayed on, saying 'If we perish, we perish with our flocks.'[6] Fear settled on the believers remaining, but there was little flinching. A great spirit of prayer possessed the Christians, and became their only refuge.

In the spring of 1947, forty pastors gathered in Pyongyang for prayer, and discussed the matter of revival. They voted to hold forty days' prayer meetings in each of the churches, starting March 1, an early morning and an evening prayer meeting in each church. Their entreaty was: 'Lord, grant us the power of the Holy Spirit and revival similar to that of forty years ago.'[7] The ministers were the first to be filled with the Spirit. The pastor of Kee Lim Presbyterian Church, Chee Hung-Soon, emerged as the leading evangelist. During the forty days, most churches experienced a great revival and ingathering, many believers experiencing the enduement of power and not a few outsiders being converted to God.

During the first week of April, a united prayer meeting was held at Central Presbyterian Church (Chang Tai Hyun). It provoked an even greater awakening. More than a thousand students at the Kim Il-Sung University professed conversion. Such was the outpouring of the Spirit upon the people that Chee Hung-Soon was forced to stop preaching by the volume of united prayer and confession of sin and of faith. Three hundred people spent two days and nights in the church in agonizing intercession. It was reported that more than ten thousand people gathered in mass prayer meetings. Hearts were being strengthened for a great tribulation.

The North Korean Communists arranged all political meetings on Sundays, and demanded that Christians attend. The North Korean Joint Presbytery announced, in the name of two thousand churches and three hundred thousand church members, that church and state should be kept separate and Sundays free for worship. The Communists infiltrated the Christian ranks and enlisted a number of collaborators who formed a Christian League, used only to pressurize the Christians.[8] The Moderator and Executive Committee of Joint Presbytery were arrested, a mock General Assembly created by the collaborators, and, within a short space of time, church workers were either prisoners, refugees in the South, on the run underground, or under ground dead.

The awakening of 1947 spread throughout North Korea. Despite intensive Communist pressure, young Christians were volunteering for the ministry, Pyongyang Seminary numbering five hundred students in the autumn of 1948.[9] In spite of increasing and unrelenting persecution, churches continued to grow until 1950, when the Korean War began. Then revival began in the South.

It was providential for the Korean nation that Syngman Rhee, its founding president, was a convinced Christian. He was born in Whanghai province on 26th April 1875, given a Chinese classical education and then a western one at a Methodist school in Seoul.[10] He became an ardent nationalist. To earn his support, he gave language lessons to Christian missionaries, observing their friendly disposition to Korea and its people.

Rhee was imprisoned by Korean authorities for reform agitation in 1897, and, while occupying a cell, he was visited by missionaries, made a study of the Bible, and was truly converted, his distaste for missionaries and hatred of the Japanese being dissipated. Released in 1904, Rhee went abroad, and earned his graduate degrees at Harvard and Princeton Universities. He returned to Korea as a Y.M.C.A. worker in 1910. He found it wise to leave Korea again, and he settled in Hawaii as director of the Korean Christian Institute. In 1919, Syngman Rhee was elected president of the Republic of Korea, and in 1948 the liberated masses in South Korea confirmed that election. Possessed by a burning desire for the liberation and then the reunification of Korea, he became a 'strongman' president, not hesitating to use police powers to maintain national liberation and to forward unification, even to occasional defiance of his allies.

A Communist uprising occurred in Yusoo in South Korea late in 1948.[11] Agents from the sealed-off North had been infiltrating the South, gathering a following among people who had no means of checking upon their promises. The Christian churches in Yusoo suffered assault for a whole week. A local pastor, released from imprisonment by the Japanese, had been serving a church there, with two sons in a local Christian school who had vocally opposed the Communist propaganda. Unable to find their father, the insurgents seized the boys, who still were insisting that the Communists were mistaken in their atheism; both of them were killed.

When the Republic of Korea Army recaptured Yusoo, the Communist students responsible for the killing of the Son brothers were arrested. Pastor Son Yang Won went to the military commander and pleaded for the life of the young ringleader. He took the student home and introduced him to his daughters as an older brother in the place of his two sons, asking them to ignore his obvious faults. Inevitably, the young man repented to become an ardent Christian.

The influx of North Korean refugees had an immediate effect upon South Korean Christians. They brought with them a spirit of prayer, and prayer meetings multiplied in churches of all denominations, among the refugees and among their hosts and in other congregations. Prayer was building up for an extraordinary awakening in the South in the terrible years ahead.

An example of North Korean refugeee influence upon the life of the Church in the South may be found in the story of Dr. Han Kyung-Chik and the Young Nak Church in Seoul. Han had worked with Dr. William Newton Blair, one of the chief missionary figures of the 1907 Revival in Pyongyang, and he studied in the Union Christian College in the northern capital. Completing his work at Emporia College in Kansas, he graduated from Princeton Theological Seminary. Though handicapped by tuberculosis, he entered the ministry in Korea and became pastor of the Second Presbyterian Church in Sin Wiju where, in 1945, he helped organize the Christian Social Democratic Party, and where the wrath of the Soviet authorities and North Korean Communists fell upon him and others.[12] Pastor Han fled south.

Han found himself without sustenance in Seoul. Meeting other destitute North Koreans, he suggested that they should gather for prayer. A score or so responded, and found the comfort of prayer so powerful that they continued to meet, until in 1946 there were five hundred of them, forming the Young Nak Church. By the summer of 1947, membership had risen to two thousand, a year later three thousand.[13] It was a congregation born in prayer and sustained by prayer —even twenty years later, when the writer visited Young Nak Church in 1970 and addressed a thousand intercessors in a regular mid-week service.

The veteran missionary, William Newton Blair, spent some time in Korea following the Liberation.[14] His heart was rejoiced to report the beginning of revival fires in the South, sparked by the northern refugees. Not only in Seoul, but in Taegu and other cities, a vast movement of people to prayer began, accelerating an ingathering of converts as well. The revival gathered momentum until the year 1950. It was thoroughly indigenous, although it came to the attention of the Western world through the visits of American youth evangelists. The revival of believers and the awakening all over Korea was a thoroughly indigenous movement, without foreign initiation though with some foreign help.

A Youth for Christ evangelist, Dr. Robert A. Pierce, accompanied by two young American athletes, Gil Dodds— a champion runner, and Robert Finley—a champion boxer, visited Korea a few weeks before the Communist invasion from the North. The Americans preached to crowds of more than ten thousand nightly, and twenty-five thousand inquirers were registered. Reported Finley, who believed that the manifestations of the Acts of the Apostles were not meant for later times:[15]

> It came as a shock to me to find Korean believers meeting for prayer every day at 5 a.m. I had never seen such discipline in America, nor had I seen such devotion to the Lord as when hundreds of persons continued all night on their knees in pure worship. . . What strange power constrained them to pour out their souls in adoration and praise?

Finley was also overwhelmed by their attitide to material things, for out of deep poverty believers were contributing half their income. Among them, he felt spiritually bankrupt. He had spoken gladly to more than seventy thousand high school students in a stadium in Taegu; but he was reluctant to address a prayer conference on Sam Kak San. He spoke to the intercessors at 4 p.m., after which a thousand people scattered to prayer groups to pray and fast all night, ringing a bell at sunrise for another united service; so they continued for three days and two nights.

Sick and afflicted people began to join the assembly, one man carrying a paralyzed boy on his back for thirty miles, the boy's right side paralyzed. Finley doubted the wisdom of leaving these incurables lying all night, but next day at daybreak the intercessors prayed for the sick. The paralyzed boy leaped to his feet and flexed his muscles—Finley, after examining his hand and foot entirely restored, found his theological prejudices shattered. The experience led to a new commitment on the American's part, leading to his work with international students and national missions. Robert Pierce too was never the same again, going back to the States to found World Vision, an organization with a burden for evangelism and social action, one of the great new developments of the mid-century Awakening.

On 25th June 1950, North Korean armies crossed the border and began to overrun the South.[16] The invasion came so suddenly that many pastors and workers were killed or imprisoned. North Korean Christians were on the run again.

The outbreak of war in 1950 provided the North Korean authorities an excuse to liquidate the pastors and elders of all congregations and to close the churches. The success of the invasion of South Korea engulfed multitudes of helpless Christians, and sent others fleeing south to the Pusan perimeter,[17] the only beachhead left to the South Korean government and its United Nations allies.

The Young Nak Presbyterian congregation dedicated its church building, seating 2200, but three weeks after the dedication service, the Korean War began, and Seoul was evacuated, then occupied. Dr. Han stayed on in hiding, but when the Communists began their systematic house-to-house searches, he slipped out of the city and made his hazardous way on foot south to Taegu.[18]

Many churches were destroyed or damaged badly. About sixty pastors were arrested in Seoul, some being executed, some dying in prison, and others shipped to North Korea, some never heard of again.[19]

Korean troops, stiffened by American contingents, made their retreat to Taegu in the south, buying time for an Allied counter-offensive. The tide of war rolled north again, the Communists resisting strongly but vainly. Seoul was retaken and Pyongyang captured. By October, the armies of North Korea had been practically destroyed, and ceased to exist as fighting units.

When the United Nations forces under McArthur landed at Inchon, the Communists gathered together imprisoned church workers and other believers and executed them.[20] A committee of North Korean Christians followed the United Nations forces into Pyongyang, and found all the churches desecrated, converted into factories, and full of machinery. Yet the Church still lived. Believers appeared and on the following Sunday came out to worship three thousand strong, a pitiable number compared to former days, but a joyful and unbroken remnant of a brave people.

By November 1950, it was clear than Communist China was massively intervening in the war. The Allies retreated. North Korean pastors and people who had returned from the South were sent fleeing again. Before the situation was stabilized at the end of actual hostilities, local Christians were forbidden to meet in congregations. Public services ceased. Christians disappeared into the population, and maintained their witness informally. The Communists killed hundreds of pastors, destroyed almost every last church.

Southwards, Seoul fell to the Chinese forces at the New Year, but was retaken by the Allies on 14th March 1951. The war dragged on throughout 1951 and into 1952. A truce was signed in July 1953.

One hundred and sixty thousand prisoners of war were held in camps in South Korea, some North Koreans and others South Koreans impressed into the Communist armies. A remarkable ministry was conducted in these camps by missionaries and Korean evangelists, Harold Voelkel being the best-known chaplain. Sixty thousand professed conversion, and, unwilling to be repatriated, were released by Syngman Rhee in unilateral action. They were soon absorbed into churches of Northern or Southern membership in South Korea, returning to army or civilian life as they chose.[21]

Night settled on North Korea. Information occasionally reaching the South suggested that there were still multiplied thousands meeting surreptitiously. No accurate count of them could be given, and no reliable information. It was estimated that there were five hundred 'cells' meeting in one city alone. Only the radio broadcasts from South Korea could penetrate the barrier of the 38th parallel. That there were believers still faithful there was confirmed.[22]

It is certain that the outbreak of revival in 1947 prepared the Church in Korea for the vicissitudes of war in 1950, in the North for martyrdom, imprisonment, repression, and dissolution so far as public services were concerned, in the South for invasion, dislocation, flight, destitution, and resistance. With the end of hostilities came rehabilitation, and with it came a new surge of advance.

The Presbyterians set aside 1952 as a year of evangelism; the Methodists dedicated 1953 thus, and both denominations united in an effort to reach all of South Korea for Christ in 1954.[23] And in 1955, Robert Pierce returned for evangelism, assisted by a team of missioners. Billy Graham came in 1956—his visit in 1952 was mainly one of encouragement to the troops—and helped glean the ripened harvest.[24]

During World War II, under Japanese restriction, there were only forty churches in the capital, Seoul; after the Liberation, their numbers grew steadily, and a dozen years later, following the Korean War,[25] there were four hundred. Likewise, in Taegu, there had been only seven churches; in 1958, there were a hundred and seventy. This amazing growth was typical of most of South Korea; the Evangelical Churches had consolidated their position in Korean life.

In 1955, the Presbyterians reported twelve hundred new churches built, the Methodists five hundred, the Holiness people two hundred and fifty, and others a hundred, a total of two thousand new buildings, to house congregations whose properties had been destroyed or new congregations coming into being.[26] The end of the Korean War brought various denominations into the country to share in the ingathering.

Strange to say, church growth continued in Presbyterian churches despite a number of splits.[27] It was said that the controversy over the shrine issue caused the divisions at first, the liberated prisoners taking to task those who had compromised. Another cause of disputation was the issue of ecumenism, compromised because of the attitudes of the World Council of Churches to revolutionary movements. In 1951 and in 1954, dissident General Assemblies were formed and another division occurred in 1959, part of those seceding re-uniting with some of those who had seceded in 1951.   An estimate of Presbyterian numbers after 1961 suggested about 325,000 in the original Presbyterian Church, 270,000 in the Reunited Presbyterian Church, 114,000 in the Presbyterian Church of the Republic of Korea, and 66,000 in the Koryo Continuing Church (1951). Dr. S. H. Moffett observed that division often followed persecution in Presbyterian history. However, the numbers of Presbyterians had grown to more than three-quarters of a million, competition being a factor in the remarkable growth, some said. There were splits in other denominations also.

Prayer conferences were arranged for Korean pastors, generally during the summer vacation. In one such rally, July 1956, a hundred pastors and Bible women spent a week in prayer at Sam Kak San, a mountain resort.[28] The Rev. Samuel Todd, a visiting American, gave a brief testimony, but was called upon for a message, then asked to return in 1957. He fasted for days while he was preaching, the local pastors in turn giving up their meals and prayerfully joining him. An outpouring of the Holy Spirit followed, transforming the ministry of many pastors, one such reporting that his Sunday morning services trebled in numbers within a few months. Local revivals continued in Korea throughout the late 'fifties, and the growth of the churches kept pace in the 1960s. Evangelism extended the movement into all the sectors of the national life, sending more missionaries and workers of Korean birth overseas, chiefly to parts of Asia, those not dominated by Communism.

The great surge of revival and evangelism in Korea was accompanied by a great extension of social service, confirming the records of history and confuting the popular notion that interest in evangelism is matched by neglect of social ministry.

Robert Pierce, a typical Youth for Christ evangelist, 'let his heart be broken' by the tragedies he saw in Korea, and returned to the United States to tell his story to the revived Christians,[29] setting up the World Vision organization which raised a multi-million dollar budget for relief as well as for evangelism.   Pierce was decorated by the Korean President.

Universities and colleges and high schools were founded or expanded in the wake of the war.[30] The dozen Christian high schools in Seoul, which formerly had operated with an average student body of five hundred, now enrolled from a thousand to twenty-five hundred.   Night schools of every type were multiplying, as the masses sought education.   As young folk prepared for ministry, ordained and unordained, Bible institutes and theological seminaries multiplied.[31] For the children, there were numerous Bible clubs, seventy thousand children attending seven thousand such clubs in association with the Presbyterians alone.

The Republic of Korea Armed Forces, alone of any nation in Asia, established a chaplain's corps with more than three hundred Christian chaplains activated by 1955.   There were likewise prison chaplains.   Korean Christians established foreign missions in other East Asian countries.[32]

Christian radio was developed, with an outreach to all of East Asia, including the Siberian and Far Eastern oblasts of the Soviet Union, where the writer encountered listeners to the broadcasts in Russian.   Christians also developed a literacy work, audio-visual projects, and the like.[33]

Christians gladly engaged in caring for the poor, the sick, and the handicapped. However, the war produced mammoth problems in these fields, and foreign aid was gladly accepted. Orphanages sprang up throughout South Korea, many begun by Christians.   Homes for widows were established.   More than twenty million pounds of food were supplied through hundreds of social welfare organizations in a typical year. Reuben A. Torrey, son of the famous evangelist, launched a rehabilitation project for amputees.[34] Special help was given victims of tuberculosis, perhaps half a million in number. Social welfare work, commenced in Korea with the work of the Salvation Army in 1918,[35] reached top gear by 1958.

In 1973, Billy Graham conducted evangelistic rallies in Seoul, using an island airfield, attracting crowds estimated by Korean police in excess of a million. Many responded among the multiplied hundreds of thousands who heard him. A Korean student evangelist gathered crowds as large. Kim Joon-Gon saw his father and mother brutally beaten to death by Communists during the Korean War, and he was himself left for dead. Burdened to reach Korean students, he came to the United States for study and there encountered Bill Bright, founder of Campus Crusade for Christ, whose simple methods of soul-winning he adapted to the Korean opportunity when he returned in January 1959.

Kim Joon-Gon recruited and trained seven full-time and thirty part-time staff workers to tackle a hundred colleges and universities in Korea. A year later, he climbed a mountain overlooking Seoul, and prayed with two hundred students for realization of a vision of Christianizing Korea.

Kim and Korean Campus Crusaders shared the commitmet to prayer so prevalent in Korea. In 1969, in Seoul, was held the first training institute for evangelism, students and laymen were trained to share their faith with inquirers and to build the converts in dedication to Christ.

In 1971, 10,564 received training in Taejon during a week long institute, and more than nine thousand went witnessing in the rain to 42,151 people; and such institutes multiplied. Fifty per cent of Korea's population live in villages, many of which possess no Christian cause. Four thousand primary school teachers and village leaders were trained in a lay institute in the capital, and returned to their villages to train others. A year later, fourteen thousand men and women representing all 1357 local districts of South Korea enrolled for sixty hours of intensive training. They were encouraged to use the Korean 'sarang-bang'—small group gathering—for Bible study, fellowship, prayer and evangelism.

Dr. Kim and other Koreans attending Dallas EXPLO returned to Korea committed to organizing a 1974 Congress—an aggregate of two million attending preliminary rallies in a score of cities. Police estimated several major rallies in excess of a million and 300,000 attended the daily training sessions. Even considering more conservative estimates of attendances, the response was unparalleled in history; it no doubt owed much to organizing ability, but owed more to the astounding progress of evangelical Christianity in a country pioneered only ninety years before.

18

THE CURTAIN FALLS IN CHINA

As the sirens sounded the all-clear and a battered people emerged from the shelters still smiling, I remember saying to myself, after a heavy Japanese air raid in Hengyang in late 1938: 'Heaven help the world if this patient people ever sided with Anti-Christ.'

Seven years later, World War II had ended. The double-dealing of the Soviet Union in Manchuria proved a boon to the Chinese Communists, and brought them added arms and a solid base for extending their control over all of China.

The defeat of Japan set the stage for a struggle for the control of China.[1] Chinese Nationalist forces, often transported by American air and naval units, took over many key cities and railways. Chinese Communist troops, moving out of guerrilla bases, occupied the hinterland in the North and Northeast. Civil war seemed inevitable.

The ill-fated American attempts to mediate between the Nationalists and those described as 'agrarian reformers' by their apologists ended in failure. On 10th January 1946, the Nationalists and Communists signed a cease-fire agreement which was totally undone within a matter of months. The civil war was fought for five years. The Nationalists took the initiative and recaptured many strategic parts of Manchuria, but they were over-extended in the face of the re-trained and re-equipped Chinese Communist armies, and in 1948 the Nationalist armies in Manchuria suffered defeat. Then began the Communist drive south.

There were three thousand returned Protestant missionaries and new recruits in China in 1947.[2] Evangelism was much in evidence throughout the country, despite the war. Peking was directly threatened by the Red tide. In 1947, Chinese Inter-Varsity students held their second summer conference, accompanied by the genuine revival of believers and evangelization of unconverted students.[3] Peking Youth for Christ directors organized the largest evangelistic campaign till then known in the city, building a temporary stadium on the polo grounds of the former embassies.

There was also urgent evangelism around the great city of Shanghai, with much activity displayed by evangelical youth organizations, such as Youth for Christ and Inter-Varsity. In fact, a conference of Christian students was in progress on the grounds of a Shanghai university when news came that the Communist armies had crossed the Yangtze River and captured Nanking.[5] Canton fell on 31st October and Chungking, the wartime capital, on 30th November 1949; the Nationalist Government retreated to Taiwan.

The fears of the missionaries and church leaders were allayed somewhat by the assurances of the Communists that religion would suffer no interference.[6] The conduct of the Communist authorities, military and civilian, seemed to confirm the impression. Government seemed to be honest and efficient, inflation was controlled, communications re-established, trade restored. For a while, the Communists had their apologists among the missionaries themselves.[7]

Communist pressure took many forms. In a fair-sized city, captured by the Communists in 1949, the services of worship in the churches and of evangelism in Youth for Christ continued for many months without interference. But, as the local officials studied the grip that Christianity had upon many lives, they began a gradual repression.[8]

A Presbyterian pastor, Wang by name, was approached with an innocent-sounding request for the use of his church building, which he granted with the proviso that there was to be no smoking permitted, nor any pictures set up. This was accepted, but the leaders promptly disregarded their promise. Pastor Wang removed the pictures and flags before the eyes of the gathering, and was accused of insulting Chairman Mao Tsetung.[9]

Before he could be arrested, Pastor Wang left the city and hid out in Shanghai.[10] Charges were made against his oldest son, who had been active in evangelical student work. He too fled to Shanghai, and both men made their way south and across the border to Hong Kong and safety. Pressure was brought on other members of the family, and upon the congregation. Attendance at the various churches began to dwindle, as believers found it safer to worship in private homes. Church members in business were arrested and accused of being capitalists. Various young people, more especially those with an investment in education, renounced their faith. Pastors began to submit their sermon material to the local police station for censorship on Fridays.

In the five years or so between the end of World War II
and the outbreak of the Korean War, one of the most active
and successful Christian service organizations in China
was the China Inter-Varsity Christian Fellowship, founded
in Chungking in July 1945. Its general secretary and chief
engineer was Chao Chûn-ying, known throughout the English-
speaking world as Calvin Chao.

In the wake of World War II, China Inter-Varsity had a
heyday, spreading to all parts of China except the three
Northeastern Provinces which passed from Japanese to
Russian control, and then to the Chinese Communists. Of
a hundred and five universities and university colleges,
aggressive evangelism was conducted in ninety-eight, from
Lanchow in the northwest, to Peking in the northeast, to
Kunming in the southwest, to Canton in the south.

China Inter-Varsity was maintained by a staff of twenty
Chinese and a dozen missionaries, among the latter David
Adeney, Paul Contento, and Leslie Lyall, seconded to the
student movement by the China Inland Mission. Its work
was extended by the enthusiastic service of a hundred or so
volunteer student evangelists. In those days of opportunity,
as many as twenty thousand outward professions of faith
were made, many of whom became active in the churches
and not a few suffered imprisonment or death in the tragic
years that followed.

So successful was the evangelistic drive of China Inter-
Varsity that the theological seminaries of the country upped
their standards of entrance from high school education to
university education, though exceptions were made. Inter-
Varsity's fame became notoriety in the eyes of the Chinese
Communist Party, and along with the indigenous fellowship
of churches, the Little Flock, and the communal fellowship,
the Jesus family, it was marked out for special attention.

Calvin Chao made his escape to Hong Kong, as did some
of the Chinese staff—and to Taiwan, where a flourishing
work was continued in the burgeoning universities of the
beautiful island. The missionaries were forced to leave,
evangelizing to the last. David Adeney stayed on as long
as possible, a marked man.

The missionaries and general secretary mentioned were
all known to the writer, and continued in strategic ministry
in the Free World. One can only conjecture what happened
to the thousands of faithful Christian students, subjected to
a flood of brain-washing and a fire of persecution.

In the early 1950s, the Christian Union of evangelical students was still operating in the universities of Shanghai. In one such college, there were a hundred believers out of two thousand students, and the average attendance at student meetings in a little church half a mile away was sixty almost every evening. Christians could not avoid being marked out, and steps were taken to correct their attitudes by frequent courses of indoctrination.[11] Persuasion corps operated in every college and university, using threats and promises, brainwashing and terror. Surveillance became more strict. A score of students in one college had been meeting at 6 a.m. for prayer, but they were discovered and the meeting ceased. Devotion was maintained privately.[12]

In May 1950, the Government leaders in Peking sent for a number of Chinese Christian leaders and discussed the place of religion, especially Christianity, in the new society. They were assured that freedom of religious belief was fully guaranteed to all Chinese citizens. However, the Chinese Church must purge itself of all overseas connections, for the missionaries were agents of imperialism.[13] A manifesto was prepared, pledging the Church to rid itself of every trace of imperialism and to obey the Government and Party. On 23rd September 1950, the Manifesto was made official by the consent, willing or cajoled, of the Christians throughout the country. Pressure was brought by Communist officials on church leaders, and by church leaders on missionaries to withdraw from the work. The Societies saw the writing on the wall, and missionaries departed month by month in larger numbers.[14] Before visas were granted, property had to be turned over to the Government, and so the Communists came into legal possession of homes, schools, universities, orphanages and hospitals, without inflicting persecution.

It is interesting to note that the Chinese Communists borrowed and perverted some of the methods of phenomenal revival used in the China-wide movement of the 1930s in their attempts to bring about submission to the will of Mao. Instead of Scripture as a court of appeal, they presented the words of Mao.[15] Instead of the accusations of conscience, they used perjured accusers of the brethren. Instead of confession of sin against God, they promoted confessions of opposition to Mao. Instead of restitution of property mis-appropriated and the reconciliation of enemies, they called for re-education in Maoist thought and the denunciation of declared 'enemies' of the regime, whether guilty or not.

Some missionaries were saddened by the fact that their Chinese colleagues accepted an obvious untruth— that they were agents of imperialism—and offered no protest against their elimination from Chinese church life. They were ready to admit their faults, which were not a few, but not to impugn their own motives in serving Christ in China.

When the Communists took over the Chinese cities, many Chinese leaders also fled to Taiwan or farther afield. In Shanghai, for example, Dorcas Gih was managing a home for sixty-five orphans.[16] Late in April the orphanage was evacuated. Dorcas Gih, whose health was broken, found a refuge in Hong Kong. The Shanghai Christians maintained the orphanage under Communist control until 1953, when it was officially disbanded and the children placed for indoctrination in ungodly homes.[17]

Andrew Gih had decided to help keep the China Biblical College in Hangchow open, even under Communist rule.[18] In 1949, when five were graduated, the seminary was enjoying a time of great revival. First to go were American helpers, then the British associates. But the college was registered with the Communist Government, and continued operation for a while. Finally it was closed, and its superintendent sent to prison, his fate unknown.

The outbreak of the Korean War in 1950 provided the Government with an excuse to crack down on Christians. In April of 1951, 158 church leaders from all over China were brought to Peking at government expense to devise ways of cutting all ties with 'American imperialism' and ensuring that the Church would become thoroughly self-governing, self-supporting, and self-propagating. Actually, this 'three-self' slogan was borrowed from missionary advocates of a generation before, in the promotion of indigenous church development.[19] What was not realized was that the Communist intention was that the 'three-self' project should end in self-liquidation. Already the official churches were under State control.[20] Their spokesmen had become voices for officials in the Government.

The first campaign of accusation was initiated in Peking by the Three-Self collaborators in April 1951.[21] A bishop, Chen Wenyuan, was accused by a fellow-Methodist bishop, Kiang Changchuan, of being a spy for the Americans; and an evangelist, Ku Jenen, was accused of crimes and recommended the death penalty by his brethren; both men went to prison.

An orgy of accusation throughout the churches followed.
There was great fear in the country, sixteen thousand people
arrested in the early hours of 27th April 1951 in Shanghai
alone. The Three-Self leaders agreed to organize a huge
accusation meeting in a Shanghai stadium, preparations
being made weeks in advance, accusers being carefully
trained, and the reaction of the delegations making up the
masses being rehearsed to perfection. Y. T. Wu opened
the accusations with a speech.[22] Then ten chief accusers
representing various denominations and organizations were
unleashed on their victims, reciting fantastic statements of
crimes against the missionaries or anyone supporting them.

The general accusation meeting was followed by special
denominational accusation meetings, through which these
denominations were to be purged of their faults. The first
to qualify was the Seventh-Day Adventist denomination which
in Allen Memorial Church in Shanghai accused its leaders,
whipping up the audience into a fury demanding the death of
three of the accused.[23] Y. T. Wu congratulated the accusers
upon their forceful demonstration. This was repeated all
over the country.[24] The local Communist cadres instructed
the accusers upon procedure; the pastor or leading worker
of the church selected was accused; all members were made
to attend; the verdict was always 'guilty,' after which the
Government took over and sentenced the accused to prison,
or even to death.[25] The procedure was varied to suit the
circumstances: sometimes children were compelled to
accuse their parents—as in the case of the daughter of the
President of Yenching University, Dr. Li Chihwei; or of the
sons of Archdeacon James Fu, who committed suicide. So
many others suffered mental break-downs.

After a year, delegates were summoned to Peking for yet
another conference, late July and early August 1954.[26] Not
content with following the Communist anti-imperialist line,
Mr. Y. T. Wu of the Y.M.C.A. denounced the most dedicated
of self-sacrificing missionaries—including Timothy Richard
and Hudson Taylor:[27]

> These missionaries misinterpreted the Scriptures, per-
> verted Christian doctrine, nurtured unspeakable reneg-
> ades within the Church, created disunion and division
> within the Church, and made Chinese Christians breathe
> in the poison of imperialist thought.

Y. T. Wu had been known as a Communist sympathizer for
many years before his enlistment in Communist service.

Evangelical Christians in China and in exile were not at all surprised to find Y. T. Wu promoting the Communist line, nor were they shocked by the adherence of some others, but they were saddened by the affiliation of Dr. Marcus Cheng, who had been active in evangelism and revival in the 1930s.

In the years of the struggle of the Communists to gain control of the churches with a minimum of force, the less visible congregations—unaffiliated with a denomination— escaped attention.[28] This was not true of the Jesus Family, a Christian commune which attracted the attention of the secular Communists and intrigued them.[29] Ching Tien-yin, one of the founders, had engaged in evangelism all over China in the revival years of the 1930s. His Sankey was Tung Henshin. The Jesus Family (Yesu Chiating) established a headquarters in Machuang, in Shantung Province. When the Communists took over the northern provinces, they were at a loss to decide what to do with the Jesus Family.

The story is told of a Jesus Family leader in jail facing trial for sheltering Nationalist soldiers. His wife was engaged in prayer in the chapel when a hen came in from the street and laid an egg. The woman disturbed got up and caught the hen, tied a note to its leg with paper money, to pay for the egg. The hen's heathen owner gossiped about the incident, and a Communist judge investigated the matter, was amazed to discover such altruistic honesty, and quashed the case against the pastor, innocent of wrongdoing.

Higher authorities in the Communist hierarchy decided that the Christian communes could not be permitted to exist. Their communal life proved too great a challenge to secular Communism based upon the class struggle. In 1953, the Jesus Family was liquidated.[30]

Far from the larger cities, unobtrusive Christians continued witnessing for Christ, engaging even in the same kind of team ministry typical of the Bethel Bands of twenty years earlier.[31] One team penetrated into China's Far Northwest, holding meetings in Sinkiang before the Chinese Communists isolated the province for atomic research and experiments. But it became impossible to catalogue the activities of local Christians. The Three-Self Movement, under the thumb of the authorities, was not interested in publicizing evangelism, and the evangelists themselves were not anxious to draw attention to themselves. There has been every reason to believe that witness continued unobtrusively, and that worship continued in private places, even in the large cities.

The Little Flock, an indigenous Chinese fellowship with separatist tendencies reminiscent of the Exclusive Brethren, was led by a very able Bible teacher, Nee Tosheng, known as Watchman Nee.[32] The Little Flock was as evangelical as any denomination, but held certain peculiar notions, such as the idea that in any given city—as small as a village or as large as a country in population—there is but one church, generally the Little Flock.

Nee Tosheng and his associates kept clear of politics as not of legitimate interest to Christians, but this did not save them from repression. Nee was operating a pharmaceutical business, supplying anti-biotics throughout China, and so became the object of a 'tiger hunt' organized to track down 'commercial tigers preying upon the people's wealth.'[33] In 1952, he was sentenced to fifteen years' imprisonment.

Four years later, thirty leaders of the Little Flock in the Shanghai area were arrested, and a couple of thousand of the members were gathered for an accusation meeting, in which the usual charges were made, while their imprisoned leader, Nee Tosheng, was accused of having seduced a hundred girls. By mid-April, the Little Flock was brainwashed.[34]

The Little Flock assemblies in Shanghai continued to meet, but none dare offer prayer for their incarcerated leader. Meanwhile, translations of his devotional writings were published throughout the Christian world, provoking much prayer on his behalf. His long, lingering imprisonment was finally ended, and he died in the faith.

In Peking, during the spring of 1954, Wang Mingtao, an outstanding evangelist and pastor of a church without any missionary connections, was accused of lack of sympathy for the Communist Government. Demands were made for his death.[35] His arrest was postponed for lack of evidence.

In 1955, Wang Mingtao conducted his largest ever gospel meetings in Peking. Many were converted, and many more in subsequent evangelistic meetings. Wang Mingtao had been noted throughout his ministry as an indigenous preacher, somewhat impatient of foreign missionaries. But he boldly denied the propaganda line that missionaries were imperialist agents, and he denounced the Christian collaborationists for being unequally yoked with atheists.[36] The storm broke, and the Christian quislings organized a nationwide attack, with fury. On 7th August 1955, Wang Mingtao preached a text, 'The Son of Man is betrayed into the hands of sinners.' He was haled to prison after midnight, his church sealed up.

Wang Mingtao was sentenced to fifteen years in prison but was released after less than fifteen months. He was subjected to incessant debate and cross-questioning, and finally broke down and 'confessed.' He read his confession in public, and it was gleefully reported in the Three-Self Movement's publication, with a tongue-in-cheek welcome to the fold. Wang Mingtao was unable to preach, obviously suffering a mental breakdown. He was reported by friends as accusing himself, shouting: 'I am Peter!' or 'I am Judas!' Only a short time passed before he decided to notify the authorities that the 'confession' was not his own, and did not represent his true convictions. He went back to prison.[37]

Wang Mingtao remained in prison for twelve years, until 1968, when he was transferred to a correction work-camp at Tatung in northern Shansi, where he died. Although his writings were not well known outside China, his name was known as a courageous dissenter to the collaborationism of pro-Communists. His protests were made, not against the Government, but against false teachers in the Church who allied themselves with atheists intent on destroying faith.

In 1957, Chairman Mao felt confident enough to borrow a Chinese proverb, 'Let a hundred flowers bloom,' to suggest that every one could feel free to express his own opinion in constructive criticism. To his surprise, an outburst of frustrated feelings exploded, leading men in Government expressing criticisms, students demonstrating, and uproar ensuing. The Government cracked down upon the dissidents. Some were executed, and many went to prison.[38]

Dr. Marcus Cheng delivered a critical speech before the Chinese People's Conference in Peking. Whether he knew that his words would cause retaliation is not known. From reports of his speech, it was recognized that churches had been closed, their buildings and furniture confiscated, and believers abused in some places. At the opening of a new bridge, a Communist official boasted that it was the work of man, and not of God, advising the Christians to throw their God in the dung heap. Marcus Cheng protested such blasphemy.[39] He protested the use of a church building in a tribal area as a stable. Protests such as these coming from Y. T. Wu's second-in-command had a stunning effect, and they led to the downfall of Marcus Cheng. A new spate of accusations was made in church rallies. Ministers, more especially those evangelical in conviction, became the target of others' criticisms, accusations of heinous crimes made.

Helen Willis, a missionary, was permitted to maintain a Christian bookshop in Shanghai until as late as spring of 1958.[40] She was kept under strict surveillance, of course, and her customers were watched. Throughout 1956, Miss Willis sold posters, books, calendars, tracts and Bibles. In 1957, a year of turmoil and repression of intellectuals, the turnover was double that of 1956. But in 1958, the sale of tracts and posters was forbidden, and accusations were being brought against the bookshop and its publications.

In 1958, Chairman Mao and his advisers announced the Great Leap Forward, aimed at the organization of China's agricultural workers into communes and the industrialization of the country. Within a couple of years' time, it was admitted that the plans had fallen far short of their objectives, with famine conditions in some areas and food shortages everywhere.[41] China was compelled to purchase huge grain shipments from Australia and Canada. In 1959, the U.S.S.R. and its satellites in Europe withdrew support of the Chinese Communists, beginning a long period of increasing tension between the Communist giants. Rebellion flared in Tibet, and was ruthlessly put down. In 1960, millions of students were ordered to the communes to share in agricultural work. Critics of Mao within China were beginning to advocate revisionist policies, modifying the Communist objectives— much to Mao's distress.

In 1960, the Peking Theological Seminary was closed and its students transferred to one at Nanking. The China Bible Society was expelled from its premises in Shanghai. The number of congregations in the great cities was reduced to a minimum, and redundant church buildings were put to other uses.[42] Three-quarters of the total number of pastors were sent to work in the factories or farms. Sunday schools were suspect as a means of counter-revolutionary action. The distribution of Bibles was sharply reduced and the sale curtailed. Christians found the everlasting discussion of politics so distasteful in church that attendance dwindled and private homes were used for worship, despite the risk of fines or imprisonment.

Yet occasional letters sent from China abroad told a story of faithful work and witness in various parts of China. Churches were regularly used for services and a few pastors still regularly preached.[43] As late as 1966, a Dutch friend of the writer found churches and Y.M.C.A.s and seminaries and bookshops open, though not well patronized.

Word was heard of a pastor in a mountain town, forced to sell vegetables for a living. On his delivery route, he visited the homes of the Christians and offered prayer and counsel.[44] The Christians bought up all his vegetables. A revival broke out in the district and his congregation grew from three hundred to three thousand. The pastor refused to join the Three-Self Movement and was hauled off to prison.

In 1965, Chairman Mao announced the Great Proletarian Cultural Revolution.[45] A battle of posters ensued, as party leaders struggled for control of China. In May 1966, Mao rallied the support of Chinese youth to overwhelm the vast opposition to his policies. The Red Guards were formed first at Tsinghua University, and on June 1st their counterparts at Peking University initiated a purge of the leadership of the University, followed by a sweep of the Peking metropolitan apparatus. By mid-June, all universities and high schools were closed down for six months, and students ordered to participate in the Cultural Revolution.

In August, the Red Guards rallied their forces in Peking, parading more than a million strong outside the Gate of the Heavenly Peace, Chairman Mao and Marshal Lin Piao taking the salute. Mao had determined to bypass the party chiefs and apparatus, and so the Red Guards were loosed upon the country nationwide to destroy the remnants of capitalism, the pockets of revisionism, and anything else that stood in the way. The Cultural Revolution sought to destroy 'the four olds'—old customs, old habits, old cultures and old thoughts. The Red Guards went on a rampage.[46]

Objection was taken to people wearing western dress; modern Chinese hair-styles were denounced; taxis were declared luxuries; elderly people were humiliated, even stripped; officials were insulted; private homes were invaded and expensive furniture thrown out on the street; art objects and antiques were smashed and pictures slashed; foreigners were reviled; physical violence became commonplace; a hundred million teenagers, provided with free travel passes, roared across the country like a flood. Sometimes factory workers armed themselves against the youth; sometimes the Army intervened.

Those Chinese Christian churches still open were often attacked and wrecked by the Red Guards, and Bibles and hymnbooks were burned in bonfires. Church leaders were roughed up and humiliated. Churches were closed finally. Islam, Taoism, Buddhism and Confucianism suffered also.

Roman Catholics suffered as much as Protestants in the Communist purges. In 1955, more than two hundred Roman Catholic priests and members of the Orders were known to be in prison, including a couple of Chinese bishops.[47] In the Red Guard rampage in 1966, a Roman Catholic Cathedral was seized in Peking, its statuary smashed and its religious symbols replaced with red flags and banners, with busts and pictures of Chairman Mao, its walls covered with posters in revolutionary red.[48]

Violence spread from city to city. The Red Guards made a shambles of churches in Canton, Swatow, Amoy, Shanghai, Nanking, Tientsin and Peking. The collaborationists fared no better than the simple evangelicals. The Three-Self Movement was liquidated. Christians were made to sit on the streets to be spat upon and derided. Ministers were marched through the streets wearing placards announcing 'I am a liar.' The persecution was so great that some both pastors and laymen took their own lives. In Hong Kong, one heard of refugees inquiring if any believers were left, as they thought that the Rapture would precede the Great Tribulation. Chinese students in the writer's classes told of receiving letters from the Mainland from parents or old friends, asking that no more letters be sent, for fear of some reprisal. By Easter of 1967, it was claimed that the Church in China had been liquidated. The future of the Church in China depended upon the multiplication of cells. Christians were continuing to meet in homes.[49]

The reaction of Christians to Chinese Communism was four-fold: (1) some fled the country, to carry on their work in Hong Kong, Taiwan, or among the Chinese dispersed in Asia or farther afield; (2) some stayed and collaborated in the Three-Self Movement, little realising that they too were marked for liquidation after their subverting of the Church was achieved; (3) some stayed and criticized the compromises between churches and State, without offering opposition to the Government itself, and suffered liquidation; (4) some stayed and ignored the political struggle for the soul of China, and suffered liquidation also. A prominent Chinese told the writer: 'My choice, if I had a choice again, would be between witnessing for the whole truth and suffering liquidation and fleeing China to survive and go back again some day to witness for the same truth. It seemed fruitless to compromise with known wrong or to ignore it.' The fact remained that centuries of mission were eclipsed.[50]

A European friend of the writer visited mainland China in the mid-1960s and reported upon his experiences.[51] To his surprise, the Chinese customs officer raised no objection to the importation of the Scriptures in Chinese. He tried giving copies away, but with little success. His interpreter returned the gift, saying that he did not have time to read it. The maid in the hotel ran after him to return a copy 'accidentally' left behind. An official in an agricultural commune told him, 'Sir, religion is for the desperate. Here we are no longer desperate.'

Of course, a Hong Kong Christian explained it by saying that, even in the safety of Hong Kong, refugees from the mainland showed extreme caution, being furtive even after months of freedom.[52] And my friend did not speak Chinese.

In the mid-sixties, there were churches still open, and Y.M.C.A.s, and theological colleges, and even Bible shops. In Shanghai, the visitor called on the friends who operated a Bible and Christian bookstore in an out-of-the-way part of town.[53] The director showed him stacks of Bibles and shelves of tracts available, but during an hour and a half not a single customer visited the shop.

Near Nanking, the tourist requested his Chinese hosts to take him to visit a theological college, where a couple of professors greeted him cordially. But when he remarked that he was a missionary, their cordiality vanished. For many years, both the government and the official church had agreed that missionaries were imperialist spies.

The highest official in the Y.M.C.A. in all of China having been enthusiastically cooperative with the Communist government in its schemes for the self-liquidation of the Church, in every city visited, he found the Y.M.C.A. open, but alas, there was little to suggest that it was for the young, for men, or Christian, for in almost every case he found old ladies there playing board games.

A church was reported open in Peking. He found there an ancient building, drab on the outside, grayer inside. He counted less than threescore people in the congregation, all elderly, as was the preacher. This was more encouraging than a Chinese friend of the writer who visited the congregation in the happier days of the seventies, and found a hastily drummed up congregation of a dozen, including a number of African students, and without a sermon at all. The depredations of the Red Guard made church attendance very unpopular indeed.[54]

Years afterwards, believers in China still spoke with distress of the bitter persecution endured by Christians at the hands of the Red Guard unleashed upon them by Mao's intransigent revolutionaries. Assault, beatings and torture were their lot.[55] It was reported that the Red Guard burst into the prison where Watchman Nee was confined and so ill-treated him that his arm was broken. Many believers were killed; others were imprisoned; Bibles were burned.

A university colleague of the writer visited Canton in the wake of the Nixon conference with Chou En-lai and Mao Tse-tung. Chinese by race and speech, he was able to make contact with Christian folk who met for fellowship and worship in homes.[56] This practice, of course, was commoner among the more evangelical fellowships of believers than the highly structured denominations.

But in 1973, an evangelical Christian from Hong Kong visited Shanghai long enough to collect and evaluate contacts thoroughly.[57] He found a centenarian Anglican priest holding eucharistic services in his hut, shunned by people living nearby but attended by elderly folk from farther away.

In another assembly, thirty-two believers met regularly on Sunday evenings for fellowship, teaching, prayer and the breaking of bread. Group meetings were held in different homes nightly, believers arriving at staggered intervals by ones and twos and departing likewise. The meetings were opened with prayer, hymns were quietly sung, Scripture was expounded for nearly an hour, then followed brief fellowship, and after a couple of hours the gathering dispersed. There were few young people present.

Few believers in Shanghai possessed a Bible of their own, more often each would share a treasured book, such as the Acts of the Apostles or the Psalms. Portions of Scripture were granted to those who were most trustworthy, and full use was made of them.

What was most amazing was that the Hong Kong visitor met many individual Christians who had been won to Christ as a result of personal witness. Open witness, it was said, was prohibited on pain of harassment and arrest. Yet there were personal soulwinners witnessing in the parks to folk they found alone. Others dared witness in the factories.

In Shanghai, it was impossible for Christians to listen to broadcasts, such as the Far East Broadcasting Company's, but they reported it as easy in the rural areas. Foreign mail coming into the country was censored.[58]

As vice-president of an almost wholly Chinese mission, the writer has visited all the countries of the Dispersion of the Chinese, from Taiwan to Singapore, as well as the perimeter of China, during the troubles in Portuguese Macao and on the northern rim, in Khabarovsk on the Amur river on the Siberian frontier.[59]

A facetious question addressed to a Russian university graduate about Chairman Mao's cross-border hostility provoked the reply: 'He's mad—like Stalin.' Conditions in China in the 'seventies resembled those prevailing in Russia in the 'thirties, when the author ventured into the frightened society of the great purges.

In 1950, there were a million or more Evangelical church members in all of China, with two thousand ordained pastors and ten thousand active evangelists.[60] A little over fifteen years later, more than ten thousand churches were closed as well as more than seven thousand evangelistic projects. The few places of worship open were show places for the convenience of tourists. Many were the homes in which Christians met unobtrusively. The experiment in easing of tensions between the United States and mainland China had little effect upon the status of Christianity.

The re-seeding of the Chinese harvest field must depend upon the faithful remnant meeting quietly wherever possible and the preparation of the dispersed believers outside the country to go in again when the opportunity is afforded.

19

TAIWAN, HONG KONG, AND OVERSEAS

The conquest of mainland China by the Red Army and the retreat of the Nationalist government to the island of Taiwan produced revolutionary changes in the political, social, and economic life of the province, which had reverted to China in 1945. An influx of two million Mainlanders speaking a Mandarin Chinese and claiming a higher degree of education and development spilled into a less sophisticated society of Taiwanese largely using the Minnan (Amoy) dialect.[1]

The new nationalist government, which had in December 1949 declared the city of Taipei the national capital, was determined to reorganize its administration, military forces, industry and agriculture, and extend education. Economic aid from the United States helped make possible the reforms. The percentage of land being cultivated by owners increased from 50% to 75%. Taiwan was on its way to becoming a model Asian economy.[2]

The President of the Republic, Chiang Kai-shek, was a professing Christian, as were many of those in government who retreated to Taiwan. While historic Chinese culture was promoted, and ancient faiths protected, Christianity was encouraged. Mme. Chiang Kai-shek established in 1950 a Chinese Christian Women's Prayer Group, which reached out to the needy, employing a score of chaplains, and within ten years ten thousand professed conversions occurred.[3]

The friendliness of national and provincial governments towards the Christian faith was of significant help to both indigenous and missionary evangelization and services. Christian service organizations—committed to aiding any and all evangelical enterprises—entered the province, including Overseas Crusades, which provided evangelism; the Pocket Testament League, which distributed Scripture; campus evangelical fellowships which witnessed to students; and various Bible and literature societies.[4] There was quite a movement for a few years in the Chinese Nationalist Army —with thousands professing conversion.[5] Taiwan enjoyed the benefits of the post-war missionary upsurge.

Many missionaries expelled from China proper followed the migration to Taiwan, and mission societies looking for new fields turned their attention thither.[6] Many directed their efforts to the Mandarin-speaking Mainlanders, some already believers, seeking new church homes, while others displayed a remarkable receptivity to the Gospel.[7]

In 1949, Southern Baptist missionaries and mainland Chinese pastors organized the first Baptist church in Taipei. Within a quarter century, there were fifty churches and an active membership of ten thousand, most of the growth occurring in early years before reaction set in.

In the 1930s, revival had been particularly intense in the province of Honan among the Lutherans, and refugees from Honan established the first Lutheran church at Kaohsiung in Taiwan—a congregation founded, organized and served by laymen.[8] In 1954, the Lutheran missions founded the Taiwan Lutheran Church, self-governing from the start, foreign missionaries concentrating upon the aggregations of Mainlanders in the larger cities. Membership in the first decade reached five thousand.

At the time of the evacuation to Taiwan, the Assembly Halls or Little Flock numbered only a handful in the island. Within ten years, twenty thousand adherents were claimed for them.[9] From their arrival, they used the 'church in the home' method of extension, relying upon their own people to support the work, though drawing from Little Flock folk in the Philippines for fraternal assistance. Watchman Nee visited the island in 1949, but elected to return to Shanghai and imprisonment, appointing Witness Lee as overseer.[10]

The Little Flock increased its size in the 1960s, growing 75% in the decade.[11] Its ministry made its appeal chiefly to Mandarin-speaking people. It was not long before it began to overflow from Taiwan to Southeast Asia and Indonesia, and then to dispersed Chinese in Europe and North America. Unlike certain other exclusive groups, the Little Flock was generous in recognizing members of other denominations as 'brethren in the Lord,' while refusing official cooperation.

The Holy Word congregations were also found in Taiwan, an outgrowth of the work of Andrew Gih in the 'Evangelize China' Fellowship, which developed after World War II and is recognized as one of the largest Third World missions[12] with three hundred national workers from Taiwan to Sumatra, three-quarters of all Indonesian-Chinese pastors having been trained in its Southeast Asia Bible College at Malang.

While upsurge in interest had begun among Mainlanders, the Presbyterians, who had worked among the Taiwanese for ninety years, came to the realization that only one per cent of Taiwan's population had become Christian in any sense. A hundred and fifty villages with populations between ten and thirty thousand were still without a Christian church. Prodded by their moderator, they launched a 'Double the Church Movement' and in ten years—1954-1964—their community strength doubled, reaching 175,000 or so, of whom 65,000 were adherents and 45,000 children.[13] This movement also developed a missionary responsibility, not only for the mountains but for overseas Chinese living in Singapore, Malaya, Thailand, Japan and even Mauritius.

During the 1920s, there were Taiwanese movements for political equality and cultural autonomy. Some Taiwanese rebels slipped across the straits to Fukien for training, and there encountered True Jesus Church enthusiasts and were converted.[14] Barnabas Chang followed them back to Taiwan for an evangelistic campaign in 1926, and founded a couple of True Jesus churches, proselytizing some Presbyterians to do so. By the end of 1945, the True Jesus Church claimed five thousand members, a quarter of them mountain tribesmen, the rest Taiwanese.[15]

The True Jesus Church in Taiwan, being pentecostal and sabbatical and sabellian in doctrine, found itself apart from orthodox Evangelicals in many ways.[16] It continued to grow, trebling its membership in the quarter of a century among the Minnan-speaking Taiwanese, while its mountain tribes members increased a dozen times over, each sector about fifteen thousand in strength.[17]

The Assemblies of God began an extensive evangelistic campaign among the Taiwanese in 1952, and twenty years of work produced a thousand communicants. The Assembly of God missionaries concentrated upon evangelism, at first among the Taiwanese, then including the Mainlanders, and then reaching out to the mountain tribes.[18] The success of the work was greatest among mountain tribes, Mainlanders and Taiwanese, in that order.

The most neglected section of the Chinese population in Taiwan appeared to be the Hakka-speaking people, who made up part of the Chinese population before the arrival of the Mainlanders.[19] Themselves earlier immigrants, like the Minnan-speaking majority, they came from Kwantung in the south where they were a distinct minority.

It was among the mountain tribes of Taiwan that the most spectacular advances were reported. The Japanese police had harried the mountaineers and had prohibited missionary work among them. In spite of stringent control, the Gospel took hold among them, and was spread during the years of repression by word of mouth, so that tribal churches in the wilderness were emerging in 1945 when liberation came.

The Taiwanese Presbyterians were surprised by the vitality of the general folk movement of the mountain tribes to Christianity. By 1957, there were nearly forty thousand tribal Presbyterians, doubling in the next decade.[20] It was recognized that preaching the Good News to the eager folk in the mountains needed to be complemented by training in the Scriptures, with a necessity for elementary education, medical services, and economic opportunity.

The Assemblies of God opened a promising work among the Tayal tribe in the north-central mountain valleys.[21] The Tayals constituted about quarter of the aboriginal population, with more than fifty thousand. The Assemblies established forty preaching chapels where scores of tribesmen attended. The 1250 adherents of the True Jesus Church among the tribes in 1945 trebled in five years to 4000, then doubled in the next five years to 8000, then increased steadily until fifteen thousand were enrolled at the end of the 1960s.[22]

Not only did folk movements move the tribes, but, with indoctrination in the Word, they became subject to revivals which originated in much prayer and produced much conviction of sin. In the local revivals among the mountain folk, there were phenomena both helpful and distressing. There were dreams, visions and trances reported, bodily prostration and exuberant activity.

Throughout Taiwan, whether among Taiwanese of Hakka or Minnan speech, Mainlanders or aboriginals, evangelism continued.[23] Chief among the national evangelists arose Wu-Yung, a Minnan-speaking Taiwanese, and Kou Shih-yung, a Mandarin-speaking Mainlander from Manchuria. Various overseas Chinese evangelists, such as Andrew Gih, visited the island.[24] Chinese leaders in Overseas Crusades and Campus Crusade likewise ministered, and the majority of the missionaries realized the value of evangelism.

The general receptivity of the Mainlanders toward the Gospel in the 1950s waned somewhat in the 'sixties, but the evangelistic outreach of the Christians continued unabated. There was no set-back in evangelism in Taiwan.

The British Crown Colony of Hong Kong survived the rigorous occupation by the imperial Japanese forces in World War II, then made an astonishingly rapid recovery. Its population was inflated many times over by a flood of refugees from the mainland, some bringing treasure and talent, and being unable to proceed further.[25]

As in Taiwan, Hong Kong also experienced an influx of Christians from the mainland churches, ebbing and flowing with the exigencies of the revolution in China. Likewise, many missionary societies, with personnel proficient in Chinese, transferred their activities to the comparative safety of British protection, finding conditions in Hong Kong congenial for living, apart from the crowding.

The British authorities welcomed the missionaries as part of the answer to the problem of educating the millions of residents. Schemes were proposed which allowed the religious bodies to establish schools in or near the vast housing complexes teeming with children.

As in Taiwan, most of the new missionary forces were evangelistic, though not neglectful of social responsibility. Evangelism was persistent, and there was a receptivity to the Christian faith as the only alternative to Communism. Evangelists of ability arose, among them Philip Teng of the Christian and Missionary Alliance. The 'Evangelize China' Fellowship maintained schools in Hong Kong, and with it were associated Holy Word congregations, hence Andrew Gih—who had ministered in Hong Kong with power in pre-war days—was a frequent visitor.

The Little Flock and the True Jesus Church established themselves in Hong Kong, alongside the historic mission-related denominations. Hong Kong, like Taiwan, became a proving ground for missionary enterprise and indigenous development. There was a strong Inter-Varsity Christian Fellowship witness in the universities.

In Vietnam and Thailand, the Chinese elements in the population showed an encouraging interest in the Gospel, the Chinese churches growing in membership. In Burma, political pressure forced many Chinese out of the country, with an understandable effect upon the Chinese churches.

Chinese emigration to the United States and Canada increased sharply and the multiplication of Chinese churches in certain cities was reported. Elsewhere, the Chinese of the Dispersion adopted open attitudes to Christianity, there being little competition offered by ancient religions.

20

CONFLICT AND REVIVAL IN SOUTHEAST ASIA

In the seven years that compassed the Vietnamese revivals of 1938 and 1942, the Church grew from 8,748 to 12,618 in communicant membership.[1] But by 1947, there were only 9,739 members in the Church, and only seven hundred were added in the two years following.[2] The cutoff of the mission subsidy and indigenous inadequacies had provoked resentment against the mission, missionaries and national leaders, according to a national authority; and 'the crisis hour' in the history of the work had arrived in 1950, according to a missionary observer.[3]

In the first week of March 1950, the annual national conference was held in Danang after an interruption of seven years.[4] The Rev. H. E. Nelson, the home secretary of the Christian and Missionary Alliance, became the vehicle of the movement of renewal which followed, his 'Spirit-filled messages' stirring the hearts of the people as rarely known for many a year. The entire front of the church building was filled with penitents, weeping and confessing their sins, while simultaneous audible prayer encompassed the meeting and not a few cried aloud for mercy and pardon.

One of the first to come to the platform was a pastor from the South.[5] He poured out his soul in confession and prayer —his heart had been filled with bitterness over the lack of funds to underwrite the work, and he asked the forgiveness of both missionaries and national Christians.

A stream of pastors, students and local Christians made their way to the platform, seeking forgiveness of God and man, receiving the prayerful sympathy of their hearers. The meeting lasted an hour after midnight. Next day, the catharsis of the Church continued in prayer and confession, in tears and brokenness.[6] Mr. Nelson spent most of his time in counsel, and even little children sought him out. Revived children were the means of reaching backslidden parents, many of whom returned to their faith and practice. Many young folk offered themselves for full-time service, including future leaders in ministry and revival.

The year 1951 witnessed a new movement in the national Evangelical Church of Vietnam.[7] A spirit of revival was rekindled in many places, and pastors became aggressively evangelistic again after a long period of defensiveness. In April, the first relatively large class was graduated from the Bible School in Danang, all of them entering the ministry, including four couples who volunteered for missionary work among the tribes. Revival was already beginning among the tribespeople, relayed by those who had been moved at Danang. The Rev. N. R. Ziemer wrote from Banmethuot:[8]

> There was strong crying with tears as many sought God for the fullness of His Spirit and were satisfied. Others confessed wrongs of various sorts with the desire to leave them . . . Others were burdened and wept for the salvation of their unsaved ones. Truly God worked in a wonderful way.

Less than ten thousand members in 1947 became more than sixteen thousand in the early 1950s in all Indo-China. It should be remembered that Indo-China was in turmoil at the time, power being transferred to Laos and Cambodia as states within the French Union, while the Viet Minh under Ho Chi-minh engaged in hostilities with the French forces.

In 1954, after the debacle of Dien Bien Phu, followed by the Geneva Accords and the vast movement of refugees, the membership of the Evangelical Church in Vietnam dropped by a couple of thousand, going down also in Cambodia and Laos,[9] despite a folk movement reported in the latter state. Numbers began to rise again the later 1950s, reaching a total of nearly twenty-seven thousand communicants in Viet Nam in 1960, only six hundred or so in Cambodia and twelve hundred or so in Laos.

During the first week of March 1966, three hundred pastors gathered in conference at Dalat, in the mountains. The visiting speakers were Dr. William Newburn of Hong Kong and Dr. Oswald Sanders of Singapore.[10] The response to the ministry was immediate—confession, restitution, reconciliation and rededication. The membership of the churches rose from 41,733 to fifty thousand in 1968.[11] The writer, who had earlier visited Hanoi, was in Saigon late in 1966, when the Vietnamese war, North against South, had become an international struggle, 700,000 South Vietnamese and 350,000 Americans resisting the North Vietnamese and insurgent Southerners' attempt to take over South Vietnam. Hostilities spilled over into Laos and Cambodia.

Among the students who had been revived during the 1950 revival at Danang were Mr. and Mrs. Truong-van-Tot, who volunteered to leave their comfortable Vietnamese homes to serve as missionaries in the mountains among tribespeople. In Dalat, the Rev. Truong-van-Tot experienced another time of quickening in 1966.[12] In 1970-71, this young missionary had his faith and vision renewed during a course on the history of Evangelical Awakenings at the School of World Mission in Pasadena, returning to the field with expectation.

> The Lord answered our prayer and a real revival broke out in the churches of our tribal district at the beginning of 1972, still going on in December 1972. The revival brought a great increase in spiritual understanding and depth in the churches. One of its main features was the exposure of animistic practices, particularly among the younger second generation Christians. Hundreds of fetishes and amulets, which had been purchased at great cost from Cambodian animistic practitioners, were turned in and abandoned. Many were sanctified, filled with joy, and dedicated completely to the Lord for His use. Many people, filled with the power of the Holy Spirit, began to serve the Lord with zeal and took the Gospel to many places. The spiritual standard of the Church rose considerably over what it had been . . .

Of the eighty-one churches which experienced revival, about a third showed no numerical increase.[13] More than a half showed a slight increase, from 1 to 16. About a dozen congregations added substantially (from 34 to 150) to their membership, thanks to outreach to distant places or more responsive groups.

A simultaneous evangelistic project was launched by the Vietnamese churches and missionaries in 1970, along the lines of Evangelism-in-Depth.[14] 'It did not catch fire with the church generally' and did not generate much dynamic. Some missionaries became burdened about revival.

In 1970, a reviving blessed the missionaries in annual conference in South Vietnam. Then a movement occurred among the American soldiers in Nhatrang.[15] A missionary, Orrel Steinkamp, commenced a series of lectures on revival at the Nhatrang Theological Institute.

The theological students invited Truong-van-Tot to address them, and some volunteered for missionary work among the tribes while all were stirred to pray for revival. The 'flash-point' flared on 3rd December 1971.[16]

For about ten minutes, the praying was normal, but then at noon a student began to weep and pray and to confess specific sins. Suddenly the room was alive with spontaneous, simultaneous prayer. . . Some students did not attend the meeting . . . Many, as soon as they entered the room, were immediately overwhelmed and fell on their knees and began crying out to the Lord to forgive their sins. . . Students began to seek each other out and confess hatred, cheating, stealing and other things to one another. . . Then spontaneous songs of praise would burst out among the students. There were healings.

The Far Eastern Broadcasting Company of Manila sent out the news of the revival to all Vietnam. On 10th December a revival broke out at Suoi Dau in a montagnard refugee village.[17] A stirring occurred among the missionaries in Saigon. Students began to return to their home towns to spread the word.[18] Ha Minh Vinh challenged the church at Phanrang where 'suddenly people began to weep, to stand up and confess their sin.' At Kondo Dame, 'the young people began to weep and tremble in the presence of the Lord . . . the session lasted until 3 a.m.' The pastor there was healed instantly of tuberculosis. Many American evangelists and pastors had visited the church at Da Ka, highlighted in the writings of Homer Dowdy. There the Rev. Ha Kar preached on 'Have I been so long with you, yet you have not known me, Philip?' The response was startling. Hundreds made confession of sin; scores were converted. . There were strange reports of tongues of fire and bright lights.

This revival occurred during the alarms of war. At Que Son, a prayer meeting was in progress one Thursday night. About midnight, rifle fire was heard, and next morning the Viet Cong appeared.[19] They were bombed, and all the houses in the vicinity except the church and parsonage were burned. Survivors ran to the parsonage for shelter. About thirty were killed in the next bomb attack.

In spite of the horrors of a dirty war, the Christians in South Vietnam continued their witness to the truth as they knew it. The withdrawal of the American forces brought about no cessation of hostilities, and the country still was being drenched in blood.[20] It seemed all the more surprising to know that the Evangelical community in Vietnam reached the hundred thousand mark. This body of believers appeared ready for whatever eventuated, whether takeover by North Vietnam Communists, or outright massacre.

Cambodia remained a country with but few Christians of any sort, a population in excess of seven millions in 1970 having but twenty thousand Roman Catholics as the fruit of a long French connection, and only six hundred Protestants after fifty years of missionary struggle against overwhelming odds. There was but little evangelism in Phnom Penh when the writer visited that beautiful capital in 1966.

Under Prince Norodom Sihanouk, there was persecution, but not of the violent sort.[21] A thousand years of monarchy ended in 1970 when a military coup upset the government and a republic was proclaimed. It was not long before a civil war was raging in the Khmer Republic, as intense as nearby in Vietnam.[22]

In early 1972, the World Vision organization, which had accomplished much good in emergency relief work throughout Indo-China, sent its director, Dr. Stanley Mooneyham, to Phnom Penh for the first public evangelistic campaign ever known in Cambodia. Crowds overflowed an auditorium that seated twelve hundred, an aggregate of ten thousand in three days attending the preaching. A couple of thousand inquirers were reported, but less than ten per cent of those interested actually joined the tiny churches, due to the novelty of both operation and follow-up.[23] Six months later, Mooneyham conducted a second Cambodian campaign, and many more made open declaration of their interest, with similar results. However, the Evangelical leaders received encouragement, and the churches began to grow in spite of, and because of the distress of war.[24]

In 1950, a folk movement began among the Meo tribes in the northern part of the Kingdom of Laos, resulting in four thousand conversions.[25] Invasion by Pathet Lao partisans, instigated by the Communist powers, interrupted the work, but it resumed in 1955 with extraordinary results. In a single year, 172 families threw away their fetishes. Three-score churches were organized by Christian and Missionary Alliance workers, with fifty preaching places.

Missionary work in Laos proved very difficult because of the see-sawing battles between the government forces and the insurgents. Hostilities hampered evangelistic enterprise. In Kengkok, for example, two girls serving with the Christian Brethren Mission were killed by the Pathet Lao;[26] missionaries were used to sudden flight by day or night. But the cause was growing, more than six thousand Evangelical church members in three million population.

In Thailand, the end of World War II heralded a return of opportunity for the Christian evangelist, whether national or missionary. As early as 1946, a missionary reported a revival in Chiengmai in the north, saying: 'The evangelistic movement in this area is one of the most wonderful things I have seen.'[27] The Rev. Tom Kham Suriyakam and the Rev. Pluang Sutikam, the Moderator of the Church of Christ in Thailand, acted as the evangelists. Some churches received a hundred or more new members.

In 1949, there were eighteen Karen churches with eight hundred or so members in the north, the fruit of American Baptist pioneering from Burma, using Karen evangelists. After a long absence from the field, the American Baptists reopened the Chiengmai work in 1950.   Immediately there was a response. A score of churches in 1955 served the needs of fourteen hundred Karens, who increased to three thousand within a dozen years, with twenty-seven churches and as many out-stations for members and inquirers.[28]

American Presbyterians reported a steady five per cent growth in the churches of the north.   First Church in the city of Chiengmai reported a thousand members in 1969, the centenary of its establishment among the Lao people there.[29] As before, the Lao converts of the Presbyterian missionaries and national pastors serving the Church of Christ in the north made up the bulk of national strength.

The displaced missionaries and new recruits of the China Inland Mission, renamed Overseas Missionary Fellowship, entered the Thai field and reported an openness among the tribespeople.[30] Alex Smith, with an evangelistic team of a score of students, reported crowds exceeding a thousand in itinerant evangelism, on one occasion in early February 1971 reporting thirteen hundred eager listeners, 'the response of the people even more astounding than the size of the crowd.' Hudson Taylor's mission soon had more missionaries in Thailand than any other organization.   An encouraging new movement was started in Chiengrai, in the far northern corner of Thailand.   Again it was among the tribes that the response was noted.

Far to the east, in territory opened by the Christian and Missionary Alliance, operating from Indo-China, there was an evangelistic thrust that won forty converts in the church at Udon.[31] A Thai evangelist from Bangkok ministered in the Roi Et province, and churches long dormant woke up and witnessed round about successfully.

In Bangkok, only one in a thousand citizens professed an evangelical faith.[32] Sophisticated Buddhists still proved resistant to the Gospel. There were, nevertheless, thriving congregations in the capital, both Chinese and Thai. In 1971, spiritual growth and numerical increase was reported in Thai and Chinese churches in South Thailand.

An Indonesian team provoked an unexpected response in the Muslim areas of South Thailand.[33] The four evangelists coming from a recognized Muslim country received a very sympathetic hearing. One, Wagijono, discussing religion with an ardent Muslim, was interrupted by a downpour of rain. He asked the Muslim to call upon Allah to stop the rain, without effect. Then, in the name of Jesus, he commanded the rain to stop, and stop it did. His Muslim friend, greatly wondering, took the evangelist to meet the priests and teachers at the mosque, and they in turn invited him to address a great crowd of students, the meeting going on till midnight, further conversation with the priests until four o'clock in the morning.

Burma, far more than Thailand, suffered from the iron-fisted Japanese military occupation during World War II. It was not long before Christian worship was forbidden, and the churches were deliberately defiled and used as stables or as breweries.[34] There were many cases of resentful Burmese Buddhists denouncing Christians to the Japanese, calling them traitors or collaborators with the British, and many were martyred for their Christian faith, though it was announced that they had been executed on political grounds. A legacy of distrust was built up between Burmese and the Karens and other tribes, so largely Christian.

At last, the war was brought to an end, and the Japanese invaders were repatriated. Burma chose independence outside the British Commonwealth, but within a few years a civil war broke out as Karens demanded autonomy. In 1948, there was a Christmas Eve massacre of two hundred Karen believers in the Mergin district gathered for worship. Revolt flared everywhere.[35]

Among the many losing their lives in the civil war was Selma Maxville, an American missionary.[36] But within a couple of years, the death-toll in the Burmese civil war exceeded that of the United States in World War II.[37] Burma was drenched in blood, due to racial, tribal, and ideological conflicts. The birthpangs of a nation were distressing, and destruction overtook whole communities.

American Baptists reported that the Bassein complex of buildings was destroyed, the Christians scattered. Mission property in Maubin was reduced to ashes.[38] In Insein, the big church was burned. Scores of churches were utterly destroyed before the end of 1950.

In 1951, fighting spread throughout the country. Many Christian villages were attacked, looted and burned, and hundreds of villagers were killed.[39] A majority of the Karen Christians resided in rebel areas, and became the target of their enemies. Meanwhile, to foster nationalism, there was a revival of Buddhism, which increased the tension.

The civil war raged through 1952, involving area after area, tribe after tribe, nationalists, rebels, Communists and even Chinese military refugees. By 1953, the issue had sharpened—Christ or Buddha. Of twelve million Burmese, only twelve thousand were Christians; whereas the Karens were two-thirds Baptists.

Tension was not lessened when the Sixth Buddhist World Council met in Rangoon in May of 1954, and continued its deliberations, year after year.[40] Missionaries were being ousted and replaced. The Burmese adopted socialism of a militant kind. Throughout the 1950s, lawlessness and tribal insurgency continued, but 85% of the Christian churches had become self-sufficient.[41] In 1959, villages were still being destroyed in the civil war.

In early 1959, World Vision leaders promoted a pastors' conference in Rangoon, with Drs. Richard Halverson, Carl Henry, Paul Rees and Han Kyung-chik participating. Of the crowds of 2500 attending, two hundred responded to the evangelistic invitation.[42] At that time, the Baptists in Burma had two hundred thousand church members and a related community of half a million, but there seemed to be a lack of Bible teaching, and moral life had slipped after World War II, with drinking, gambling, smuggling, bribery, and sexual laxity all too prevalent.

In 1961, the constitution of Burma was amended, to give —according to the letter of the law—full protection and rights to practice the Christian and other minority faiths, hitherto jeopardized in the Buddhist revival. This gave a fuller scope to a five-year evangelistic advance begun in October 1960, when civil order seemed reviving. Buddhism was still maintained as the state religion. The evangelistic outreach continued with unflagging zeal, H. G. Tegenfeldt serving notably as field secretary of the Mission.[43]

In 1965, insurgency was still the major problem, but in evangelical circles there was much cause for thanksgiving for successful evangelism.[44] Burma then had a population of 23,664,000, with a Christian community of 1,137,084 of whom 463,974 were Protestant church members, meeting in 5667 churches, mostly Baptist. Suddenly, all Christian schools were nationalized, including 49 Roman Catholic, 16 Baptist, 10 Anglican, 7 Methodist and 3 others.[45] And, in the next year, in a move to appease the Buddhist hierarchy, all foreign missionaries—three hundred in all—were forced to leave Burma.

The Protestant Churches being cut off, attempts were made to negotiate a union of denominations. The quarter of a million Baptists were increasingly restricted.[46] Chinese Communist agents wooed the leaders of Christian tribes, seeking to exploit their undoubted grievances.

In the 1970s, restrictions were eased for foreigners who desired to visit Burma.[47] Where only twenty-four to forty-eight hour passes were granted, now visas available for seven days were granted, and foreigners were welcomed in church congregations but not in private homes. Christians still suffered tight travel restrictions, and meetings in the homes were virtually banned.

It seemed amazing to visitors to find the Evangelical churches not only subsisting but thriving under such severe repression. The period of war had lasted thirty years, but —while it had prevented a nationwide revival of Christian faith—it had not hindered steady church growth.

Conclusion

AWAKENINGS IN EASTERN ASIA

The major concern of the fifteenth century awakening—
that of the Lollards, who followed the teaching of Wycliffe
and his helpers—was the dissemination of the Scriptures
in the language of the people and the authority of the Word
of God thus conveyed. The major concern of the sixteenth
century awakening—that of the Reformers, Luther, Calvin,
Cranmer and the Radicals—was the reform of the Church
according to the Word of God. The major concern of the
seventeenth century awakening—that of the Puritans—was
the restatement of theology by a Church reformed according
to the Word of God. The major concern of the eighteenth
century awakening—that of Wesley and Whitefield, and of
the Pietists and Moravians—was the experience of an
assurance of salvation and commitment based upon biblical,
reformed theology. It was not until such an experience of
'a warm heart' became the possession of common people
rather than of a cloistered few that the age of missions
dawned in evangelical Christendom.

The mission of the Church to the non-Christian world
was a minor concern of Evangelical Christianity even during
the First General Evangelical Awakening, which ran from
1725 for half-a-century. It was not until the coming of the
Second General Evangelical Awakening, which began as a
union of prayer in the churches in the 1780s and broke out
as a phenomenal revival following the French Revolution,
that the missionary burden became general, and with it the
birth of the denominational missionary societies, working
together in evangelical comity.

The first objective of the missions was the South Seas,
but attempts were made before long to extend the enterprise
begun by Pietists and Moravians in India and South Africa,
and to enter Latin America and especially China.

William Carey, pioneer to India, possessed an eager
urge to evangelize China, initiating translation of the Holy
Scripture into Chinese and promoting an attempt to reach
China overland through the Indo-China peninsula. Robert

Morrison, as much a product of the Second General Revival as Carey, finally secured a foothold in China's far south.

It was the Second General Awakening in Evangelical Christendom that sent the pioneers to Eastern Asia, to the lands of the Buddha. The Third General Awakening, begun in 1830, reinforced the tentative missionary landing in China, bringing pioneers from Europe and North America, but as yet the Celestial Empire was highly resistant, and the ocean frontiers of Japan and Korea were impenetrable. One of the unanswered questions of history involved the indigenous, semi-Christian movement, the T'aip'ing revolt against the Manchurian emperor—what would have happened had this folk movement been evangelized?

The Fourth General Awakening began in the United States and Great Britain in 1858 and 1859, and spread throughout the world for forty years. It produced great evangelists in the West and reinforced the missions in the East, more particularly raising up the China Inland Mission under Hudson Taylor as an expression of interdenominational and evangelical missionary passion, 'unique in the entire history of the expansion of Christianity,' said Latourette. The same years saw sporadic revivals in the tiny churches of Chinese believers, as well as the opening of Japan to the influence of the West, which transformed a hermit kingdom into a modern power. The 1860s, 'seventies, 'eighties and 'nineties all saw recurring waves of revival and missionary enterprise, especially the 1880s, which produced the Student Volunteers who flocked to the mission field by the thousands.

The 1880s also witnessed the outbreak of a phenomenal revival in Japan, sweeping the evangelical schools and colleges and touching all the tiny congregations of believers —producing seven years of renewal and rapid growth, the first such movement in the Orient to touch the whole body of believers in a nation. Alas, imported Christo-humanism brought about a decade of decline until the end of the century.

The major factors in the evangelization of the peoples and the growth of the Church in Eastern Asia, as elsewhere, have been pioneer evangelism, folk movements, translation of the Scriptures, revivals or quickening of the body of believers, mass evangelism, and indigenous missionary outreach. The cycle is then repeated.

Fortunately, Eastern Asia suffered no such repression of common humanity and impediment of evangelization as the caste system of India. Folk movements in Eastern

Asia, therefore, were tribal. It is interesting to note that the initiation of such people movements to Christ seemed related to the evangelical awakenings, worldwide or local. Often the missionary pioneer, and as often the indigenous forerunner, arose from a time of revival when the prayers of the saints bespoke the movings of the Spirit, the Lord of the Harvest, the dynamic of evangelism and engineer of folk movements.

As early as the 1830s, when a worldwide moving of the Spirit was manifest, a significant folk movement began among the Karens of Burma. Boardman's evangelism was a necessary factor, extended by the witness of Ko Tha-Byu; but neither missionary nor indigenous evangelist would have achieved very much had not the Karens been prepared as a people for a movement towards Christ.

Likewise, in Thailand, the 1858-59 Revival thrust out Daniel McGilvary, and a folk movement among the Lao occurred in the 1860s, the greatest factor in the growth of the Church in Thailand, whose major people was resistant. As yet, there were no such movements in China, Korea or Japan, in the main resistant to the Gospel.

Just as the 1905 Revival produced an acceleration of folk movements in eastern India, triggering phenomenal growth among the Khasis, Mizos and other tribes, so the same awakening heralded folk movements in Burma, the great ingathering among the Lahus in the Shan States being most outstanding. In China, a phenomenal ingathering gained momentum among the tribes of the Southwest, again an accompaniment of revival in the sending countries as well as in all of China.

But the greatest impact of the 1905 Revival, the Fifth General Awakening triggered by the extraordinary revival in Wales, was felt not in South-East Asia but in China, Korea and Japan. Chinese, Korean and Japanese societies were stratified by class distinctions, but tribal enclaves were rare in these countries of ancient civilization. The major thrust of the movement occurred through a revival of the believing Church, an awakening of the masses—in Korea taking on the appearance of a national folk movement.

Chronologically, the blessing of a movement of the Spirit occurred first in Japan, in 1900, ahead of the general moving of the waters throughout the world. Some awakenings have followed in the wake of war, as in South Africa at the turn of the century; but the movement in Japan preceded by a

number of years the outbreak of the Russo-Japanese War,
a turning point in the history of Japan and all of Asia, an
all-engrossing national struggle during which a revival
could scarcely have arisen, but once under way continued.
Taikyo Dendo was first a movement of prayer before it
became aggressive evangelism. It mobilized the whole of
the spiritual strength of the infant Japanese churches, and
in that way, it anticipated by half-a-century the Evangelism-
in-Depth of Latin America. It is surely ironic to think that
the organizers of Sodoin Dendo in the 1960s—a movement
inspired by Evangelism-in-Depth—seemed unaware of the
prototype of 1900 in Taikyo Dendo in their own country.

Taikyo Dendo added five new members for every eight
in Japan, and was succeeded by Taisho Dendo, a greater
movement of evangelism which lasted through World War I,
and spawned a number of indigenous evangelical movements
which rapidly caught up with the mission-related Churches.
Then came the rise of militarism in Japan, with repression
at home and oppression abroad.

The extent of the evangelical revivals and awakening in
China in the years between the Boxer Revolt and the 1911
Revolution is unrealised by most Chinese Christians. As
early as 1900, sporadic revivals were occurring in China,
often accompanied by martyrdom. By 1903, awakenings
were reported from colleges, north, central and south. By
1905, the evangelical awakening was becoming general, and
by 1908, every province in China was experiencing revival
in the churches and an ingathering of souls. Although there
were missionaries outstanding as evangelists in the movement, such as Goforth and Lutley, by far the major burden
of evangelization was taken up by Chinese evangelists, such
as Ting Li-mei. Chinese Evangelicalism had come of age.
The missionaries were still a major force in China, but
their disciples were now being called and equipped for a
nationwide mission.

The Revolution in China was followed by national chaos.
The humiliation of China by the Powers continued, while
ambitious warlords struggled for control of provinces. The
Communists, abetted by a militant revolution in Russia,
made a determined effort to capture the national movement.
They were thwarted by Chiang Kai-shek, but the Churches
continued to suffer, and the missionary body was largely
evacuated to Shanghai and other protected points on the east
coast, some going home permanently.

It was then, in the late 'twenties, that an extraordinary revival of evangelical religion occurred, almost wholly indigenous, though delighting the heart of the missionaries. It was thoroughly interdenominational, and fully widespread. There were several missionaries outstanding in the general movement, notably Marie Monsen and Anna Christensen, Norwegian and Danish. But the movement was spearheaded by the Bethel Band, led by Andrew Gih. His chief associate, John Sung, achieved his national usefulness first as a Bethel evangelist, and then as a freelance. Sung was noted for his eccentricities, but remembered for his thoroughness. The Bethel Band became hundreds of Bethel Bands of eager witnesses, roaming China throughout its vastness in spite of the gathering clouds of war. For twelve years, revival in phenomenal proportions swept China. It lasted until the beginning of World War II.

The corresponding years in Korea were marked by few revivals, as national repression and religious persecution became the way of life of a generation of Christians. The folk movement slackened, but never died out; the Church continued to win the heart of many patriots; many there were who suffered imprisonment rather than compromise their consciences, refusing to give to Cæsar what belonged to God. There was light in Korea's darkest days.

In Japan, the rise of militarism and the resurrection of State Shinto as a means of thought control blighted the life of the Church, for the identification of the oppressors with ardent patriotism posed problems for many a citizen. Thus there was much more compromise by Japanese Christians in conforming to political pressure.

The body of believers continued to grow in Burma in the 1920s and 'thirties, but the resistance of Buddhism among Burmese and Thais continued strong, though there were lesser revivals reported in Thailand, and in Vietnam where Evangelical Christianity at last had secured a foothold.

World War II was fought, and the uneasy peace disturbed by a confrontation of Communism and Democracy provoked the revolutionary struggles of the 1950s. The greatest upheaval occurred in China, where the Red Armies seized control of the sub-continent from the tired Nationalists. As in Germany, where the Christ-humanists were the first to collaboarate with the National Socialists, the liberal leaders enabled the Communists to gain control of the organized denominations, ostensibly to become independent of Western influences, self-governing, self-supporting, and self-propagating. By wicked accusation and unrelenting terror, the Christians were forced to destroy themselves. The movement became self-liquidating. True believers betook themselves to house churches, meeting quietly, and waiting for the storm to blow over. In the 1960s, it rose to hurricane force, as the wrath of Mao Tse-tung and his Red Guards fell upon an already helpless body of believers. By the end of the decade, ten thousand evangelical churches had been closed, and the faithful remnant met secretly.

In the providence of God, the island of Taiwan and the colony of Hong Kong were spared the holocaust of demonic persecution. Into Taiwan, as into the others countries of free Eastern Asia, flowed a tide of evangelical resurgence, renewed denominational missionaries, ardently evangelical new societies, evangelical service organizations, such as Overseas Crusades, Pocket Testament League, Campus Crusade, and the like, reinforcing evangelical organizations already there, such as the Bible Societies and Inter-Varsity Christian Fellowship. In Taiwan, as elsewhere, indigenous Christianity was resurgent, both in missionary-related denominations and in independent organizations and churches. This factor, together with a Church made pure by violent persecution on the mainland, brought hope of the re-seeding of the China harvest field in the coming years.

Korea was also called upon to suffer, the North being overwhelmed by Communist dictatorship which obliterated the visible Church, and the South by war which raged across the country in tides of misery before South Korea was finally secured for freedom. Phenomenal revival began in the North just before the agony of torment began; it spread to South Korea ahead of the Korean War. The folk movement continued in the South, aided by sporadic revival, continuing evangelism, and the influx of evangelical missions, both denominational and service organizations. The Korean missionary outreach was extended, and the social ministry of the Church found glorious opportunities in the upheaval.

Evangelical Christianity in Japan experienced a happy resurgence in the days of a benevolent occupation, then continued to grow in the face of a revival of national sentiment —including the vast expansion of a militant Buddhism, Soka Gakkai, millions strong and anti-Christian. Japanese Evangelicals bravely undertook the evangelization of their booming society.

Vietnam was devastated by a war between North and South, one backed by the Communist Powers, the other by United States intervention. In spite of unbearable human misery, the Evangelical Church was strengthened and a measure of revival undergirded church growth. Burma too was ravaged by civil war, more losing their lives therein than were lost by the United States in World War II. Yet the Churches grew, chiefly in the ethnic minorities touched by the folk movements of the past. Thailand, affected but not involved in war, witnessed a widening of evangelistic opportunity. In Cambodia, the outbreak of civil war was followed by an open door to the Gospel in the non-Communist territories, as in the kingdom of Laos.

In social service, the Evangelical Churches made their contribution to the nations they served in Eastern Asia. Timothy Richard, a convert of the Revival of 1859 in Wales, was a prime instigator and dedicated engineer of the China-wide system of higher education. Missionaries contributed to secondary and primary education also. Evangelical missionaries, in the wake of the 1858-59 Revival, pioneered a system of medical services in their respective countries. In Japan, the modern educational system owed much to the missionary example, the same being true of Korea. The early pioneers were famed for their excellence in teaching.

Christian influence in social services was many times greater than its numerical strength seemed to warrant. In the countries of Eastern Asia, Evangelicals were a tiny minority. In Korea, they were a rising percentage in the population, a significant sector of society. Evangelicals dominated church life, before and after independence, and their social service was nothing to be ashamed of—even in a more evangelistic organization such as World Vision. It is worth noting that disasters such as the upheaval in China in the 1920s and the war in Korea in the 1950s increased the evangelical representation and decreased that of the Christo-humanists in the missionary body.

What of the future? All the signs point to another time of extraordinary revival and awakening wherever the Good News may be freely preached. The closed society of the Chinese People's Republic— and, to a lesser extent, that of North Korea and North Vietnam—has presented the Church with its greatest challenge of all time. The hope of gaining an entrance to China lies with the reviving Christians of the Chinese Dispersion, when the opportunity is afforded.

Christians in Japan, Korea, China, Vietnam, Cambodia, Laos, Thailand, and Burma have much to learn from the lessons of the past. They may evangelize in season or out, use this method or that technique, follow this plan or that, but their greatest achievement will be made when the winds of the Spirit blow through their congregations in revival, at the same time awakening the masses of their fellow-citizens, moving classes and tribes alike towards Christ, and presenting them as subjects for evangelism.

NOTES

Notes on Chapter 1: AWAKENINGS AND PIONEERS, 19th Century

1   Malaysia, including the peninsula and island territories, is treated as part of Greater Oceania, rather than East Asia.
2   The nineteenth century here is the extended nineteenth century, from the French Revolution in 1789 until the outbreak of World War I.
3   K. S. Latourette, A HISTORY OF THE EXPANSION OF CHRISTIANITY, Volume III, p. 454.
4   See W. W. Sweet, THE STORY OF RELIGION IN AMERICA, p. 224.
5   The impact of the 'turn of the nineteenth century revivals' is treated in detail in the author's work, THE EAGER FEET, the first of a trilogy dealing with the Great Century.
6   See Francis Wayland, MEMOIR OF ADONIRAM JUDSON.
7   See Alonzo King, MEMOIR OF GEORGE DANA BOARDMAN.
8   See Francis Mason, THE KAREN APOSTLE: MEMOIR OF KO THAH-BYU.
9   G. B. McFarland, HISTORICAL SKETCH OF PROTESTANT MISSIONS IN SIAM, pp. 35ff.
10 E. F. Irwin, WITH CHRIST IN INDO-CHINA, pp. 25ff.
11 S. Pearce Carey, WILLIAM CAREY, pp. 405ff.
12 H. B. Morse, CHRONICLE OF THE EAST INDIA COMPANY TRADING TO CHINA, 1635-1834, Volume II, pp. 227, 251.
13 See Marshall Broomhall, ROBERT MORRISON, A MASTER BUILDER: and other biographies.
14 John Kesson, THE CROSS AND THE DRAGON, pp. 221ff.
15 K. S. Latourette, A HISTORY OF THE EXPANSION OF CHRISTIANITY, Volume VI, pp. 304-305.
16 See Islay Burns, MEMOIR OF THE REV. W. C. BURNS.
17 W. J. Hail, THE TAIPING REBELLION.
18 The story of the 1858-59 Awakening is told in the author's work, THE FERVENT PRAYER, based upon original research in both Chicago and Oxford, the second of a trilogy dealing with the Great Century, the third being THE FLAMING TONGUE.
19 E. Stock, HISTORY OF THE CHURCH MISSIONARY SOCIETY, Volume II, p. 34.
20 MISSIONARY HERALD, Boston, 1867, p. 67.
21 See W. E. Soothill, TIMOTHY RICHARD OF CHINA.
22 K. S. Latourette, HISTORY OF CHRISTIAN MISSIONS IN CHINA, p. 382.
23 H. & G. Taylor, HUDSON TAYLOR IN EARLY YEARS, p. 499.
24 See J. Edwin Orr, THE FERVENT PRAYER, pp. 132 & 217.
25 J. Edwin Orr, THE LIGHT OF THE WORLD, pp. 187ff.
26 K. S. Latourette, A HISTORY OF THE EXPANSION OF CHRISTIANITY, Volume VI, p. 336.
27 National Bible Society of Scotland, ANNUAL REPORT, 1865.
28 Otis Cary, A HISTORY OF CHRISTIANITY IN JAPAN, Volume II, pp. 41ff.
29 J. D. Davis, A SKETCH OF THE LIFE OF REV. JOSEPH HARDY NEESIMA.
30 American Baptist Missionary Union, ANNUAL REPORT, 1873.
31 Otis Cary, A HISTORY OF CHRISTIANITY IN JAPAN, Volume II, p. 104.

32 See H. & G. Taylor, HUDSON TAYLOR AND THE CHINA INLAND MISSION, passim.
33 CHINA'S MILLIONS, London, 1906.
34 K. S. Latourette, A HISTORY OF THE EXPANSION OF CHRISTIANITY, Volume VI, pp. 341-342.
35 Otis Cary, A HISTORY OF CHRISTIANITY IN JAPAN, Volume II, p. 167.
36 C. W. Iglehart, A CENTURY OF PROTESTANT CHRISTIANITY IN JAPAN, p. 73.
37 Otis Cary, Volume II, chapter IV.
38 C. W. Iglehart, A CENTURY OF PROTESTANT CHRISTIANITY IN JAPAN, p. 75.
39 The phrase is that of Iglehart.
40 Otis Cary, A HISTORY OF CHRISTIANITY IN JAPAN, Volume II, p. 216.
41 See L. G. Paik, THE HISTORY OF PROTESTANT MISSIONS IN KOREA, 1832-1910.
42 D. McGilvary, A HALF CENTURY AMONG THE SIAMESE AND THE LAO, passim.

Notes on Chapter 2: THE FIFTH GENERAL AWAKENING

1 Sigmund Freud, THE FUTURE OF AN ILLUSION, 1928.
2 1st July 1916. The Ulster Division was decimated in 'going over the top' of the trenches at the Battle of the Somme.
3 F. C. Ottman, J. WILBUR CHAPMAN, p. 272.
4 A distinction is made between evangelism based upon organization and publicity and evangelism undergirded by revival of the churches.
5 This observation is based on thirty years' experience in evangelism on all six continents.
6 Keir Hardie died in 1915.
7 STATESMAN'S YEARBOOK, 1905 & 1911 data.
8 STATESMAN'S YEARBOOK, 1905 & 1909 figures.
9 Minutes, South African Methodist Conference, 1901-10, Cape Town.
10 INTERNATIONAL REVIEW OF MISSIONS, 1912, p. 28, cf. YEAR BOOK OF MISSIONS IN INDIA, 1912.
11 92nd Annual Report, American Baptist Missionary Union, pp. 99 & 119; cf. 93rd Annual Report, Boston.
12 R. E. Shearer, WILDFIRE: CHURCH GROWTH IN KOREA.
13 CHINA MISSION YEAR BOOK, 1915.
14 see ATLAS OF PROTESTANT MISSIONS, 1903, and WORLD ATLAS OF CHRISTIAN MISSIONS, 1911.
15 Malagasy figures are deducted from the totals.
16 Is not the best sense the scriptural one, the Ephesian verses?
17 Every Welsh authority consulted, as well as Pentecostal leaders in Britain converted in the Welsh Revival, affirmed that the first glossolalic outbreak recorded in the wake of the Welsh Revival occurred at Waunllwyd, near Ebbw Vale, 22nd December 1907, as a result of a visit of A. H. Post, from Azusa Street in Los Angeles.
18 See pp. 49 & 97-99, for documentation.
19 K. S. Latourette, A HISTORY OF THE EXPANSION OF CHRISTIANITY, Volume IV, Chapter XI.
20 Preface to Gabriel Vahanian's THE DEATH OF GOD, 1961.
21 J. Edwin Orr, THE SECOND EVANGELICAL AWAKENING IN BRITAIN, pp. 35ff, 207 & 269ff. The numbers added to the Welsh churches in the Revival of 1904 matched those of 1859.

Notes on Chapter 3: TAIKYO DENDO IN JAPAN

1 Otis Cary, A HISTORY OF CHRISTIANITY IN JAPAN, Volume II, pp. 164ff.
2 Student Volunteer Movement Report, Toronto, 1902, pp. 390ff.
3 see P. M. Kanamori, KANAMORI'S LIFE STORY & MISSIONARY REVIEW OF THE WORLD, 1900, p. 689.
4 MISSIONARY HERALD, Boston, June 1900.
5 MISSIONARY HERALD, October 1901.
6 J. H. DeForest, SUNRISE IN THE SUNRISE KINGDOM, p. 194.
7 JAPAN EVANGELIST, July 1901, p. 227.
8 see JAPAN EVANGELIST, 1901 onwards.
9 JAPAN EVANGELIST, June 1901, p. 195.
10 JAPAN EVANGELIST, July 1901, p. 226.
11 Student Volunteer Movement Report, Toronto, 1902, pp. 390ff.
12 JAPAN EVANGELIST, April 1902, pp. 109ff.
13 J. H. DeForest, SUNRISE IN THE SUNRISE KINGDOM, p. 194.
14 BAPTIST MISSIONARY MAGAZINE, 1907, p. 406.
15 MISSIONARY HERALD, 1907, pp. 80ff.
16 C. W. Iglehart, A CENTURY OF PROTESTANT CHRISTIANITY IN JAPAN, p. 119.
17 A. Ebisawa, NIPPON KIRISTOKYO HYAKUNENSHI, p. 168.
18 A. Ebisawa, NIPPON KIRISTOKYO HYAKUNENSHI, p. 169.
19 C. W. Iglehart, PROTESTANT CHRISTIANITY, p. 128.
20 MISSIONARY REVIEW OF THE WORLD, 1907, p. 325.
21 Basil Matthews, JOHN R. MOTT, World Citizen, p. 183.
22 MISSIONARY REVIEW OF THE WORLD, 1908, p. 3.
23 ALLIANCE WEEKLY, New York, 1906-1907, p. 235.
24 ASSEMBLY HERALD, Philadelphia, 1908, pp. 405ff.
25 MISSIONARY REVIEW OF THE WORLD, 1910, p. 598.
26 JAPAN EVANGELIST, November 1901, pp. 338ff.
27 Edinburgh MISSIONARY CONFERENCE, 1910, Volume I, p. 36.
28 cf. MISSIONARY REVIEW, 1903, p. 521; 1909, p. 74.
29 T. Yanagita, HISTORY OF CHRISTIANITY IN JAPAN, p. 63.
30 Buddhists strove to form by way of response a Buddhist Evangelistic Association, cf. JAPAN EVANGELIST, February 1902, pp. 46ff.
31 see K. Aoyoshi, DR. MASAHISA UEMURA, passim.

Notes on Chapter 4: THE KOREAN PENTECOST

1 A. W. Wasson, CHURCH GROWTH IN KOREA, p. 29.
2 Report of the Methodist Episcopal Church, South, 1904, pp. 23-24.
3 Hazel T. Watson, 'Revival and Church Growth in Korea,' 1884-1910, pp. 145-146.
4 O. C. Grauer, FREDRIK FRANSON, pp. 160ff; cf. D. B. Woodward, AFLAME FOR GOD, p. 155.
5 A. W. Wasson, CHURCH GROWTH IN KOREA, p. 31.
6 A. W. Wasson, CHURCH GROWTH IN KOREA, p. 32.
7 O. C. Grauer, FREDRIK FRANSON, p. 161.
8 W. N. Blair, GOLD IN KOREA, Chapter XV.
9 MISSIONARY REVIEW, 1905, pp. 474-475, 555ff, 955.
10 Annual Meeting, Korea Mission of the Presbyterian Church in the U.S.A., Seoul 1906. Johnston addressed meetings also in Pyongyang and Taegu, telling of the Awakenings in Wales and India.
11 cf. THE KOREA MISSION FIELD (II: 12:228), & MISSIONARY REVIEW OF THE WORLD, 1906, p. 395.

12 G. T. Brown, MISSION TO KOREA, p. 59.
13 MISSIONARY REVIEW OF THE WORLD, 1906, p. 556.
14 cf. R. E. Shearer, WILDFIRE: CHURCH GROWTH IN KOREA;
    & MISSIONARY REVIEW OF THE WORLD, 1907, p. 15.
15 MISSIONARY REVIEW OF THE WORLD, 1907, p. 15.
16 MISSIONARY REVIEW OF THE WORLD, 1907, p. 323.
17 G.H. Jones & W.A. Noble, THE KOREAN REVIVAL, an account
    of the 1907 movement.
18 MISSIONARY REVIEW OF THE WORLD, 1907, p. 323.
19 Microfilm Report, George McCune, Pyongyang, 15 January 1907,
    Archives of the Presbyterian Church in the U.S.A.
20 MISSIONARY REVIEW OF THE WORLD, 1907, p. 168.
21 W. N. Blair, GOLD IN KOREA, Chapter XVI.
22 The details were still vivid in the mind of a 90-year-old survivor,
    William Newton Blair, interviewed sixty years later by the writer.
    Dr. Blair is since deceased.
23 G. McCune, Pyongyang, 15 January 1907. Mrs. Watson supposed
    that praying simultaneously and audibly is an oriental custom, but
    the writer has heard this phenomenon among European, African
    and American peoples, in times of spiritual revival.
24 L.G. Paik, THE HISTORY OF PROTESTANT MISSIONS IN KOREA,
    p. 357.
25 William L. Swallen, Pyongyang, 18 January 1907, in the microfilm
    reports of the Presbyterian Church in the U.S.A., Philadelphia.
26 W. N. Blair, GOLD IN KOREA, p. 64.
27 L.G. Paik, PROTESTANT MISSIONS IN KOREA, p. 357.
28 L.G. Paik, PROTESTANT MISSIONS IN KOREA, p. 359.
29 1908 Report, Board of Missions, Methodist Episcopal Church, South.
30 A. H. Wasson, CHURCH GROWTH IN KOREA, p. 420.
31 The missionary journal, KOREAN MISSION FIELD, featured 32
    different reports from observers in the field.
32 W. N. Blair, GOLD IN KOREA, p. 64.
33 There was a surprising unanimity of agreement.
34 Student Volunteer Movement, STUDENTS AND THE MODERN
    MISSIONARY CRUSADE, 1910, p. 307; & A. W. Wasson, p. 419;
    & INTERNATIONAL REVIEW OF MISSIONS, July, 1912.
35 S.V.M., STUDENTS & THE MISSIONARY CRUSADE, 1910, p. 307.
36 JOURNAL of the Methodist Episcopal Church, South, 1908.
37 L. G. Paik, PROTESTANT MISSIONS IN KOREA, p. 364.
38 G. T. Ladd, IN KOREA WITH MARQUIS ITO, 1908.
39 see WHO WAS WHO, 1947, Volume II, p. 599.
40 G. T. Ladd, IN KOREA WITH MARQUIS ITO, p. 408.
41 ANNALS OF THE AMERICAN ACADEMY, January–June 1909, p. 197.
42 A. W. Wasson, CHURCH GROWTH IN KOREA, p. 53.
43 W. N. Blair, GOLD IN KOREA, pp. 67ff.
44 A. W. Wasson, CHURCH GROWTH IN KOREA, p. 54.
45 F. C. Ottman, J. WILBUR CHAPMAN, p. 197.
46 J. E. Adams, Annual Personal Report, Board of Foreign Missions,
    Presbyterian Church in the U.S.A., (Taegu, 1910-1911).
47 C.A. Clark, THE KOREAN CHURCH & NEVIUS METHODS, p. 155.
48 cf. R. E. Shearer, WILDFIRE, figures 3 & 16.
49 Dr. Han Kyung-Chik, Young Nak Church, Seoul.
50 Edinburgh MISSIONARY CONFERENCE, 1910, Volume I, p. 77.
51 cf. R. E. Shearer, WILDFIRE: CHURCH GROWTH IN KOREA.
52 W. N. Blair, PENTECOST IN KOREA, passim.
53 See C. A. Clark, THE KOREAN CHURCH, pp. 73-74.

Notes on Chapter 5: THE CHINESE QUICKENING

1 A. H. Smith, CHINA IN CONVULSION, passim.
2 ENCYCLOPEDIA BRITANNICA, 1970, China, history.
3 see A. E. Glover, A THOUSAND MILES OF MIRACLE IN CHINA
   & Marshall Broomhall, editor, MARTYRED MISSIONARIES OF
   THE CHINA INLAND MISSION.
4 P. A. Varg, MISSIONARIES, CHINESE AND DIPLOMATS, p. 86.
5 D. MacGillivray, A CENTURY OF PROTESTANT MISSIONS IN
   CHINA, pp. 277-278.
6 MISSIONARY REVIEW OF THE WORLD, 1900, p. 652.
7 D. MacGillivray, A CENTURY OF PROTESTANT MISSIONS IN
   CHINA, p. 211.
8 CHINESE RECORDER, Shanghai, 1905, p. 221.
9 ASSEMBLY HERALD, February 1903.
10 MISSIONARY REVIEW OF THE WORLD, 1909, p. 483.
11 D. MacGillivray, PROTESTANT MISSIONS IN CHINA, p. 58; cf.
   MISSIONARY REVIEW OF THE WORLD, 1909, p. 483.
12 MISSIONARY REVIEW OF THE WORLD, 1905, p. 936.
13 CHINA'S MILLIONS, 1906, p. 141.
14 CHINA'S MILLIONS, 1907, p. 14.
15 MISSIONARY REVIEW OF THE WORLD, 1907, p. 485.
16 MISSIONARY REVIEW OF THE WORLD, 1906, p. 802.
17 CHINA'S MILLIONS, 1906, p. 141.
18 MISSIONARY REVIEW OF THE WORLD, 1906, p. 643.
19 CHINA'S MILLIONS, 1906, p. 141.
20 MISSIONARY HERALD, 1906, p. 357.
21 MISSIONARY HERALD, 1905, pp. 80-81.
22 CHINA'S MILLIONS, 1906, p. 143.
23 MISSIONARY REVIEW, 1907, p. 642 & 1908, p. 451.
24 ALLIANCE WEEKLY, 1906, pp. 234 & 318; CHINA'S MILLIONS,
   1906, p. 154.
25 S. R. Clarke, AMONG THE TRIBES IN SOUTHWEST CHINA,
   pp. 140ff.   26 CHINA'S MILLIONS, 1907, pp. 10ff.
27 MISSIONARY REVIEW OF THE WORLD, 1907, pp. 207ff.
28 R. E. Kendall, THE EYES OF THE EARTH (The Diary of Samuel
   Pollard), p. 73.
29 R. Toliver, unpublished research on the Awakenings of 1905 among
   the Tribes of Southwest China, School of World Mission, Pasadena.
30 Rosalind Goforth, GOFORTH OF CHINA, passim.
31 Jonathan Goforth, 'BY MY SPIRIT,' pp. 33ff.
32 Jonathan Goforth, 'BY MY SPIRIT,' pp. 74ff.
33 J. Webster, THE REVIVAL IN MANCHURIA, passim; cf. Austin
   Fulton, THROUGH EARTHQUAKE, WIND AND FIRE, Church &
   Mission in Manchuria, 1867-1950, pp. 47ff.
34 K. S. Latourette, A HISTORY OF THE EXPANSION OF CHRIS-
   TIANITY, Volume VI, p. 344.
35 CHINESE RECORDER, 1908, p. 333.
36 MISSIONARY REVIEW OF THE WORLD, 1913, pp. 529ff.
37 Edinburgh MISSIONARY CONFERENCE, 1910, Vol. I, pp. 36-39.
38 MISSIONARY REVIEW OF THE WORLD, 1908, pp. 16ff.
39 CHINA'S MILLIONS, 1909, pp. 74, 147 & passim.
40 CHINA'S MILLIONS, 1909, passim.
41 CHINA'S MILLIONS, 1910, p. 22.   42 1909, p. 9.
43 see MISSIONARY REVIEW OF THE WORLD, 1909, pp. 884ff,
   & BAPTIST MISSIONARY MAGAZINE, 1909, p. 355.

44 MISSIONARY HERALD, 1910, p. 51.   45 1910, p. 51.
46 CHINA'S MILLIONS, 1909, p. 123.
47 ALLIANCE WEEKLY, 1909, p. 173.
48 RECORD OF CHRISTIAN WORK, 1907, p. 371.
49 CHINA'S MILLIONS, February 1911.   50 May 1911.
51 Edinburgh MISSIONARY CONFERENCE, 1910, Volume I, p. 37.
52 L. T. Lyall, A BIOGRAPHY OF JOHN SUNG, passim.
53 Donald Gee, THE PENTECOSTAL MOVEMENT, pp. 43, 48, 85.
54 TRUE JESUS CHURCH, Taichung, 1967.
55 Conversations with Leland Wang, Simon Meek, and others.
56 Angus Kinnear, AGAINST THE TIDE, passim.
57 K. S. Latourette, A HISTORY OF THE EXPANSION OF CHRIS-
     TIANITY, Volume VI, pp. 441ff.

Notes on Chapter 6: SOUTH EAST ASIA 1900—

1 American Baptist Missionary Union, ANNUAL REPORT, 1905,
    pp. 55-56.
2 E. N. Harris, A STAR IN THE EAST: AMERICAN BAPTIST
    MISSIONS TO THE KARENS IN BURMA; American Baptist
    Missionary Union, ANNUAL REPORT, 1906, pp. 55ff.
3 A.B.M.U., ANNUAL REPORT, 1905, pp. 102, 107, 116, 121.
4 A.B.M.U., ANNUAL REPORT, 1906, p. 106.
5 Business was largely in British, Chinese, and Indian hands. See
    A.B.M.U., ANNUAL REPORT, 1905, pp. 47, 55, 86, 92.
6 A.B.M.U., ANNUAL REPORT, 1906, p. 99.
7 A.B.M.U., ANNUAL REPORT, 1907, pp. 56ff.
8 On Ko San Ye, see ANNUAL REPORT, 1908, pp. 77ff.
9 A.B.M.U., ANNUAL REPORT, 1909, p. 52; 1910, p. 58; 1911,
    p. 53.
10 Dickason and Sowards, BURMA BAPTIST CHRONICLE, p. 409.
11 MISSIONARY REVIEW OF THE WORLD, 1906, pp. 163, 307;
    A.B.M.U., ANNUAL REPORT, 1906, p. 119.
12 A.B.M.U., ANNUAL REPORT, 1907, p. 56.
13 Dickason and Sowards, BURMA BAPTIST CHRONICLE, p. 413;
    American Baptist Missionary Union, ANNUAL REPORT, 1907,
    p. 81; 1908, pp. 84-85; 1909, p. 55; 1911, p. 57.
14 A.B.M.U., ANNUAL REPORT, 1910, pp. 55, 58; 1911, p. 53.
15 Dickason and Sowards, BURMA BAPTIST CHRONICLE, p. 348;
    A.B.M.U., ANNUAL REPORT, 1910, pp. 61, 63, 65.
16 A.B.M.U., ANNUAL REPORT, 1911 and 1921 statistics.
17 See L. B. Hughes, THE EVANGEL IN BURMA, p. 153; also
    Dickason and Sowards, p. 215.
18 Dickason and Sowards, BURMA BAPTIST CHRONICLE, p. 309ff.
19 INTERNATIONAL REVIEW OF MISSIONS, 1908, p. 334; see
    K. S. Latourette, A HISTORY OF THE EXPANSION OF CHRIS-
    TIANITY, Volume VI, pp. 240-241.
20 Daniel McGilvary, A HALF CENTURY AMONG THE SIAMESE
    AND THE LAO, passim.
21 See John H. Freeman, AN ORIENTAL LAND OF THE FREE,
    pp. 163ff.
22 cf. W. A. Brown, MISSIONARY REVIEW OF THE WORLD, 1908,
    pp. 334ff; and A. J. Brown, 1908, pp. 339ff.
23 INTERNATIONAL REVIEW OF MISSIONS, 1913, p. 27; and 1914,
    p. 29; and 1915, p. 51.
24 E. F. Irwin, WITH CHRIST IN INDO-CHINA, pp. 25ff.

Notes on Chapter 7: YEARS OF WAR IN JAPAN

1 MISSIONARY REVIEW OF THE WORLD, 1910, pp. 652-653;
cf. Reports on Japan, in WORLD MISSIONARY CONFERENCE,
1910, at Edinburgh.
2 See THE CHRISTIAN MOVEMENT IN JAPAN, 1914, statistical
tables; Basil Mathews, JOHN R. MOTT: WORLD CITIZEN.
3 C. W. Iglehart, A CENTURY OF PROTESTANT CHRISTIANITY
IN JAPAN, pp. 149-150. Latourette described the effort as 'One
of the outstanding features of Protestant Christianity in Japan in
the years immediately following 1914,' A HISTORY OF THE
EXPANSION OF CHRISTIANITY, Volume VII, p. 386.
4 See NIHON KIRISUTO KYODANSHI, (Nihon Kirisuto Kyodan
Shuppambu, Tokyo, 1967), p. 73.
5 MISSIONARY REVIEW OF THE WORLD, 1914, pp. 655-660,
citing the Rev. S. H. Wainwright.
6 MISSIONARY REVIEW OF THE WORLD, 1914, p. 953. The
Japanese press gave a very friendly coverage of the campaign.
7 MISSIONARY REVIEW OF THE WORLD, 1915, p. 484.
8 W. R. Wheeler, A MAN SENT FROM GOD: A BIOGRAPHY
OF ROBERT E. SPEER, p. 104; MISSIONARY REVIEW OF
THE WORLD, 1915, p. 629.
9 MISSIONARY REVIEW OF THE WORLD, 1916, p. 143.
10 Count Shigenobu Okuma, quoted in MISSIONARY REVIEW OF
THE WORLD, 1916, p. 825.
11 INTERNATIONAL REVIEW OF MISSIONS, 1922, p. 204. See
Beach and Fahs, WORLD MISSIONARY ATLAS, p. 82.
12 See B. Godfrey Buxton, THE REWARD OF FAITH (Biography
of Barclay F. Buxton); and T. Miyakoda, BUXTON TO SONO
DESHITACHI (Buxton and His Disciples), a more recent work.
13 MISSIONARY REVIEW OF THE WORLD, 1916, p. 338; see
A. Ebisawa, NIPPON KIRISTOKYO HYAKUNENSHI, pp. 168-169.
14 P. M. Kanamori, KANAMORI'S LIFE STORY, pp. 84-87. (His
Japanese name was Kanamori Tsurin).
15 SALVATION ARMY YEARBOOK, 1969, p. 142; see also JAPAN
CHRISTIAN QUARTERLY, October 1962, pp. 223ff, 'Yamamuro
Gumpei, an Officer of the Salvation Army.'
16 Isamu Yoneda, NAKADA JUJI DEN (A Biography of Juji Nakada),
pp. 296; 418.
17 Mildred Morehouse, 'Awakenings and Church Growth in Japan,'
unpublished paper, p. 10.
18 See William Axling, KAGAWA (the standard biography); Toyohiko
Kagawa, BEFORE THE DAWN (part-autobiographical novel);
INTERNATIONAL REVIEW OF MISSIONS, XXI, pp. 19ff; and
XXIII, p. 7; JAPAN MISSION YEARBOOK, 1929, pp. 94ff; 1930,
pp. 139ff; R. H. Drummond, A HISTORY OF CHRISTIANITY
IN JAPAN, pp. 235-236.
19 D. C. Holtom, MODERN JAPAN AND SHINTO NATIONALISM,
p. 97. See also INTERNATIONAL REVIEW OF MISSIONS,
XXIX, pp. 161ff; 305ff.
20 R. H. Drummond, A HISTORY OF CHRISTIANITY IN JAPAN,
pp. 260-262; R. T. Baker, DARKNESS OF THE SUN, pp. 34ff.
21 The writer read the offical dossier in S.C.A.P. H.Q. in Tokyo in
1945, and discussed the details with various missionaries.
22 Toyohiko Kagawa, David Tsutada and others told their stories to
the writer in Tokyo in 1945.

Notes on Chapter 8: KOREA'S DARKEST DAYS

1 R. E. Shearer, WILDFIRE: CHURCH GROWTH IN KOREA, pp. 62ff; A.W.Wasson, CHURCH GROWTH IN KOREA, pp. 98ff.
2 A. D. Clark, HISTORY OF THE KOREAN CHURCH, pp. 168ff.
3 W. N. Blair, GOLD IN KOREA, pp. 77ff.
4 ANNUAL REPORT OF THE BOARD OF FOREIGN MISSIONS OF THE PRESBYTERIAN CHURCH IN THE U.S.A., 1922 & 1923, Philadelphia.
5 MISSIONARY REVIEW OF THE WORLD, 1920, p. 862.
6 MISSIONARY REVIEW OF THE WORLD, 1921, p. 668.
7 See R. E. Shearer, WILDFIRE: CHURCH GROWTH IN KOREA, pp. 80ff; Chae Eun-Soo, 'Revival in Korea,' unpublished paper, School of World Mission, Pasadena, California, pp. 4-5.
8 Chulla Province lay to the southwest, Kyungsang to the southeast—rice-growing areas—A.D.Clark, pp. 3-4; see Chae Eun-Soo in 'Revival in Korea,' p. 5.
9 See L. G. Parker, HISTORY OF PROTESTANT MISSIONS IN KOREA, p. 21; Chae Eun-Soo, 'Revival in Korea,' p. 5.
10 Cf. W. N. Blair, Annual Personal Report, Pyongyang, 1925; and Chae Eun-Soo, 'Revival in Korea,' pp. 1-2.
11 Chae Eun-Soo, 'Revival in Korea,' p. 2.
12 MISSIONARY REVIEW OF THE WORLD, 1921, pp. 346; Clark, HISTORY OF THE KOREAN CHURCH, p. 174.
13 Cf. H. G. Underwood, Evangelistic Report to the Board, 1914 & W. N. Blair, GOLD IN KOREA, pp. 88ff.
14 MISSIONARY REVIEW OF THE WORLD, 1921, p. 810.
15 MISSIONARY REVIEW OF THE WORLD, 1921, p. 154.
16 Koh Won Yong, 'A Brief History of Evangelical Awakenings in Korea since 1920,' unpublished paper, School of World Mission, Pasadena, California, p. 1.
17 The Rev. Koh Wong Yong, a Presbyterian minister, was himself a witness of events in North Korea.
18 MISSIONARY REVIEW OF THE WORLD, 1929, p. 412.
19 Report in MISSIONARY REVIEW OF THE WORLD, 1929, p. 27.
20 MISSIONARY REVIEW OF THE WORLD, 1928, p. 381.
21 Report in MISSIONARY REVIEW OF THE WORLD, 1929, p. 392.
22 MISSIONARY REVIEW OF THE WORLD, 1929, p. 392.
23 A. D. Clark, HISTORY OF THE KOREAN CHURCH, pp. 193ff; R. E. Shearer, WILDFIRE, pp. 70-76.
24 See W. N. Blair, GOLD IN KOREA, pp. 99ff; INTERNATIONAL REVIEW OF MISSIONS, XX, p. 12.
25 See R. E. Shearer, WILDFIRE: CHURCH GROWTH IN KOREA, pp. 75-76.
26 W. N. Blair, GOLD IN KOREA, pp. 102ff.
27 A. D. Clark, HISTORY OF THE KOREAN CHURCH, p. 202; cf. Annual Report of the Board of Foreign Missions, 1946, p. 20.
28 INTERNATIONAL REVIEW OF MISSIONS, XXVIII, p. 11. See R. E. Shearer, WILDFIRE, pp. 207-208.
29 A. D. Clark, HISTORY OF THE KOREAN CHURCH, p. 203; cf. Yang Sun Kim, HISTORY OF THE KOREAN CHURCH, p. 1.
30 Harold Voelkel, A REVIVAL AMONG MISSIONARIES IN KOREA, privately published booklet.
31 J. Edwin Orr, I SAW NO TEARS, pp. 86ff.
32 Harold Voelkel, A REVIVAL AMONG MISSIONARIES IN KOREA, provides the only printed source.

Notes on Chapter 9: DESPAIR AND RECOVERY IN CHINA

1   See Chang Kuo-tao, THE RISE OF THE COMMUNIST PARTY, 1921-1927, pp. 422ff.
2   CHINESE RECORDER, LVIII, September 1927, p. 604.
3   See CHINESE RECORDER, LVIII, January 1927, p. 4; Gustav Carlberg, CHINA IN REVIVAL, p. 21.
4   Andrew Gih, CHINA'S WONDERFUL REVIVING, p. 11. There are many accounts of this conference in print.
5   Gustav Carlberg, CHINA IN REVIVAL, p. 22.
6   CHINESE RECORDER, LVIII, March 1927, p. 223.
7   Yang Ching-Siao, quoted in Gustav Carlberg, CHINA IN REVIVAL, pp. 30ff.
8   MISSIONARY REVIEW OF THE WORLD. G. T. B. Davis served with Torrey and Alexander in China a generation earlier.
9   Quoting Dr. Marcus Cheng, Changsha, Gustav Carlberg, CHINA IN REVIVAL, p. 29.
10 CHINA CHRISTIAN YEARBOOK, 1929, p. 152.
11 MISSIONARY REVIEW OF THE WORLD, 1932, p. 468.
12 CHINESE RECORDER, LXIV, April 1933, editorial; MISSIONARY REVIEW OF THE WORLD, 1933, pp. 67 & 125; 1934, p. 247. There are many supporting opinions.
13 Gustav Carlberg, CHINA IN REVIVAL, pp. 45ff.
14 Leslie Lyall, COME WIND, COME WEATHER, pp. 52ff. Wang Ming-dao became a hero of Christian nonconformity to Maoism.
15 MISSIONARY REVIEW OF THE WORLD, 1935, p. 133; Gustav Carlberg, CHINA IN REVIVAL, pp. 37ff.
16 Gustav Carlberg, CHINA IN REVIVAL, pp. 84ff.
17 Personal knowledge of Leland Wang and Simon Meek, two of the famous trio in Foochow that included Watchman Nee. Wang Tsai—the former's Chinese name—and his conversion are well described in Angus Kinnear, AGAINST THE TIDE, pp. 39ff.
18 Gustav Carlberg, CHINA IN REVIVAL, pp. 51-52.
19 Gustav Carlberg, CHINA IN REVIVAL, p. 72.
20 Marie Monsen, THE AWAKENING, pp. 23-24.
21 Personal acquaintance; see Leslie T. Lyall, in Marie Monsen, THE AWAKENING, p. 20; also p. 110.
22 See J. Edwin Orr, THROUGH BLOOD AND FIRE IN CHINA, pp. 53-54.
23 Andrew Gih, LAUNCH OUT INTO THE DEEP, p. 14.
24 J. Edwin Orr, THROUGH BLOOD AND FIRE IN CHINA, p. 54.
25 Leslie T. Lyall, JOHN SUNG, p. 73.
26 William E. Schubert, I REMEMBER JOHN SUNG, p. 2.
27 Leslie T. Lyall, JOHN SUNG, pp. 29ff.
28 John Sung, in Andrew Gih, INTO GOD'S FAMILY, p. 57.
29 Leslie T. Lyall, JOHN SUNG, pp. 31-32.
30 John Sung, in Andrew Gih, INTO GOD'S FAMILY, p. 58.
31 Leslie T. Lyall, JOHN SUNG, pp. 45-46.
32 William E. Schubert, I REMEMBER JOHN SUNG, p. 12.
33 This assessment of John Sung was confirmed by those who knew him—conceded by his friends, affirmed by his critics.
34 Information from many colleagues and sponsors.
35 Philip Lee, in Andrew Gih, INTO GOD'S FAMILY, pp. 43ff.
36 Frank Lin, in Andrew Gih, INTO GOD'S FAMILY, pp. 32ff.
37 Lincoln Nieh, in Andrew Gih, INTO GOD'S FAMILY, pp. 11ff.
38 John Shih, in Andrew Gih, INTO GOD'S FAMILY, pp. 18ff.

Notes on Chapter 10: AWAKENING BEYOND THE WALL

1 Gustav Carlberg, CHINA IN REVIVAL, p. 67.
2 Marie Monsen, THE AWAKENING, pp. 50ff.
3 Gustav Carlberg, CHINA IN REVIVAL, pp. 109-110.
4 MISSIONARY REVIEW OF THE WORLD, 1929, p. 947.
5 MISSIONARY REVIEW OF THE WORLD, 1933, p. 277.
6 Leslie T. Lyall, JOHN SUNG, pp. 76-77.
7 Andrew Gih, CHINA'S WONDERFUL REVIVING, p. 16.
8 Leslie T. Lyall, JOHN SUNG, pp. 79ff.
9 Leslie T. Lyall, JOHN SUNG, pp. 83ff.
10 Andrew Gih, LAUNCH OUT INTO THE DEEP, pp. 18-19.
11 Andrew Gih, CHINA'S WONDERFUL REVIVING, p. 18.
12 Leslie T. Lyall, JOHN SUNG, pp. 87-88.
13 MISSIONARY REVIEW OF THE WORLD, 1932, p. 672.
14 CHINESE RECORDER, December 1933.
15 Gustav Carlberg, CHINA IN REVIVAL, p. 116.
16 Gustav Carlberg, CHINA IN REVIVAL, p. 116.
17 MISSIONARY REVIEW OF THE WORLD, 1935, p. 612.
18 K. S. Latourette, ADVANCE THROUGH STORM, p. 368.
19 T. R. Morton, TODAY IN MANCHURIA, pp. 65ff.
20 CHINA'S MILLIONS, Philadelphia, May 1933.
21 Andrew Gih, LAUNCH OUT INTO THE DEEP, pp. 43ff.
22 Leslie T. Lyall, JOHN SUNG, pp. 112ff.
23 CHINA'S MILLIONS, February 1933.
24 Leslie T. Lyall, JOHN SUNG, pp. 116ff; cf. William E. Schubert,
    I REMEMBER JOHN SUNG, p. 12; Bethel Band informants.

Notes on Chapter 11: AWAKENINGS IN NORTH CHINA

1 Marie Monsen, THE AWAKENING, pp. 53-55.
2 C. L. Culpepper, THE SHANTUNG REVIVAL, pp. 11-14.
3 Southern Baptist North China Mission meetings, Chefoo, 1930.
4 ANNUAL REPORT of the North China Mission, 1932.
5 Andrew Gih, LAUNCH OUT INTO THE DEEP, pp. 16ff.
6 MISSIONARY REVIEW OF THE WORLD, 1932, p. 468.
7 ANNUAL REPORT of the North China Mission, 1932.
8 Leslie T. Lyall, JOHN SUNG, p. 68.
9 Andrew Gih, LAUNCH OUT INTO THE DEEP, p. 43.
10 MISSIONARY REVIEW OF THE WORLD, 1933, p. 197.
11 Gustav Carlberg, CHINA IN REVIVAL, pp. 121-124.
12 MISSIONARY REVIEW OF THE WORLD, 1933, p. 67.
13 Gustav Carlberg, CHINA IN REVIVAL, pp. 124-125.
14 MISSIONARY REVIEW OF THE WORLD, 1933, p. 67.
15 Leslie T. Lyall, JOHN SUNG, pp. 99-100.
16 Paul Abbott, in CHINA CHRISTIAN YEARBOOK, 1932.
17 Leslie T. Lyall, JOHN SUNG, p. 88.
18 Andrew Gih, LAUNCH OUT INTO THE DEEP, p. 47.
19 Leslie T. Lyall, JOHN SUNG, p. 125.
20 Marie Monsen, THE AWAKENING, pp. 57ff.
21 Marie Monsen, A PRESENT HELP: & Carlberg, pp. 76ff.
22 Leslie T. Lyall in Marie Monsen, THE AWAKENING, p. 21.
23 Andrew Gih, LAUNCH OUT INTO THE DEEP, p. 17.
24 Leslie T. Lyall, JOHN SUNG, pp. 108-109.
25 CHINA'S MILLIONS, February 1933.
26 MISSIONARY REVIEW OF THE WORLD, 1933, p. 71.

27 Leslie T. Lyall, JOHN SUNG, pp. 101-104.
28 MISSIONARY REVIEW OF THE WORLD, 1933, p. 417.
29 Andrew Gih, CHINA'S WONDERFUL REVIVING, pp. 24ff.
30 Marie Monsen, THE AWAKENING, pp. 88-89.
31 Leslie T. Lyall, JOHN SUNG, p. 104.
32 Leslie T. Lyall, JOHN SUNG, pp. 125-126.
33 CHINA'S MILLIONS, June 1933.
34 CHINA'S MILLIONS, March 1933.
35 Leslie T. Lyall, JOHN SUNG, pp. 109-110.
36 CHINA'S MILLIONS, July 1934.
37 Andrew Gih, BANDS OF SOLDIERS FOR WAR, pp. 21ff.
38 MISSIONARY REVIEW OF THE WORLD, 1935, p. 154.
39 CHINA'S MILLIONS, March 1935.
40 Andrew Gih, BANDS OF SOLDIERS FOR WAR, pp. 26ff.
41 MISSIONARY REVIEW OF THE WORLD, 1935, p. 612.
42 Gustav Carlberg, CHINA IN REVIVAL, pp. 51-52.

Notes on Chapter 12: SHANGHAI AND CENTRAL CHINA

1 Personal knowledge. The writer edited many of Gih's books.
2 Andrew Gih, LAUNCH OUT INTO THE DEEP, p. 15.
3 Dr. Betty Hu, long-time associate, informant.
4 Leslie T. Lyall, JOHN SUNG, p. 90.
5 Dr. Betty Hu, informant.
6 John Shih, in Andrew Gih, INTO GOD'S FAMILY, pp. 18ff.
7 Leslie T. Lyall, JOHN SUNG, p. 124.   8 JOHN SUNG, p. 127.
9 Leslie T. Lyall, JOHN SUNG, p. 127.
10 MISSIONARY REVIEW OF THE WORLD, 1935, p. 377.
11 Gustav Carlberg, CHINA IN REVIVAL, pp. 129ff.
12 Marie Monsen, THE AWAKENING, pp. 97-100.
13 Gustav Carlberg, CHINA IN REVIVAL, pp. 129-130.
14 Andrew Gih, LAUNCH OUT INTO THE DEEP, p. 43 & Lyall,
   JOHN SUNG, p. 108.   15 JOHN SUNG, p. 114.
16 Frank Lin, informant.
17 Gustav Carlberg, CHINA IN REVIVAL, pp. 133-138.
18 CHINA'S MILLIONS, May 1933.   19 May 1933.
20 CHINA'S MILLIONS, June 1933.
21 CHINA'S MILLIONS, October 1933.
22 CHINA'S MILLIONS, May 1934.   23 May 1934.
24 CHINA'S MILLIONS, February 1935.
25 CHINA'S MILLIONS, June 1936, July 1936.
26 LUTHERAN HERALD, Minneapolis, 20 March 1934.
27 Gustav Carlberg, CHINA IN REVIVAL, pp. 138-139.
28 Andrew Gih, LAUNCH OUT INTO THE DEEP, pp. 50-53.
29 Marcus Cheng, 12 April 1934, in Gustav Carlberg, pp. 167-168.
30 Gustav Carlberg, CHINA IN REVIVAL, pp. 164-165.
31 Fritz Peterson, COVENANT WEEKLY, 29 January 1935.
32 D. R. Wahlquist, 19 October 1934, UNGDOMSVANNEN, Stockholm.
33 Gustav Carlberg, CHINA IN REVIVAL, pp. 171-172.
34 V. E. Swenson, in LUTHERAN COMPANION, Rock Island; see
   Gustav Carlberg, pp. 155-160.
35 NORSK MISSIONSTIDENE, Stavanger, 19 August 1933.
36 MISSIONSTIDNING FOR FINLAND, Helsinki, October 1933.
37 Leslie T. Lyall, JOHN SUNG, pp. 114ff.
38 China Inland, Mission Covenant, and Presbyterian Missions.
39 Leslie T. Lyall, JOHN SUNG, pp. 117-119.

Notes on Chapter 13: REVIVAL IN THE SOUTH AND WEST

1 Andrew Gih, CHINA'S WONDERFUL REVIVING, p. 40.
2 Andrew Gih, LAUNCH OUT INTO THE DEEP, p. 38.
3 CHINESE RECORDER, LX, 1929, p. 402.
4 Andrew Gih, TWICE BORN AND THEN? pp. 41-42.
5 John Sung, in Andrew Gih, INTO GOD'S FAMILY, p. 60.
6 Andrew Gih, TWICE BORN AND THEN? p. 43.
7 Andrew Gih, CHINA'S WONDERFUL REVIVING, pp. 42-44.
8 Andrew Gih, TWICE BORN AND THEN? p. 40.
9 CHINESE RECORDER, LX, 1929, p. 402.
10 Leslie T. Lyall, JOHN SUNG, pp. 51ff.
11 Andrew Gih, TWICE BORN AND THEN? pp. 44-46.
12 Leslie T. Lyall, JOHN SUNG, p. 96.
13 MISSIONARY REVIEW OF THE WORLD, 1933, p. 162.
14 Leslie T. Lyall, JOHN SUNG, pp. 128-131.
15 MISSIONARY REVIEW OF THE WORLD, 1935, p. 314.
16 Leslie T. Lyall, JOHN SUNG, pp. 61-64.
17 William E. Schubert, I REMEMBER JOHN SUNG, pp. 9-10.
18 CHINA'S MILLIONS, September 1933.
19 See J. Edwin Orr, THROUGH BLOOD AND FIRE IN CHINA, pp. 17-18, 140ff.
20 CHINA'S MILLIONS, February 1935.
21 Andrew Gih, LAUNCH OUT INTO THE DEEP, pp. 38-39.
22 See J. Edwin Orr, THROUGH BLOOD AND FIRE IN CHINA, pp. 14-17.
23 MISSIONARY REVIEW OF THE WORLD, 1933, p. 277.
24 Leslie T. Lyall, JOHN SUNG, pp. 93-94.
25 Principal Vera Shen, Bethel High School, Kowloon.
26 Leslie T. Lyall, John Sung, p. 95.
27 Again at the Peniel Mission in Kowloon.
28 Leslie T. Lyall, JOHN SUNG, p. 126.
29 See J. Edwin Orr, THROUGH BLOOD AND FIRE IN CHINA, pp. 52ff.
30 INTERNATIONAL REVIEW OF MISSIONS, XXI, p. 25.
31 See Beach & St. John, WORLD STATISTICS OF CHRISTIAN MISSIONS, p. 62; & Joseph I. Parker, INTERPRETATIVE STATISTICAL SURVEY, p. 33.
32 MISSIONARY REVIEW OF THE WORLD, 1938, p. 127.
33 INTERNATIONAL REVIEW OF MISSIONS, XXX, p. 13; XXXI, p. 12. See A. J. Swanson, TAIWAN, p. 87.
34 Hollington Tong, CHRISTIANITY IN TAIWAN, p. 76.
35 Sheldon Sawatzky, 'Awakenings in Taiwan,' pp. 2-3.
36 George Vicedom, FAITH THAT MOVES MOUNTAINS, pp. 35-38.
37 CHINA'S MILLIONS, February 1933.
38 CHINA'S MILLIONS, March 1934.
39 CHINA'S MILLIONS, May 1934.
40 CHINA'S MILLIONS, September 1935.
41 Andrew Gih, BANDS OF SOLDIERS FOR WAR, pp. 16ff; 34ff.
42 Andrew Gih, LAUNCH OUT INTO THE DEEP, pp. 54ff.
43 CHINA'S MILLIONS, January 1935.
44 CHINA'S MILLIONS, May 1934.
45 CHINA'S MILLIONS, November 1935.
46 CHINA'S MILLIONS, January 1935.
47 Andrew Gih, BANDS OF SOLDIERS FOR WAR, pp. 38-43.
48 Andrew Gih, BANDS OF SOLDIERS FOR WAR, pp. 44-51.

Notes on Chapter 14: CHINA IN REVIVAL, 1927-1939

1   CHINA'S MILLIONS, Philadelphia, February 1935.
2   Andrew Gih, CHINA'S WONDERFUL REVIVING, pp. 70-71.
3   Andrew Gih, LAUNCH OUT INTO THE DEEP, p. 68.
4   CHINA'S MILLIONS, 1926, Editorial.
5   K. S. Latourette, ADVANCE THROUGH STORM, p. 346.
6   ANNUAL REPORT, Associated Boards for Christian Colleges in China, 1943.   7   CHINA'S MILLIONS, July 1933.
8   Leslie T. Lyall, JOHN SUNG, p. 97.
9   Andrew Gih, BANDS OF SOLDIERS FOR WAR, 1939.
10 Leslie T. Lyall, JOHN SUNG, p. 97.
11 Andrew Gih, LAUNCH OUT INTO THE DEEP, p. 62.
12 Andrew Gih, CHINA'S WONDERFUL REVIVING, p. 66.
13 Conversation in China, 1938.
14 Andrew Gih, CHINA'S WONDERFUL REVIVING, p. 25.
15 Anglicans, Baptists, Lutherans, Methodists and Presbyterians so reported.   16 Andrew Gih, LAUNCH OUT, pp. 34-35.
17 Andrew Gih, CHINA'S WONDERFUL REVIVING, p. 64.
18 Allen J. Swanson, TAIWAN, pp. 54-57.
19 Angus Kinnear, AGAINST THE TIDE, pp. 86ff.
20 F. P. Jones, THE CHURCH IN COMMUNIST CHINA, p. 17.

Notes on Chapter 15: SOUTH-EAST ASIAN REVIVALS, 1920—

1   R. E. Reimer, 'The Evangelical Church in Vietnam,' pp. 3 & 16.
2   E. F. Irwin, THE CALL OF FRENCH INDO-CHINA, April-June 1924, pp. 4-6.
3   R. E. Reimer, 'The Evangelical Church in Vietnam,' p. 16.
4   Leslie T. Lyall, JOHN SUNG, p. 162.
5   See Le-Huang-Phu, 'The Evangelical Church of Vietnam,' p. 32.
6   ALLIANCE WEEKLY, 19 November 1938, pp. 744-746.
7   Mrs. D. I. Jeffrey, in ALLIANCE WEEKLY.
8   Le-Huang-Phu, 'The Evangelical Church of Vietnam,' pp. 33-35.
9   E. F. Irwin, in ANNUAL REPORT of the Indo-China Mission Field, 1939.
10 Truong-van-Tot, 'Revivals in Vietnam,' unpublished paper, 1972, School of World Mission, Pasadena, California, pp. 10ff.
11 See J. Edwin Orr, THROUGH BLOOD AND FIRE IN CHINA, pp. 148ff.
12 Letter of Andrew Gih, 1971, to the Rev. Truang-van-Tot.
13 Le-Huang-Phu, 'The Evangelical Church of Vietnam,' p. 44.
14 Joseph I. Parker, INTERPRETATIVE STATISTICAL SURVEY, p. 53; & Beach & Fahs, WORLD MISSIONARY ATLAS, p. 101.
15 MISSIONARY REVIEW OF THE WORLD, 1925, p. 320.
16 Leslie T. Lyall, JOHN SUNG, pp. 160ff.
17 MISSIONARY REVIEW OF THE WORLD, 1939, pp. 341-342.
18 INTERNATIONAL REVIEW OF MISSIONS, XXXIII, p. 25.
19 MISSIONARY REVIEW OF THE WORLD, 1922, p. 999.
20 INTERNATIONAL REVIEW OF MISSIONS, 1922, pp. 586ff.
21 American Baptist Foreign Mission Society, REPORT, 1921.
22 MISSIONARY REVIEW OF THE WORLD, 1923.
23 INTERNATIONAL REVIEW OF MISSIONS, 1928.
24 MISSIONARY REVIEW, 1931, pp. 626-627 & p. 549.
25 American Baptist Foreign Mission Society, REPORT, 1931.
26 WORLD DOMINION, January-February 1945.

Notes on Chapter 16: POST-WAR EVANGELISM IN JAPAN

1 J. Edwin Orr, I SAW NO TEARS, pp. 114 & 118.
2 Haruichi Yokoyama, KAGAWA TOYOHIKO DEN, pp. 436-440.
3 J. M. L. Young, TWO EMPIRES IN JAPAN, p. 137.
4 Of the 2710 Protestant missionaries assigned to Japan in 1957 (see JAPAN CHRISTIAN YEARBOOK, 1958, 'Protestant Missions in Japan,' Olaf Hansen), the great majority were avowed Evangelicals.
5 E. Stanley Jones, 'Evangelism in Japan after the Occupation,' in JAPAN CHRISTIAN QUARTERLY, Summer 1953.
6 See Tomio Muto, LACOUR CRUSADE (Kirisuto Shimbun), 1959.
7 The movement began among the Evangelical Alliance Mission team, but affected only a couple of hundred foreigners and nationals.
8 Tomio Muto, LACOUR CRUSADE, pp. 29ff.
9 WORLD VISION MAGAZINE, February 1959.
10 There was criticism of the foreign sponsorship of the Crusade, see C. H. Germany, editor, THE RESPONSE OF THE CHURCH IN CHANGING JAPAN, p. 82.
11 CHRISTIAN YEAR BOOK (Kirisuto Kyo Nenkan), 1969, p. 78.
12 Paul K. Ariga, Notes on Sodoin Dendo, Pasadena, California, 1972.
13 CHRISTIAN YEAR BOOK (Kirisuto Kyo Nenkan), 1969, p. 69.
14 Paul K. Ariga, Notes on Sodoin Dendo, 1972.
15 John Mizuki, 'Great Crusades in Post-War Japan,' unpublished paper, Pasadena, California, 1974.
16 NIPPON TIMES, Tokyo, 12 October 1951.
17 NIPPON TIMES, Tokyo, 17 October 1951.
18 See Philip Tsuchiya, 'Shakabuku— Soka Gakkai's Apologetics Evangelism,' published paper, Pasadena, California, 1970.
19 Harry Thomsen, NEW RELIGIONS OF JAPAN, p. 82.
20 SHOKUN (Magazine), Tokyo, May 1970, p. 72.
21 SHOKUN (Magazine), Tokyo, May 1970, p. 79.
22 Noel Brannen, SOKA GAKKAI, p. 80.
23 See Tsunesaburo Makaguchi, SOKA KYOIKUGAKU TAIKEI.
24 For a summary, see Philip Tsuchiya, 'Shakabuku—Soka Gakkai's Apologetics Evangelism,' 1970.

Notes on Chapter 17: THE 1947 REVIVAL IN KOREA

! J. Edwin Orr, I SAW NO TEARS, pp. 120-121.
2 Allen D. Clark, HISTORY OF THE KOREAN CHURCH, pp. 206ff.
3 Kim Yang Sun, HISTORY OF THE KOREAN CHURCH IN THE TEN YEARS SINCE LIBERATION, translated by A. D. Clark.
4 Allen D. Clark, HISTORY OF THE KOREAN CHURCH, p. 212; cf. Kim Yang Sun.
5 Koh Won Yong, 'A Brief History of Evangelical Awakenings in Korea since 1920,' unpublished paper, School of World Mission, Fuller Theological Seminary, Pasadena, California, p. 2.
6 See R. E. Shearer, WILDFIRE: CHURCH GROWTH IN KOREA, p. 209; cf. Koh Won Yong, 'A Brief History,' pp. 4-5.
7 Koh Won Yong, 'A Brief History of Evangelical Awakenings in Korea since 1920,' p. 5.
8 Allen D. Clark, HISTORY OF THE KOREAN CHURCH, pp. 213ff; Kitok Kyo Kyoto Yun Maing.
9 Koh Won Yong, 'A Brief History,' p. 6.
10 Republic of Korea, SYNGMAN RHEE, Seoul, 1956.

11 Allen D. Clark, HISTORY OF THE KOREAN CHURCH, pp. 217ff.
12 Information from a classmate, Dr. W. Wyeth Willard; A.D.Clark, HISTORY OF THE KOREAN CHURCH, pp. 211ff.
13 Rene Monod, THE KOREAN REVIVAL, pp. 58-60.
14 W. N. Blair, GOLD IN KOREA, pp. 108ff.
15 Robert Finley, 'Revival in Korea,' in CHRISTIAN LIFE, 1950, YOUTH FOR CHRIST, ALLIANCE WITNESS, etc.
16 Allen D. Clark, HISTORY OF THE CHURCH IN KOREA, p. 219.
17 See Kim YangSun, HISTORY OF THE KOREAN CHURCH IN THE TEN YEARS SINCE LIBERATION, passim.
18 Rene Monod, THE KOREAN REVIVAL, p. 59.
19 R. E.Shearer, WILDFIRE: CHURCH GROWTH IN KOREA, p. 209.
20 Kim YangSun, passim. Information from the Rev. J.T.Underwood.
21 Allen D. Clark, HISTORY OF THE KOREAN CHURCH, p. 228.
22 Rene Monod, THE KOREAN REVIVAL, pp. 46-48.
23 Allen D. Clark, HISTORY OF THE KOREAN CHURCH, pp. 221ff.
24 Kim YangSun, HISTORY OF THE KOREAN CHURCH IN THE TEN YEARS SINCE LIBERATION, passim.
25 Allen D. Clark, HISTORY OF THE KOREAN CHURCH, pp. 222ff.
26 Cf. R. E. Shearer, p. 210; Allen D. Clark, pp. 222-223.
27 S. H. Moffett, THE CHRISTIANS OF KOREA, p. 116.
28 Koh Won Yong, 'A Brief History,' pp. 6-7.
29 Richard Gehman, LET MY HEART BE BROKEN, New York, 1960. Robert Pierce deserves a definitive biography.
30 Allen D. Clark, HISTORY OF THE KOREAN CHURCH, pp. 223ff.
31 Allen D. Clark, A SEMINARY SURVEY, p. 159.
32 Allen D. Clark, HISTORY OF THE KOREAN CHURCH, p. 227.
33 The writer crossed Siberia in 1967.
34 Allen D. Clark, HISTORY OF THE KOREAN CHURCH, p. 244.
35 For a sketch of the Salvation Army in Korea, see pp. 249-254.

Notes on Chapter 18: THE CURTAIN FALLS IN CHINA

1 See J. Leighton Stuart, FIFTY YEARS IN CHINA, passim.
2 INTERNATIONAL REVIEW OF MISSIONS, XXXVIII, p. 16.
3 Leslie T. Lyall, COME WIND, COME WEATHER, pp. 15-16.
4 David Adeney, of the China Inland Mission, was seconded to the Inter-Varsity Fellowship of Evangelical Unions.
5 Leslie T. Lyall, COME WIND, COME WEATHER, pp. 17.
6 K. S. Latourette, CHRISTIANITY IN A REVOLUTIONARY AGE, Volume V, p. 397.
7 See Mary A. Endicott, FIVE STARS OVER CHINA, 1953. A well-publicized example was that of Dryden Phelps, A.B.F.M.S.
8 Mary Wang, THE CHINESE CHURCH THAT WILL NOT DIE, pp. 15ff.
9 The Communists so desecrated a cathedral in Peking.
10 Mary Wang, THE CHINESE CHURCH, pp. 44ff.
11 The Christian students were almost all evangelical by conviction.
12 Mary Wang, THE CHINESE CHURCH, pp. 63 & 75.
13 Leslie T. Lyall, COME WIND, COME WEATHER, p. 19.
14 H. R. Williamson, BRITISH BAPTISTS IN CHINA, p. 185.
15 Leslie T. Lyall, COME WIND, COME WEATHER, p. 38.
16 Andrew Gih, THE CHURCH BEHIND THE BAMBOO CURTAIN, p. 24. Personal information from Dorcas Gih.
17 Dissolution was the experience of all Christian orphanage——as of all Christian social service.

18 Andrew Gih, THE CHURCH BEHIND THE BAMBOO CURTAIN, pp. 36-37. The mission lost contact with its personnel in China.
19 Helen Ferris, THE CHRISTIAN CHURCH IN COMMUNIST CHINA, pp. 8ff; Leslie T. Lyall, COME WIND, COME WEATHER, p. 27.
20 W. C. Merwin & F. P. Jones, DOCUMENTS OF THE THREE-SELF MOVEMENT, pp. 19ff & 34ff.
21 Leslie T. Lyall, COME WIND, COME WEATHER, pp. 39ff.
22 See Helen Ferris, THE CHRISTIAN CHURCH IN COMMUNIST CHINA, pp. 8 & 9.
23 Leslie T. Lyall, COME WIND, COME WEATHER, pp. 42-43.
24 G. N. Patterson, CHRISTIANITY IN COMMUNIST CHINA, passim.
25 Leslie T. Lyall, COME WIND, COME WEATHER, p. 46.
26 W. C. Merwin & F. P. Jones, DOCUMENTS OF THE THREE-SELF MOVEMENT, pp. 27ff.
27 Leslie T. Lyall, COME WIND, COME WEATHER, p. 31.
28 It is impossible to estimate how many such congregations existed in Mainland China.
29 CHINA'S MILLIONS, London, January 1951; D. Vaughn Rees, THE JESUS FAMILY IN COMMUNIST CHINA, pp. 30ff.
30 Leslie T. Lyall, COME WIND, COME WEATHER, p. 30.
31 Christian Workers' Mission, July 1954 Report cited in Leslie T. Lyall, COME WIND, COME WEATHER, pp. 66-68.
32 Angus Kinnear, AGAINST THE TIDE, pp. 143ff; see CHINA'S MILLIONS, London, November 1951, p. 101.
33 LIBERATION DAILY, Shanghai, 1 February 1956.
34 Angus Kinnear, AGAINST THE TIDE, pp. 168ff.
35 Leslie T. Lyall, COME WIND, COME WEATHER, pp. 49ff.
36 See TIEN FENG (Heavenly Wind), 31st July 1974.
37 Leslie T. Lyall, COME WIND, COME WEATHER, pp. 79ff.
38 CHINA BULLETIN, Hong Kong, 20 October 1958.
39 Reported in PEOPLE'S DAILY, Peking, 25 March 1957.
40 See Helen Willis, THROUGH ENCOURAGEMENT OF THE SCRIPTURES: TEN YEARS IN COMMUNIST SHANGHAI, passim.
41 National People's Congress, Peking, 10 April 1959.
42 See Leslie T. Lyall, RED SKY AT NIGHT, passim.
43 Some letters have reached the writer's desk.
44 Mary Wang, THE CHINESE CHURCH, p. 76.
45 Colin Mackerris & Neale Hunter, CHINA OBSERVED, 1964-67, Chapters XII-XIV.
46 Leslie T. Lyall, RED SKY AT NIGHT, passim.
47 MISSION BULLETIN, Hong Kong, January 1956, pp. 223, 224.
48 Leslie T. Lyall, RED SKY AT NIGHT, passim.
49 Also information from 'Evangelize China' Fellowship sources.
50 Opinions given the writer by prominent Chinese Christians.
51 CHINA NEWS AND VIEWS, November-December 1966, pp. 7-8.
52 Consolidated reports, Hong Kong.
53 Brother Andrew, 'Behind the Bamboo Curtain,' GUIDEPOSTS, July 1966.
54 Consolidated reports, Hong Kong.
55 Angus Kinnear, AGAINST THE TIDE, p. 172.
56 A professor in the University of California at Los Angeles.
57 ECHOES OF SERVICE, Exeter, July 1973, pp. 134ff.
58 Christian broadcasters receive occasional letters.
59 March 1966 in Siberia; October 1967 in Macao.
60 Mary Wang, THE CHINESE CHURCH, p. 9.
 * Documentation of affairs Chinese is extremely limited.

Notes on Chapter 19: TAIWAN, HONG KONG, AND OVERSEAS

1 C. M. Hsieh, TAIWAN—ILHA FORMOSA, p. 184.
2 Allen J. Swanson, TAIWAN, p. 67; C. M. Hsieh, p. 286.
3 H. K. Tong, CHRISTIANITY IN TAIWAN, p. 124. (The writer addressed Mme. Chiang Kai-shek's group in 1967.
4 Overseas Crusades enrolled hundreds of thousands in its Bible correspondence courses; the Pocket Testament League distributed Gospels by the million; Campus Crusade evangelized the students.
5 This movement continued for a number of years, until Jehovah's Witnesses were reported trying to encourage 'army pacifism.'
6 WORLD CHRISTIAN HANDBOOK, 1957. (Most of the new societies were avowedly evangelical.)
7 TAIWAN CHRISTIAN YEARBOOK, 1960, p. 15; cf. TAIWAN BAPTIST CONVENTION REPORT, 1970.
8 Allen J. Swanson, TAIWAN, pp. 122-124.
9 H. K. Tong, CHRISTIANITY IN TAIWAN, p. 114.
10 Allen J. Swanson, TAIWAN, pp. 190ff.
11 TAIWAN CHRISTIAN YEARBOOK, 1960, p. 85.
12 This point was made in MISSIONS FROM THE THIRD WORLD, edited by Wong, Church Growth Study Center, 1972.
13 C. H. Hwang, 'P. K. U. and the Centenary Year in Formosa,' in THEOLOGY AND THE CHURCH, V, pp. 3-23.
14 True Jesus Church, EVANGELISM IN TAIWAN, Taichung, 1956, p. 6.
15 Tribal statistics, p. 30.
16 In other words, tongues-speaking, seventh-day keeping, and 'Jesus only'—an acceptance of the deity of Christ, a denial of the Trinity.
17 True Jesus Church, DESCRIPTION OF TRUE JESUS CHURCH, 1967, pp. 6-7.
18 Christine Carmichael, TAIWAN: Foreign Missions Department of the Assemblies of God, 1964, p. 6; see TAIWAN CHRISTIAN YEARBOOK, 1968, p. 27.
19 David Liao, THE RESPONSIVE: RESISTANT OR NEGLECTED? The Hakka Chinese in Taiwan, 1972.
20 See George Vicedom, FAITH THAT MOVES MOUNTAINS, 1967; original report: 'A People Find God,' 1957.
21 Robert J. Bolton, 'China Assemblies of God through 1969,' paper (unpublished), School of World Mission, Pasadena, California.
22 True Jesus Church, DESCRIPTION OF TRUE JESUS CHURCH, pp. 6-7.
23 See Allen J. Swanson, TAIWAN, p. 92, n. 11.
24 The writer preached in Taiwan with his former Bethel Band leader, Andrew Gih, in 1967.
25 K. S. Latourette, CHRISTIANITY IN A REVOLUTIONARY AGE, Volume V, p. 405.

Notes on Chapter 20: CONFLICT IN SOUTH-EAST ASIA

1 Truong-van-Tot, 'Revivals in Vietnam,' unpublished paper, 1971, School of World Mission, Pasadena, California, p. 16.
2 Christian and Missionary Alliance Statistics, 1945-1970, p. 13.
3 Mrs. D. I. Jeffrey, 'Spiritual Refreshing in Indo-China,' CHILD EVANGELISM, June 1950; Le-Hoang-Phu, 'The Evangelical Church of Vietnam,' unpublished thesis, Wheaton College, p. 82.
4 Mrs. D. I. Jeffrey, 'Spiritual Refreshing in Vietnam,' June 1950.

5   Truong-van-Tot, 'Revivals in Vietnam,' p. 17.
6   Mrs. D. I. Jeffrey, 'Spiritual Refreshing in Vietnam,' June 1950.
7   Le-hoang-Phu, 'The Evangelical Church of Vietnam,' p. 83.
8   N. R. Ziemer, 'Banmethuot District and Bible School,' in THE
    CALL OF INDO-CHINA, 1951, pp. 24-25; see Christian and
    Missionary Alliance statistics, 1947-1950.
9   Christian and Missionary Alliance Statistics, 1945-1970, p. 13.
10 Truong-van-Tot, 'Revivals in Vietnam,' pp. 19-20.
11 Christian and Missionary Alliance Statistics, 1966-1968.
12 O. N. Steinkamp, THE HOLY SPIRIT IN VIETNAM, p. 27.
13 CHURCH GROWTH BULLETIN, March 1973, p. 297; ALLIANCE
    WITNESS, 16 August 1972.
14 O. N. Steinkamp, THE HOLY SPIRIT IN VIETNAM, pp. 17-18.
15 ALLIANCE WITNESS, 2 February 1972.
16 O. N. Steinkamp, THE HOLY SPIRIT IN VIETNAM, pp. 7ff.
17 ALLIANCE WITNESS, 29 March 1972.
18 O. N. Steinkamp, THE HOLY SPIRIT IN VIETNAM, pp. 40ff.
19 ALLIANCE WITNESS, 22 November 1972.
20 Communicants numbered more than 60,000 in 1972, community
    calculated at two-and-a-half times that figure.
21 WORLD VISION, May 1972, p. 4.
22 1 November 1970, inauguration of the Khmer Republic, following a
    coup d'etat by the Cambodian armed forces.
23 WORLD VISION, May 1972, pp. 4ff.
24 Report of January 1973, WORLD VISION.
25 R. H. Glover & J. H. Kane, THE PROGRESS OF WORLD-WIDE
    MISSIONS, p. 124.
26 EAST ASIA MILLIONS, Philadelphia, February-March 1973.
27 J. W. Gustafson, 'Syncretistic Thai Buddhism,' unpublished thesis,
    School of World Mission, Pasadena, California, 1970, p. 164.
28 J. E. Hudspith, 'Tribal Highways and Byways: Church Growth
    Study in North Thailand,' unpublished thesis, School of World
    Mission, Pasadena, California, 1969, pp. 310ff.
29 Eleventh Annual Report, Commission on Ecumenical Mission and
    Relations, United Presbyterian Church in the U. S. A., May 1969.
30 EAST ASIA MILLIONS, Philadelphia, May 1971.
31 Report from Udon, Christian and Missionary Alliance.
32 EAST ASIA MILLIONS, October 1971.
33 EAST ASIA MILLIONS, June 1971.
34 WORLD DOMINION, September-October 1946, pp. 262ff.
35 ALONG KINGDOM HIGHWAYS, 1949, p. 3.
36 ALONG KINGDOM HIGHWAYS, 1950, p. 4.
37 ALONG KINGDOM HIGHWAYS, 1951, p. 3.
38 Special Edition, ALONG KINGDOM HIGHWAYS, 1951, p. 10.
39 ALONG KINGDOM HIGHWAYS, 1952, p. 10.
40 ALONG KINGDOM HIGHWAYS, 1954, p. 9.
41 ALONG KINGDOM HIGHWAYS, 1955, p. 3; 1957, p. 4; 1959, p. 3.
42 CHRISTIANITY TODAY, 31 August 1959, p. 35.
43 CHRISTIANITY TODAY, 10 November 1961; ALONG KINGDOM
    HIGHWAYS, 1961 & 1962, Reports on Burma.
44 ALONG KINGDOM HIGHWAYS, 1965, p. 9; CHRISTIANITY
    TODAY, 30 June 1965 (WORLD CHRISTIAN HANDBOOK, 1962
    —H. W. Coxill & Kenneth Grubb, editors.
45 CHRISTIANITY TODAY, 7 May 1965, 27 May 1966.
46 CHRISTIANITY TODAY, 13 October, 22 December 1967.
47 CHRISTIANITY TODAY, 19 January 1973.

BIBLIOGRAPHY

Aoyoshi, K., DR. MASAHISA UEMURA, Tokyo, 1940.
Axling, William, KAGAWA, New York, 1946.
Baker, R. T., DARKNESS OF THE SUN, New York, 1947.
Beach and Fahs, WORLD MISSIONARY ATLAS, New York, 1925.
Beach and St. John, WORLD STATISTICS OF CHRISTIAN MISSIONS, New York, 1916.
Blair, W. N., PENTECOST IN KOREA, New York, 1910.
Blair, W. N., GOLD IN KOREA, Topeka, 1948.
Brannen, Noah S., SOKA GAKKAI, Richmond, 1968.
Broomhall, Marshall, ROBERT MORRISON, A MASTER BUILDER, London, 1924.
Broomhall, Marshall, Editor, MARTYRED MISSIONARIES OF THE CHINA INLAND MISSION, London, 1901.
Brown, G. T., MISSION TO KOREA, Nashville, 1962.
Burns, Islay, MEMOIR OF THE REV. W. C. BURNS, London, 1885.
Buxton, B. Godfrey, THE REWARD OF FAITH (Biography of Barclay F. Buxton), London, 1953.
Carey, S. Pearce, WILLIAM CAREY, New York, 1953.
Carlberg, Gustav, CHINA IN REVIVAL, Rock Island, 1936.
Carmichael, Christine, TAIWAN, Springfield, Missouri, 1964.
Cary, Otis, A HISTORY OF CHRISTIANITY IN JAPAN, New York, 1909.
Chang, Kuo-tao, THE RISE OF THE COMMUNIST PARTY, 1921-1927. (By a former member of the Chinese Communist Party).
Clark, A. D., HISTORY OF THE KOREAN CHURCH, Seoul, 1961.
Clark, C. A., THE KOREAN CHURCH AND THE NEVIUS METHODS, New York, 1930.
Clarke, S. R., AMONG THE TRIBES IN SOUTHWEST CHINA, London, 1911.
Coxill, H. W. & Kenneth Grubb, Editors, THE WORLD CHRISTIAN HANDBOOK, London, 1962.
Culpepper, C. L., THE SHANTUNG REVIVAL, Dallas, 1968.
Davis, J. D., A SKETCH OF THE LIFE OF REV. JOSEPH HARDY NEESIMA, Chicago, 1894.
DeForest, J.H., SUNRISE IN THE SUNRISE KINGDOM, New York, 1904.
Dickason and Sowards, BURMA BAPTIST CHRONICLE, Rangoon, 1963.
Drummond, R. H., A HISTORY OF CHRISTIANITY IN JAPAN, Grand Rapids, 1961.
Ebisawa, A., NIPPON KIRISTOKYO HYAYUNENSHI, Tokyo, 1959.
Endicott, Mary A., FIVE STARS OVER CHINA, Toronto, 1953.
Ferris, Helen, THE CHRISTIAN CHURCH IN COMMUNIST CHINA, Lackland A.F.B., 1956.
Freeman, John H., AN ORIENTAL LAND OF THE FREE, (SIAM), Philadelphia, 1910.
Freud, Sigmund, THE FUTURE OF AN ILLUSION, London, 1928.
Fulton, Austin, THROUGH EARTHQUAKE, WIND AND FIRE, Church and mission in Manchuria, 1867-1950, London, 1965.
Gee, Donald, THE PENTECOSTAL MOVEMENT, London, 1949.
Gehman, Richard, LET MY HEART BE BROKEN, New York, 1960.

Germany, C. H., Editor, THE RESPONSE OF THE CHURCH IN CHANGING JAPAN, New York, 1967.

Gih, Andrew, BANDS OF SOLDIERS FOR WAR, London, 1939.

Gih, Andrew, CHINA'S WONDERFUL REVIVING, London, 1935.

Gih, Andrew, THE CHURCH BEHIND THE BAMBOO CURTAIN, London, 1961.

Gih, Andrew, INTO GOD'S FAMILY, London, 1937.

Gih, Andrew, LAUNCH OUT INTO THE DEEP, London, 1938.

Gih, Andrew, TWICE BORN AND THEN? London, 1936 & 1954.

Gih, Andrew, WHEN WAR COMES, London, 1964.

Glover, A. E., A THOUSAND MILES OF MIRACLE IN CHINA, London, 1901.

Glover, R. H. & J. H. Kane, THE PROGRESS OF WORLD-WIDE MISSIONS, New York, 1960.

Goforth, Jonathan, 'BY MY SPIRIT,' London, undated.

Goforth, Rosalind, GOFORTH OF CHINA, London, undated.

Grauer, O. C., FREDRIK FRANSON, Chicago, 1960.

Gustafson, J. W., 'Syncretistic Thai Buddhism,' unpublished thesis, School of World Mission, Pasadena, California, 1970.

Hail, W. J., THE TAIPING REBELLION, New Haven, 1927.

Harris, E. N., A STAR IN THE EAST: AMERICAN BAPTIST MISSIONS TO THE KARENS IN BURMA, New York, 1920.

Holtom, D. C., MODERN JAPAN AND SHINTO NATIONALISM, Chicago, 1943 & 1949.

Hsieh, C. M., TAIWAN—ILHA FORMOSA, Washington, 1964.

Hudspith, J. E., 'Tribal Highways and Byways: Church Growth Study in North Thailand,' unpublished thesis, School of World Mission, Pasadena, California, 1968.

Hughes, L. B., THE EVANGEL IN BURMA, Rangoon, 1926.

Iglehart, C. W., A CENTURY OF PROTESTANT CHRISTIANITY IN JAPAN, Tokyo, 1959.

Irwin, E. F., WITH CHRIST IN INDO-CHINA, Harrisburg, 1937.

Jones, F. P., THE CHURCH IN COMMUNIST CHINA, New York, 1962.

Jones, G. H. & W. A. Noble, THE KOREAN REVIVAL, New York, 1906.

Kagawa, Toyohiko, BEFORE THE DAWN (a part-autobiographical novel), New York, 1924.

Kanamori, P. M., KANAMORI'S LIFE STORY, Philadelphia, 1921.

Kendall, R. E., THE EYES OF THE EARTH (The Diary of Samuel Pollard), London, 1954.

Kesson, John, THE CROSS AND THE DRAGON, London, 1854.

Kim, Yang Sun, HISTORY OF THE KOREAN CHURCH IN THE TEN YEARS SINCE LIBERATION, Seoul, 1962.

King, Alonzo, MEMOIR OF GEORGE DANA BOARDMAN, Boston, 1834.

Kinnear, Angus, AGAINST THE TIDE, THE STORY OF WATCH-MAN NEE, London, 1973.

Ladd, G. T., IN KOREA WITH MARQUIS ITO, New York, 1910.

Latourette, K. S., ADVANCE THROUGH STORM, New York, 1947.

Latourette, K. S., CHRISTIANITY IN A REVOLUTIONARY AGE, Volume V, London, 1962.

Latourette, K. S., HISTORY OF CHRISTIAN MISSIONS IN CHINA, New York, 1929.

Latourette, K. S., A HISTORY OF THE EXPANSION OF CHRIS-TIANITY, Volumes III, IV, VI, New York, 1938, 1941, 1946.

Le-Hoang-Phu, 'The Evangelical Church of Vietnam during the Second World War and the War of Independence,' unpublished thesis, Wheaton College, 1967.

Liao, David, THE RESPONSIVE: RESISTANT OR NEGLECTED? The Hakka Chinese in Taiwan, Grand Rapids, 1972.

Lyall, Leslie T., A BIOGRAPHY OF JOHN SUNG, London, 1954.

Lyall, Leslie T., COME WIND, COME WEATHER, London, 1961.

Lyall, Leslie T., RED SKY AT NIGHT, London, 1969.

McFarland, G. B., HISTORICAL SKETCH OF PROTESTANT MISSIONS IN SIAM, Bangkok, 1928.

MacGillivray, D., A CENTURY OF PROTESTANT MISSIONS IN CHINA, Shanghai, 1907.

McGilvary, D., A HALF CENTURY AMONG THE SIAMESE AND THE LAO, New York, 1912.

Mackerris, Colin & Neale Hunter, CHINA OBSERVED, 1964-1967, London, 1967.

Mason, Francis, THE KAREN APOSTLE: MEMOIR OF KO THAH-BYU, Boston, 1843.

Matthews, Basil, JOHN R. MOTT, World Citizen, New York, 1934.

Merwin, W. C. & F. P. Jones, DOCUMENTS OF THE THREE-SELF MOVEMENT, New York, 1963.

Miyakoda, T., BUXTON TO SONO DESHITACHI (Buxton and His Disciples), Tokyo, 1964.

Moffett, S. H., THE CHRISTIANS OF KOREA, New York, 1962.

Monod, Rene, THE KOREAN REVIVAL, London, 1971.

Monsen, Marie, THE AWAKENING, London, 1961.

Morse, H. B., CHRONICLE OF THE EAST INDIA COMPANY TRADING TO CHINA, 1635-1834, Volume II, Boston, 1927.

Morton, T. R., TODAY IN MANCHURIA, London, 1939.

Muto, Tomio, LACOUR CRUSADE (Kirisuto Shimbun), Tokyo, 1959.

Orr, J. Edwin, THROUGH BLOOD AND FIRE IN CHINA, London, 1939.

Orr, J. Edwin, I SAW NO TEARS, London, 1948.

Orr, J. Edwin, THE SECOND EVANGELICAL AWAKENING IN BRITAIN, London, 1949.

Orr, J. Edwin, THE LIGHT OF THE NATIONS, Exeter, 1965.

Orr, J. Edwin, THE FLAMING TONGUE, Chicago, 1973.

Orr, J. Edwin, THE FERVENT PRAYER, Chicago, 1974.

Orr, J. Edwin, THE EAGER FEET, Chicago, 1975.

Ottman, F. C., J. WILBUR CHAPMAN, New York, 1920.

Paik, L. G., THE HISTORY OF PROTESTANT MISSIONS IN KOREA, Pyongyang, 1929.

Parker, Joseph I., INTERPRETATIVE STATISTICAL SURVEY, New York, 1928.

Patterson, G. N., CHRISTIANITY IN COMMUNIST CHINA, Waco, 1969.

Rees, D. Vaughn, THE JESUS FAMILY IN COMMUNIST CHINA, London, 1954.

Republic of Korea, SYNGMAN RHEE, Seoul, 1956.

Sawatzky, Sheldon, 'Awakenings in Taiwan,' an unpublished paper, School of World Mission, Pasadena, California, 1969.

Schubert, William E., I REMEMBER JOHN SUNG, unpublished typescript, by a close collaborator in China.

Shearer, Roy E., WILDFIRE: CHURCH GROWTH IN KOREA, Grand Rapids, 1966.

Smith, A. H., CHINA IN CONVULSION, Chicago, 1901.

Soothill, W. E., TIMOTHY RICHARD OF CHINA, London, 1924.
Steinkamp, O. N., THE HOLY SPIRIT IN VIETNAM, Carol Stream, Illinois, 1973.
Stock, E., HISTORY OF THE CHURCH MISSIONARY SOCIETY, London, 1899ff.
Stuart, J. Leighton, FIFTY YEARS IN CHINA, New York, 1954.
Swanson, Allen J., TAIWAN, MAINLINE VERSUS INDEPENDENT CHURCH GROWTH, South Pasadena, 1970.
Sweet, W. W., THE STORY OF RELIGION IN AMERICA, New York, 1950.
Taylor, H. & G., HUDSON TAYLOR IN EARLY YEARS, London, 1912.
Taylor, H. & G., HUDSON TAYLOR AND THE CHINA INLAND MISSION, London, 1919.
Thomsen, Harry, NEW RELIGIONS OF JAPAN, Tokyo, 1963.
Tong, Hollington, CHRISTIANITY IN TAIWAN, Taipei, 1960.
True Jesus Church, DESCRIPTION OF THE TRUE JESUS CHURCH, Taichung, 1967.
True Jesus Church, EVANGELISM IN TAIWAN, Taichung, 1956.
Truong-Van-Tot, 'Revivals in Vietnam,' unpublished paper, School of World Mission, Pasadena, California, 1971.
Tsuchiya, Philip, 'Shakabuku: Soka Gakkai's Apologetics Evangelism, unpublished paper, Pasadena, California, 1970.
Vahanian, Gabriel, THE DEATH OF GOD, New York, 1961.
Varg, Paul A., MISSIONARIES, CHINESE AND DIPLOMATS, Princeton, 1953.
Vicedom, George, FAITH THAT MOVES MOUNTAINS, Taipei, 1967.
Voelkel, Harold, A REVIVAL AMONG MISSIONARIES IN KOREA, privately published booklet.
Wang, Mary, THE CHINESE CHURCH THAT WILL NOT DIE, London, 1971.
Wasson, A. W., CHURCH GROWTH IN KOREA, New York, 1934.
Watson, Hazel T., 'Revival and Church Growth in Korea, 1884-1910,' unpublished thesis, School of World Mission, Pasadena, California, 1968.
Wayland, Francis, MEMOIR OF ADONIRAM JUDSON, Boston, 1853.
Webster, James, THE REVIVAL IN MANCHURIA, London, 1910.
Wheeler, W. R., A MAN SENT FROM GOD: A BIOGRAPHY OF ROBERT E. SPEER, London, 1956.
Williamson, H. R., BRITISH BAPTISTS IN CHINA, 1845-1952, London, 1957.
Willis, Helen, THROUGH ENCOURAGEMENT OF THE SCRIP-TURES: TEN YEARS IN COMMUNIST SHANGHAI, Hong Kong, 1961.
Wong, James, Editor, MISSIONS FROM THE THIRD WORLD, South Pasadena, 1972.
Woodward, D. B., AFLAME FOR GOD, Chicago, 1966.
Yanagita, T., SHORT HISTORY OF CHRISTIANITY IN JAPAN, Sendai, 1957.
Yokoyama, Haruichi, KAGAWA TOYOHIKO DEN, Tokyo, 1952.
Yoneda, Isamu, NAKADA JUJI DEN (A biography of Juji Nakada), Tokyo, 1959.
Young, J. M. L., TWO EMPIRES IN JAPAN, London, 1959.

Abbott, Paul 71
Adams, James E. 32
Adeney, David 122
Alexander, Charles M. 14, 32
Ariga, Paul 105
Ballagh, James 10
Barber, Margaret E. 41
Berggrav, Eivind 15
Bevan, Aneurin 15
Blair, William Newton 33, 51, 113
Boardman, George 3
Booth, William 24, 48
Broomhall, Marshall 7
Burns, W. C. 4, 6
Buxton, Barclay 25, 48
Calvin, John 149
Carey, William 3, 149, 150
Cary, Otis 10
Cassels, W. W. 9, 39
Cecil, Lord William 28
Chang, Barnabas 137
Chang, Hsueh-Liang 64
Chang, James 75, 77, 86
Chang, Ling-Sheng 41, 96
Chang, Tso-Lin 64
Chao, Chun-Ying (Calvin) 122
Chapman, J. Wilbur 12, 14, 24, 32
Chee, Hung-Soon 111
Chen, Wen-Yuan 124
Cheng, Marcus 60, 80, 126, 128
Chi, O-Ang 88
Chiang, Kai-Shek 9, 36, 135, 152
Chiang, Mme Mei-Ling 85, 135
Chiba, Yugoro 46
Ching, Tien-Yin 126
Chou, En-Lai 133
Chow, Hope 86
Christensen, Anna 29, 61, 74, 153
Coffin, Henry Sloan 62
Cole, W. B. 83
Contento, Paul 122
Cowman, Charles 25
Cox, Josiah 8
Culpepper, C. L. 69, 70
Davis, G. T. B. 59
Dodds, Gil 114
Ebina, Danjo 23
Feng, Yu-Hsiang 60
Finley, Robert 114
Finney, Charles G. 1, 8, 32, 104
Franson, Fredrik 26, 36
Freud, Sigmund 12
Fu, James 125
Garr, A. G. 40

Getesarn, Boon Mark 100
Gih, Tsu-Wen (Andrew) 61, 62, 65
66, 68-70, 72, 73, 75-78, 81, 83-
86, 90, 92-96, 99, 124, 136, 138
Gih, Dorcas 61, 89, 124
Gilmour, James 7
Gladden, Washington 19
Goble, Jonathan 8
Goforth, Jonathan 17, 37-39
60, 66, 91
Goforth, Rosalind 38, 152
Graham, Billy 105, 116
Grant, Willard 86
Grey, Sir Edward 12
Gutzlaff, Karl 3, 4
Ha Minh-Vinh 143
Haldane, Robert & James 2
Halverson, Richard 147
Han, Kyung-Chik 113, 115, 147
Hardie, Keir 15
Hardie, R. A. 26, 28
Harris, C. M. 30
Hauge, Hans Nielsen 2
Henry, Carl F. H. 147
Ho Chi-Minh 141
Honda, Koji 105
Hsieh, Meng-Tse 60, 65, 80
Hu, Betty 89
Hughes, Jennie 93
Hung, Hsiu-Chuan 4
Iglehart, C. W. 10
Ito, Prince 30
Jacobsz, Aletta 56
Jaffray, R. A. 97
Jensen, Emil 64
John, Griffith 7
Johnston, Howard Agnew 27
Jones, E. Stanley 85, 101, 104
Jones, George Heber 27
Joyce, F. S. 39, 79
Joyce, Raymond 89
Judd, F. H. 93
Judson, Adoniram 2, 3, 42
Kagawa, Toyohiko 77, 103
Kanamori, Paul 48
Keil, San-Ju 33
Kiang, Chang-Chuan 124
Kim, Ik-Tu 53, 54
Kim, Joon-Gon 119
Kim, Il-Sung 109
Kishi, Nobosuke 108
Ko San Ye 43
Koh Tha Byu 3, 151
Koo, John 86, 89, 90

Kou, Shih-Yung 138
Ku, Cheng-Hung 57
Ku, Jen-En 124
Kung, H. H. 9, 85
Lacour, Lawrence 104, 105
Ladd, George T. 30, 31
Lan, Alice 89
Latourette, K. S. 1, 8
Le, Van-Thai 99
Lee, Philip 63, 66, 73, 85
Lee, Sung-Bong 110
Lee, Y. S. 39
Lee, Yong-Do 53
Leynse, James P. 73
Li, Chih-Wei 125
Lie, Olaf 80
Lin, Frank 63, 66, 73, 81, 84, 90
Liu, Tao-Sheng 60, 75, 77-80, 89
Lloyd, Llewellyn 34
Lunde, Albert 15
Lutley, Arthur 39, 152
Lyall, Leslie 61, 72, 74, 122
Mao, Tse-Tung 121, 123, 129-131
133, 134, 154
McGilvary, Daniel 45, 151
McWhirter, James 66
Meek, Simon (Miao Shou-Hsun) 41
Milne, William 3
Moffett, S. A. 27
Moffett, S. H. 117
Monsen, Marie 61, 69, 72
73, 78, 79
Moody, D. L. 5, 8, 18
Mooneyham, Stanley 144
Morrison, Robert 3, 150
Morton, Ralph 66
Mott, John R. 24, 27, 46
Muller, George 7
Nakada, Juji 23, 25, 48
Nee, To-Sheng (Watchman) 41
96, 127, 133, 136
Neesima, Joseph Hardy 8
Nelson, H. E. 140
Newburn, William 141
Nieh, Lincoln 63, 66, 73
Nordhaug, Knut 80
Octavianus, Petrus 106
Orr, J. Edwin (Ou I-Wen) 86, 99
Pearse, George 6, 7
Pierce, Robert 105, 114, 116, 118
Ramsey, Paul 20
Rees, Paul S. 147
Rhee, Syngman 112, 116
Richard, Timothy 6, 125
Ridout, George 82
Roberts, Evan 14, 39

Robertson, D. T. 67
Rutherford, Dorothy 66
Sanders, J. Oswald 141
Sasao, Tetsusaburo 25
Saunders, Alexander 93
Schubert, W. E. 84
Shen, Vera 86
Shih, John 63, 75, 77, 86, 89
Smebye, Einar 81
Smith, Alex 145
Smith, Gipsy Rodney 14
Sook, Pong-Sanoi 100
Speer, Robert E. 47
Spurgeon, C. H. 5
Stam, John & Betty 79
Stearns, Thornton 71
Stone, Mary 76
Sun Yat-Sen 9, 41
Sung, John 46, 62, 63, 66, 68-71
73-75, 77, 78, 80-87, 95
96, 98, 100, 101, 153
Suriyakam, Tom Kham 145
Sutikam, Pluang 145
Tako, Weilam 88
Taylor, Hudson 6-8, 40, 125, 145
Tegenfeldt, H. G. 147
Teng, Philip 139
Thomas, R. J. 8
Thompson, R. Ernest 73
Ting, Li-Mei 39, 152
Tippett, C. F. 61, 91
Toda, Josei 107, 108
Todd, Samuel 117
Torrey, R. A. 14, 24
Toynbee, Arnold 12
Truong-Van-Tot 142
Uemura, Masahisa 23, 25
Vahanian, Gabriel 20
Voelkel, Harold 56, 116
Wagijono, Evangelist 146
Wahlquist, D. R. 81
Wang, Chang-Lai 39
Wang, Ming-Tao 60, 65, 127, 128
Wang, Tsai (Leland) 41, 60, 75, 76
85, 89, 96
Wedderburn, L. D. M. 66
Whitefield, George 1, 20
Wesley, John 1, 2, 12, 18, 20, 83
Wilkes, Paget 48, 58, 61, 76
Wilson, J. R. 50, 81
Wu, Tjen-Ming 78, 81
Wu, Y. F. 125, 126, 128
Yamamuro, Gumpei 48, 126
Yao, S. S. 39, 86
Young, William 17, 43
Ziemer, N. R. 141

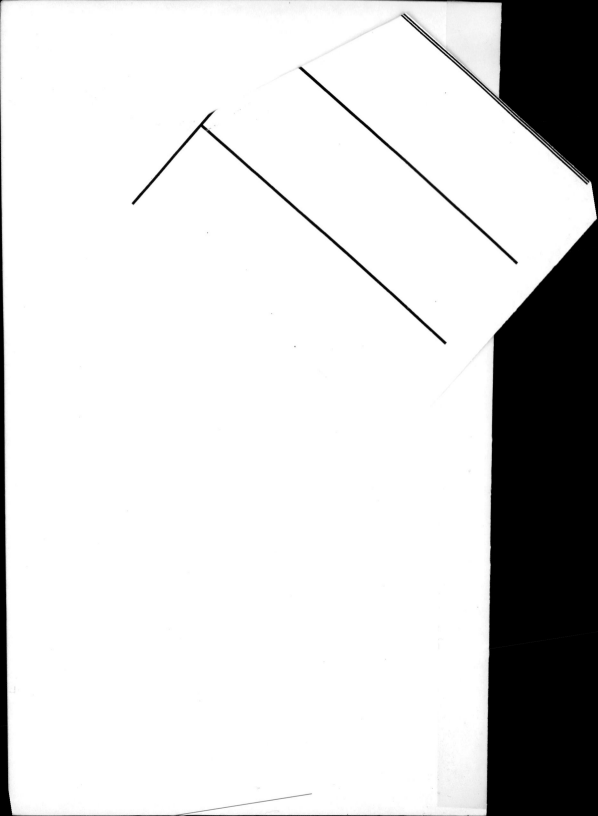